WITHDRAWN

WOMEN ON DEADLINE
A Collection of America's Best

WOMEN ON DEADLINE

A Collection of America's Best

Sherry Ricchiardi and Virginia Young

Iowa State University Press / Ames

Sherry Ricchiardi has been a reporter, *Sunday Magazine* writer, and international travel columnist for the *Des Moines Register.* After receiving a Ph.D. from Iowa State University in May 1986, she took a job as city editor for the *Columbia Missourian,* a newspaper produced at the University of Missouri School of Journalism, where she also was a professor. She joined the faculty at the Indiana University School of Journalism at Indianapolis in fall 1989 and is a director of the National Institute for Advanced Reporting there. She is in the process of gathering information for a book about top women photojournalists.

Virginia Young has worked for 14 years as a reporter, editor, and journalism professor in Missouri. After receiving a master's degree in journalism, she started her career at the *Columbia* (Missouri) *Daily Tribune.* She then joined the faculty at the University of Missouri School of Journalism for five years. She now covers state government in Jefferson City, Missouri for the *St. Louis Post-Dispatch.*

© 1991 Iowa State University Press, Ames, Iowa 50010

Manufactured in the United States of America
⊗ This book is printed on acid-free paper.

First edition, 1991

Library of Congress Cataloging-in-Publication Data

Women on deadline : a collection of America's best / Sherry Ricchiardi and Virginia Young.
    p. cm.
    Includes index.
    ISBN 0–8138–1687–4. ISBN 0–8138–1688–2 (pbk) (acid-free paper)
    1. Women journalists—United States—Bibliography. 2. Journalism—United States—History. 3. Women—United States—History. I. Ricchiardi, Sherry. II. Young, Virginia.
PN4872.W66 1991
070′.92′273—dc20
[B]
                             90–41648

PN
4872
.W66
1991

To our parents

Rose and John Ricchiardi • Cordelia and Richard Young

CONTENTS

FOREWORD

For generations, American women have tap-tap-tapped out their stories in newsrooms around the country. Their presence is nothing new, but as recently as the 1960s women were rarities in the newsroom. A female reporter was never really one of the boys. Often she didn't even sit with the boys.

The newsroom was considered no place for a lady before World War I, so even such stars as Emma Bugbee and Ishbel Ross worked down the hall instead of in the newsroom at the *New York Herald Tribune*. Kay Harris of the Associated Press drew top assignments because the men in the San Francisco bureau were uncomfortable with her presence in the office. And Jean Sharley Taylor recalls the day her typewriter was finally carried from the women's section to the main newsroom at the *Detroit Free Press*.

The women who went before us had no one after whom they could fashion their conduct. So they worked by themselves in New York, Baton Rouge, Omaha, and points west, setting their own standards, keeping their own counsel. If they were crusty, it was because they had to be. But, oh, they could spin out a story and jerk a tear with the best of them. Some of their spiritual descendants live in these pages.

Journalism thrives on those rare reporters who seem to have put aside their notes, sat down to write, and spun out a seamless tale. Their journalism is far from effortless, but their grace makes it seem so. They take you where they have been. They may take you into Dachau with the liberation forces, as Marguerite Higgins did. Or they may take you into Herbert Hoover's White House in a day when the First Family's private lives were little covered, as Bess Furman did when she sneaked in with a troop of caroling Girl Scouts.

For many years, virtually all those stars were men. Now there is Christine Brennan taking us into the Washington Redskins locker room and Molly Ivins drawing portraits of Texas good ol' boys who fairly swagger from the page. And there is Jacqui Banaszynski: If you are not drawn in by the love and pain in her AIDS stories, you are not breathing.

This book is important not only because these outstanding journalists get the recognition they deserve, but also because readers beyond the reach of Bella Stumbo and the *Los Angeles Times* or Cynthia Gorney and the *Washington Post* have a chance to share the passion and insights these women bring to their work. And it is important to trace, as the interviews with these journalists do, the influences that have made each of the women the fine writers they are. You can get angry all over again at some of the sexist decisions editors made regarding their assignments or their copy, and you can cheer at their breakthroughs. Through this book, their lives are now part of the historical record of our profession.

And there is a history to record.

Women made modest breakthroughs in Washington in the 1930s when Eleanor Roosevelt decided only women could cover her news conferences. That First Lady made news so every newspaper and wire service — and there were several more then — had to hire or keep at least one woman on the payroll despite Depression layoffs.

World War II opened the door to countless Rosie the Reporters, who found there was nothing magical about doing this job — they had the talent — but something magical about the work itself. Getting their start at United Press during the war, for example, were Helen Thomas, later its White House bureau chief; Eileen Shanahan, who went on to become a premier economics correspondent for the *New York Times;* Charlotte Moulton, who covered the U.S. Supreme Court; and Marj Paxson, who later became a Gannett newspaper publisher.

In the 1950s and early 1960s, the same kind of women who had been welcome at the news desk during World War II could no longer get by the front desk. A few pioneers — Jean Taylor, Betsy Wade Boylan, Nan Robertson, and Dorothy Gilliam among them — started their careers, but it was not until the 1960s and 1970s, when the civil rights movement begat the women's movement, that hiring practices really changed.

So what? As more and more women entered the newsroom, they saw countless stories that had gone uncovered, especially because more and more women were entering the work force in general and changing its face. The women in the newsroom covered the women's movement seriously for the first time. They wrote about women in politics. They spotted the lack of child care as a problem. They highlighted the difficulty poor women have in getting prenatal care. They could write a column or an editorial from the perspective of a mother. They gave women a place in the news.

The next task ahead for women is to secure top editing jobs in some reasonable proportion to their numbers in the journalistic work force. They aren't there yet and won't be until more publishers and editors recognize the benefits that diversity brings to their newspapers. They aren't there, but they are knocking on the doors.

Only with many sacrifices did women as a whole get to the point where some among them could have the luxury or the opportunity to write the stories in this collection. The women not represented in this book who sued major newspapers and news organizations risked their careers so that others who followed might flourish. I want to dedicate at least my part of this effort to those who were brave beyond belief, to those women who worked alone in all-male newsrooms, to those who felt the thrill of the story was enough despite all odds. We—these writers and I—stand on their shoulders.

Kay Mills
Editorial writer, *Los Angeles Times,*
and author of *A Place in the News: From the
Women's Pages to the Front Page*

PREFACE
Why and How We Did It

When I landed my first newspaper job, I wore the title "Food Editor." It didn't matter that I didn't know how to cook or that my real love was covering the newsier side of life.

The features editor, a pudgy, middle-aged man, tagged nicknames onto the women in his department. For some unknown reason, I was dubbed Little Bear. The editor made a ritual of pulling a bottle of aspirin out of his desk drawer and pretending to dispense birth control pills. "Don't want these gals to miss any work," he would say to reporters within earshot.

He would snicker; the male reporters would snicker. The women in the department did not.

It didn't occur to us that this behavior was blatantly sexist and that we should have taken a stand. After all, we were lucky to have a job in the newsroom.

The year was 1966.

Twenty years later, many of us had moved off the women's pages onto the front pages with stories about prison violence and misappropriation of funds in the governor's office. Some of us covered the legislature and the police beat. Some of us won Pulitzer prizes or worked on Pulitzer teams.

The generation of women who followed bowled their way into NFL locker rooms and into the thick of Olympic coverage; they roamed the Third World back alleys to document the human condition, from brothels in Bangkok to Iraqi battlefields.

They forced corrupt politicians out of office and helped to put drug dealers behind bars. They wrote stories about wife and child abuse; about AIDS in the heartland and pregnant women ordered into caesareans against their will.

Yet, check the winners' lists of the American Society of Newspaper Editors (ASNE) newswriting competition prior to 1990 and the message is clear—it's not easy to spot the great women at work in America's newsrooms.

This book started the way many journalistic projects do—with the feeling that something was amiss. As professors at the University of Missouri School of Journalism back then, Virginia Young and I were seeking a textbook for a reporting class. The Best Newspaper Writing series, featuring winners from the ASNE competition, appeared an excellent choice. It is beautifully edited; the writing is superb.

A crucial element was missing. No women were featured among the winners in 1986, the edition we were considering. Maybe next year.

But the trend continued. In 1987, 1988, and 1989 the book remained an exclusive all-male club. Since the contest began in 1978, the tally of winners stands at males, 43; females, 7.

Anthony Day, who ran the ASNE competition from 1986 to 1988, believes the situation soon will be remedied. Day predicts that as the number of top women in America's newsrooms increases, so will the number of ASNE winners.

"The men have been at it longer and more men are entered in the contest," said Day from his office at the *Los Angeles Times* where he is editorial page director. "In the future there will be no problem."

Day singled out two-time ASNE winner Greta Tilley of the *Greensboro News and Record* as "one of the best newspaper writers in the country." Tilley, who won ASNE writing awards in 1983 and 1985, was the last female listed among top winners until 1990.

There are other points to consider: maybe women aren't routinely assigned to beats where they are likely to do hard-hitting, prize-winning work; maybe editors, the majority of them men, aren't entering stories by female reporters as often as they enter those written by male staffers.

But those are problems for another time.

Nationwide, 66 percent of all journalism graduates are women; it seemed only fair to us that the work of top female journalists should be showcased in the classroom.

We began asking colleagues, Who are some of the top women writers in the country? Usually, the names of the pioneers surfaced. Among them: Flora Lewis, foreign affairs columnist, the *New York Times;* Ellen Goodman, columnist, the *Boston Globe;* Helen Thomas, reporter, UPI; Edna Buchanan, crime reporter, the *Miami*

Herald; Mary Hargrove, Director of the investigative team and managing editor of the *Tulsa Tribune.*

We decided to go after those who had achieved excellence but were not known nationally.

First, we set the criteria. We considered whether they held a major prize, like the Pulitzer; had a major fellowship like Harvard's Neiman; played a leadership role in a national media organization; or have been groundbreakers.

We wrote to the managing editors of 25 major newspapers, asking for suggestions. We networked with journalism educators and researchers, with directors of professional organizations within the industry, and with other women journalists.

Out of the six-month search 150 names surfaced from newspapers like *Newsday* and the *Chicago Tribune;* the *Pittsburgh Press* and the *Seattle Times;* the *Miami Herald* and *Boston Globe.*

The first round of letters went out only to women who met one of the four criteria. The response rate was close to 70 percent. The women sent samples of their work and letters encouraging continuation of the project.

A panel of five journalists advised us on the final choices. Included on the panel were Deborah Howell, formerly vice-president and editor, *St. Paul Pioneer Press Dispatch* and currently Washington Bureau Chief, Newhouse News Service; Kay Mills, editorial writer for the *Los Angeles Times* and author of *A Place in the News;* Michael Gartner, president of NBC news; Carl Sessions Stepp, senior editor, the *Washington Journalism Review* and journalism professor at the University of Maryland; and Carolyn Matalene, English professor, South Carolina University.

We supplied the panel with a set of criteria, including such questions as: Is the story idea fresh? Is the focus clear? Is the reporting solid? The writing compelling? Is the language alive, human, precise? Does the story reveal human character and leave an impression on the reader? Panelists did not judge entries from their own papers.

Based on their consensus rankings, we chose nine women as the mainstay of the book. All the interviews except one were conducted in person and lasted an average of four hours. The tapes were edited heavily for clarity and brevity. In some cases, the questions were re-composed.

We set out to discover what beats those women cover; what kinds of stories they write. We wondered whether being a woman held them back and how they coped. Or was being female, in some instances, an advantage in their career? Have they encountered sexism? If so, what kind?

Do they feel they have to work harder than their male colleagues to succeed? How did they rise to stardom in a male-dominated industry?

We plan for "Women on Deadline" to become an on-going project to be periodically updated as new female stars emerge.

Sherry Ricchiardi

ACKNOWLEDGMENTS

We wish to thank Don Fry of the Poynter Institute, who took time in the beginning to hear us out and remained a guiding light throughout the project, and Associate Dean for Graduate Studies Ed Lambeth, who offered encouragement and a grant from the University of Missouri School of Journalism to fund research and travel for the interviews.

Our prestigious panel of five offered insight and professional savvy in helping us make the final selections. We are grateful to Deborah Howell, Carolyn Matalene, Kay Mills, Michael Gartner, and Carl Sessions Stepp for the countless hours they spent reading stories submitted by the women and providing invaluable feedback.

Two University of Missouri journalism students, Jennifer Cobb and Joël Brenner, assisted with typing, phone calls, and compiling information. Leonard Fischer, a student at the Indiana University School of Journalism, served as consultant for computing services.

Lastly we are grateful to our husbands, Frank Folwell and Joe Holt, for their constant support during this project, and to 18-month-old Zachary Young Holt, who patiently accompanied his mother on the interviews.

INTRODUCTION

Virginia Young berated me for an hour while we sat on a sofa in the Indiana University Student Union. She wanted me, as the editor of *Best Newspaper Writing*, to justify the virtual exclusion of women from the winners of the American Society of Newspaper Editors Distinguished Writing Awards. I lamely defended myself by pointing out that editors do the nominating, that neither I nor the Poynter Institute have anything to do with the judging, that the juries include some women, and so on, the usual litany of a sexist world and profession. What could I say when men have won 43 out of 50 prizes in a contest open to all journalists, regardless of sex?

The second hour went better, as she picked my brain about an idea of redress, a *Best Newspaper Writing* exclusively for women that she was working on with Sherry Ricchiardi. I endorsed the project enthusiastically, not just to get myself off the hot spot, but also because I consider myself a feminist. What could serve the purpose better than an anthology of selections by women picked by women, framed by women, and edited by women? Well, I can think of one better solution: more women winning the ASNE contest, but that's another campaign.

Such a volume transcends regret and recrimination. Such a collection deserves praise and celebration, not only of these women and of all women journalists, but also of good newswriting itself.

What do we mean by "good newswriting?" First and foremost, good newswriting must meet our most basic professional standards: accuracy, balance, completeness, and fairness. Second but equally important, good newswriting always results from good reporting.

Good newswriting focuses on people and lets the reader see them. We need look no further than Alice Steinbach's "A Boy of Unusual Vision" to find this quality, as in this scene:

> Calvin can read and spell and do fractions and follow the classroom work in his specially prepared braille books. He is smart and he can do everything the rest of his class can do. Except see.

"What's the next word, Calvin?" Mrs. Jackson asks.

"Eleven," he says, reading from his braille textbook.

"Now tell us how to spell it—without looking back at the book!" she says quickly, causing Calvin's fingers to fly way from the forbidden word.

"E-l-e-v-e-n," he spells out easily.

"Letting the reader see" does not require long, literary descriptions. Steinbach lets us "see" Calvin with a few choice details, mostly sounds. She frames those details in clear, simple, precise, bright sentences. She takes the reader to the scene without the reader noticing the journey.

Steinbach keeps her focus on the subject, so the reader does not notice her style. We glimpse that style in her lead, which begins: "First, the eyes: . . ." We know instinctively that a master writer has taken us in hand for a journey through complex, even hazardous materials. Her first three words set a tone of assurance, and we trust her voice. That voice releases us in the kicker: " 'Well,' said the father, trying to comfort the mother, 'we'll do what we have to do and Calvin will be fine.' He is. And so are they." And so are we.

Good newswriters transcend mere recording by explaining things to readers. Steinbach follows the math scene with this reflection:

> It all seems so simple, the ease with which Calvin follows along, the manner in which his blindness has been accommodated. But it's deceptively simple. The amount of work that has gone into getting Calvin to this point—the number of teachers, vision specialists and mobility instructors, and the array of special equipment is staggering.

Steinbach could let the reader just float along in the great American myth of the heroic handicapped, but she explains the immense support system behind Calvin's apparently effortless adaptations. And she explains it by letting us see more people.

Good newswriting surprises the reader, respects the reader, and courageously carries the reader into new experiences, as in this extraordinary passage:

> It's spring vacation and Calvin is out in the alley behind his house riding his bike, a serious looking, black and silver two-wheeler. "Stay behind me," he shouts to his friend Kellie Bass, who's

furiously pedaling her bike down the one-block stretch of alley where Calvin is allowed to bicycle.

Now: Try to imagine riding a bike without being able to see where you're going. Without even knowing what an "alley" looks like. Try to imagine how you navigate a space that has no visual boundaries, that exists only in your head. And then try to imagine what Calvin is feeling as he pedals his bike in that space, whooping for joy as the air rushes past him on either side.

The reader gasps at the idea of a blind boy who can ride a bike at all, only to be drawn into an empathetic attempt to capture blindness for all sighted persons. Yet this tour de force does not tell us too much, leaving the details and emotions to our imaginations.

Finally, good newswriting empowers the reader. It gives readers the information they need to live and to make decisions, and it shows them models of conduct and hope in a harsh world. The reader will not accept such models if they seem too goody-goody, and Steinbach balances the essential goodness of her characters with their stresses, labor and sorrowful memory.

I could track these characteristics of good newswriting through all nine writers we celebrate here, but I leave that to you, the reader, female or male. Study their dedication and their work and their craft, and learn from them.

Don Fry
Associate Director
Poynter Institute for Media Studies
St. Petersburg, Florida

WOMEN ON DEADLINE

1 Lucy Morgan

DEADLINE/INVESTIGATIVE ■ *St. Petersburg Times*

AS an investigative reporter, Lucy Morgan specialized in covering drug smuggling, public corruption, and organized crime. The hard-hitting stories she wrote sparked threats against members of her family and some of her key sources. They also sparked a murder contract on her life.

In 1985 she was rewarded with a Pulitzer Prize—the first woman to win a Pulitzer in the investigative category. That honor, shared with Jack Reed of the *St. Petersburg Times,* was for a series of stories that led to the firing of the Pasco County sheriff and his cronies.

In 1982 she was Pulitzer runner-up for local reporting on drug smugglers operating in Dixie and Taylor counties. Her stories caught the attention of federal officials. The result: More than 200 indictments.

Morgan, 50, moved on to become *Times* bureau chief in Tallahassee and continues to be a reporter. She grew up in Hattiesburg, Mississippi, and graduated from Pasco-Hernando Community College. She has been with the *Times* for 23 years.

In 1973 Morgan was sentenced to eight months in jail for refusing to reveal confidential sources. The Florida Supreme Court later overturned her sentence, creating a landmark press-freedom case that still stands.

Following is an investigative piece on the Pasco County Sheriff's Department, part of the Pulitzer package, and two stories written on deadline.

SOME DEPUTIES HAD RECORDS BEFORE BEING HIRED

NEW PORT RICHEY—Some Pasco County sheriff's deputies know about law enforcement from both sides of the badge. Before joining the force, several had arrest records. Some had been convicted.

And some did not tell the truth about their criminal records when they applied to work for the Pasco County Sheriff's Department.

For its part, the department's background checks were often so superficial that the false statements of the would-be officers were not caught. Of those people, some were hired even though they had been arrested and convicted of crimes within Pasco County in the last 10 years.

A *St. Petersburg Times* investigation shows that today, among the 195 sworn officers serving the department run by Pasco Sheriff John Short:

— At least one in every eight officers has an arrest record — and the ratio could be higher.

— More than half of those officers with arrest records signed statements falsely swearing that they had never been arrested or charged with a crime, or they did not correctly list all their arrests.

— At least one in every 13 officers was convicted of a misdemeanor before joining the force.

These facts raise questions about the integrity of some of the people who enforce the law in Pasco County and of the administrative ability of the sheriff's department to meet its own standards, which say that deputies must keep their lives "untainted as an example to all."

State Attorney James T. Russell must prosecute the cases made by Pasco deputies. When told the results of the *Times* review of Pasco Sheriff's Department personnel, Russell said: "I don't think that's right. I think the sheriff's office owes a duty to the county to be certain that the people who are the protectors of our society are qualified to do so. If what you are telling me is correct, the sheriff has an obligation to explain what he is doing."

On Feb. 14 and several times since, the *Times* asked Sheriff Short for an interview so that he could answer questions about his department and tell his side of the story.

Short refused. He asked a reporter to "put her questions in writing. I will respond in writing to the questions I wish to answer." The *Times* submitted 29 detailed questions to Short Wednesday morning. He refused to answer any of them. Because he has forbidden his employees to talk with the press, the *Times* asked for interviews with those to be mentioned in the stories to be printed today. A spokesman for Short said none of the people wanted to talk.

'GOOD MORAL CHARACTER'

Before hiring anyone to be a law enforcement officer, the state demands that a police or sheriff's department certify that the applicant has been subject to a "thorough background investigation" and is "satisfied" that the person is of "good moral character."

The Pasco County Sheriff's Department made just such a certification when it hired:

— A former Monroe County deputy to work in the department's canine unit in 1982. The man had been charged with stealing the police dog he intended to use in Pasco County. The charges against him were dropped the day he started work after he agreed to pay for the dog. He is no longer a Pasco deputy.

— An auxiliary deputy who had been charged with armed robbery in neighboring Hillsborough County. The charges against him were dropped after he testified against a codefendant who received a 45-year prison term. The deputy, who is still on the force, did not tell the truth about his prior arrest record in a sworn affidavit filed with Florida's Police Standards and Training Commission.

An arrest or a conviction on most misdemeanor charges does not automatically exclude an applicant from consideration. But the state wants to know about it. (A felony conviction is grounds for exclusion as is conviction on a misdemeanor involving "moral turpitude.")

The *Times* review found no Pasco sheriff's personnel with felony convictions.

In addition to their police records, applicants are asked about such things as whether they have ever been fired from a job or have a history of drug or alcohol abuse.

Applicants must swear their answers are true.

But law enforcement agencies aren't supposed to take their word for it.

Everything from the applicant's age and physical condition to their fingerprints and police records is to be checked. Written explanations are required when, for instance, an applicant acknowledges having been arrested or fired from a job. The state suggests that agencies look at all available records, interview neighbors and associates and take "such other means necessary and proper to complete its investigation."

Then, somebody from the agency must certify that this was done.

BACKGROUND CHECKS

The *Times* has found, however, that on numerous occasions, the background checks conducted by the Pasco County Sheriff's Department met neither the letter nor the spirit of the state requirements.

Some applicants were apparently subject to no background checks whatsoever.

One of those apparently was John T. Moorman, the millionaire part-time deputy who has helped Short profit from a series of real estate transactions.

Short signed a statement advising the state that he had conducted a background investigation and could vouch for Moorman's good moral character. But personnel files in Short's office include no background report.

The *Times* talked with Sheriff Gerry Coleman of Pinellas County, where Moorman was registered as an auxiliary deputy from Sept. 14, 1976 to June 16, 1977.

Coleman said Moorman was forced to resign after he abused his authority as a reserve deputy during a confrontation with Moorman's girlfriend and another man.

In 1980, Ronald Roppolo signed affidavits swearing that he had never been arrested or convicted of a crime. He was hired. The department's background check did not turn up two misdemeanor convictions in Pasco County, one of them just three months earlier.

In 1982, Rick Parrillo swore on his application that he had never been arrested. His initial state certification was rejected when an arrest record was discovered. Parrillo then said that since the charges against him were later dismissed, he thought he had not been arrested.

While Sheriff Short is not talking, spokesmen for other departments say they take the background checks very seriously—especially when it comes to an applicant's arrest record.

THE IMPORTANCE OF ARREST RECORDS

Just because somebody was arrested for a crime doesn't, of course, mean that he did it.

But speaking in the context of evaluating potential law enforcement officers, police officials point out that the absence of a criminal conviction may not mean that the person was innocent. Sometimes a person escapes a conviction by pleading no contest and having a judge withhold a formal adjudication of guilt.

Other times criminal charges are dropped by prosecutors for reasons that have nothing to do with a person's guilt or innocence.

"Checking arrest records is a vital part of determining whether a man should be a police officer," says Tampa Police Chief Robert L. Smith.

"We check all arrests," says Pinellas County Sheriff's Capt. W. H. Hagans. "We're not holding something against those that experimented once with marijuana, but we're looking at theft, heavy use of drugs, violent crimes."

And what if the background check turns up an arrest the applicant didn't admit to?

"We think that is a serious problem," Hagans said. In such cases, the applicant is invited in to discuss the false answer. Sometimes it can be explained away, he said, but a deliberate lie would disqualify the person from being employed.

Hagans also said, "I had a fellow in here recently tell me he didn't remember being arrested. Come on now, it's hard for me to believe that he didn't remember being handcuffed and fingerprinted and locked up."

A law enforcement officer can lose his state certification if it is found that he gave a false answer about his background on his application.

In addition, Florida law makes it a misdemeanor to knowingly give a false written statement to a public agency.

In Pasco County, several men with arrest records have been hired as sheriff's deputies even though the department discovered the men swore falsely that they had no previous arrests.

A number of other Florida sheriff's departments questioned by the *Times* do extensive background checks that include psychological examinations, agility tests, polygraph tests and interviews with neighbors. None of these were part of the Pasco department's routine background checks in files examined by the *Times*.

THE DONAHUE CASE

Last spring, the *St. Petersburg Times* disclosed that Sheriff Short never checked the background of the man he placed in charge of the department's organized crime unit.

When the *Times* checked the credentials of former Sheriff's Capt. Joe Donahue, it discovered that Donahue had falsely claimed to be a 20-year veteran of the New York police department.

Donahue never worked for the department. Instead, he had been a plumber in Queens, N.Y. before moving to Florida.

Donahue was indicted on racketeering charges last year with alleged Mafia leader Santo Trafficante and others. Donahue was found dead, with a gunshot wound in his head, last April.

It was the Donahue case that led the *Times* to review the records of hundreds of men and women who carry guns and badges in Pasco County.

A *Times* reporter reviewed the records of more than 500 current and former deputies, corrections officers and auxiliary deputies hired by the Pasco County Sheriff's Department since John Short became sheriff in 1977. Those records are on file at the State Criminal Justice Standards and Training Commission in Tallahassee. The *Times* also obtained from the sheriff's department the personnel files of about 200 employees.

The *Times* examined the employees' statements about their arrest records and compared them with public records in a number of Florida counties. While the *Times* review was far more limited than a thorough background investigation, it does show that:

— At least 40 of the sworn personnel hired by Short had arrest records for misdemeanors and felonies at the time they were hired. The charges ranged from gambling and petty larceny to armed robbery. Twelve applicants, eight of them still on the force, had been arrested by the Pasco County Sheriff's Department, and a number of others had arrest records in neighboring counties. Six of the 40 officers with arrest records left the department while the *Times* was examining their backgrounds.

— Nineteen of the 40 did not tell the truth about their arrest records on sworn applications on file in the department, or on affidavits filed with the state, or both.

— Twenty of the 40 were convicted or pleaded guilty to the charge for which they were arrested. The disposition of the charges against four others could not be determined.

There are about 195 sworn officers in the 360-person Pasco County Sheriff's Department. Of those 195 officers, the *Times'* investigation shows that on the force today are: at least 25 with previous arrest records; at least 14 who swore falsely on their applications that they had never been arrested or charged with a crime, or they failed to list all their arrests; at least 15 with previous misdemeanor convictions. (The actual figures could be much higher. The *Times* checked the arrest records of only about half the sworn personnel, and the check included records available in only a few Florida counties.)

The *Times'* review found that some of the references questioned during the background investigation done by the sheriff's department were the fathers, brothers or other relatives of the applicants. The department sometimes ignored a state requirement to check with all other law enforcement agencies that employed the officer.

In one instance, Roger Michels, the administrator who conducted many of the recent background investigations, was listed as a reference by an applicant. Michels listed himself on a document spelling out the results of the applicants reference check. In effect, he interviewed himself. On the same document were the names of two of Michels' close friends. Based on those references and others, he hired the son of a third friend.

The problems at the Pasco County Sheriff's Department are not limited to personnel.

Sheriff Short has placed much of the real authority within the department in the hands of his former secretary, Donna Lewis, and Michels, a longtime friend and campaign worker.

When Short took office in 1977 he hired two respected police administrators, Maj. Gil Thivener, director of operations, and Maj. Lee Henley, director of administrative services. Both men are still there, but often take a back seat when it comes to decision-making.

Mrs. Lewis, director of administration, and Michels, deputy director of administration, have no other law enforcement background or training. Short's increasing reliance on them has irritated some employees.

Short keeps a tight rein on the department and has threatened employees with polygraph tests and dismissal if they talk to outsiders, especially reporters.

Short's control of the department is bolstered by the fact that Florida law allows sheriffs to hire and fire their deputies at will.

Sheriff's deputies are exempt from the Policeman's Bill of Rights, a state law that gives municipal officers certain basic rights when they are confronted with adverse personnel decisions or dismissal.

TAX DEAL CUT OVER PIZZA AND BEER AT MYSTERY TOWN HOUSE

TALLAHASSEE — Florida's best and brightest leaders reached final accord on a giant tax deal over pizza and beer in a secret late night session a few miles away from the State Capitol.

A day later none of them could remember where the town house apartment was where they met or who owned it. But most of them recalled sealing the deal with a few drinks at Studebaker's, a local watering hole a short distance away.

Senate President John Vogt, House Speaker Jon Mills and Lt. Gov. Bobby Brantley could all remember the pizza and beer they shared, but they had trouble remembering a few of the other details.

Vogt, Mills, Brantley and about 15 other legislators met until midnight Wednesday before agreeing on the biggest single tax increase in Florida history.

"It was in a town house," said Brantley. "The owner wasn't there, they said we were just supposed to lock the door when we left."

"It weren't mine," said House Appropriations Chairman Sam Bell, D-Ormond Beach.

"I don't know whose town house it was," said Mills. "But we had pepperoni and extra cheese on the pizza. It was just a happening. It wasn't a planned event."

"There was a map, and they said follow the map," said Sen. Robert Crawford, D-Winter Haven.

"Somebody gave me directions," said House Majority Leader Ron Silver, D-Miami. "I don't remember who, it must have been Mills that called me."

Silver brought the first round of pizza, the ones with the pepperoni and extra cheese.

"I don't know whose town house it was," Vogt said. "I won't tell you where it was. We might want to meet there again."

Vogt denied reports that the town house was owned by lobbyist Prentiss Mitchell, saying it was provided by "another interest."

Rules Committee Chairman Dempsey Barron said, "people met everywhere and talked everywhere."

"Finally there was a spontaneous gathering together," Barron said. "Then we went to a juke joint."

"I don't know where I was," said House Rules Chairman Carl Carpenter, D-Plant City. "They told me how to get there, and people just drifted in and out."

Before the night was over, between 15 and 20 legislators met with Brantley and J. M. "Mac" Stipanovich, chief of staff for Gov. Bob Martinez. Brantley and Stipanovich arrived in tuxedos after being called away from a reception at the governor's mansion.

"I've contracted a severe memory loss," said Stipanovich when asked Thursday. "It's probably a CIA safe house that we have access to. I don't hardly even remember being there."

"I can't remember who was there or where it was," said Senate Appropriations Chairman Jim Scott, R-Fort Lauderdale. "All I know is, it was too close to Studebaker's because I wound up there when it was over."

Barron said he saw a sign that said Studebaker's "and my car was choking up so I thought I could get it fixed there. It did run better after I left or I didn't notice as much."

House Finance and Tax Committee Chairman Winston "Bud" Gardner, D-Titusville, said he was about to sit down to dinner at the Governor's Club when Mills summoned him to the meeting. When he arrived, Gardner said about six others were already there.

Thursday night about 8, before darkness had fallen across Tallahassee, Martinez had signed the new tax bill into law. He did it on the sun porch at the governor's mansion, rejecting a plea from photographers who asked to be present.

LOBBYISTS OWN TOWN HOUSE USED BY LEGISLATORS

TALLAHASSEE—The mysterious Tallahassee town house that became the site of a historic sales tax agreement this week is home to some of Florida's best-known sugar lobbyists.

The apartment at Holland Townhouses is owned by the U.S. Sugar Corp. of Clewiston and is now occupied by corporate lobbyist Robert E. Coker. Another U.S. Sugar lobbyist, Robert C. Lee, has also lived there.

Senate President John Vogt admitted Friday that it was Coker's apartment after a *Times* reporter traced its location and ownership. More than 15 legislative leaders met at the town house Wednesday night to hammer out a final deal on a giant tax increase that breezed through the Legislature the next day.

All day Thursday, the legislators who attended the late-night session at Coker's apartment on Holland Drive insisted that they did not know where the apartment was or who owned it.

"I really didn't know who owned it," Vogt said Friday. "All I know is that I found the key under the doormat."

Vogt said he had aide Clint Smawley find a place where the legislators could meet. Smawley also was told to provide maps for those who planned to attend.

"I didn't know whose place it was until I got there," Vogt said.

The meeting, like many a legislative deal-making session, was held behind closed doors without scrutiny of the press or public. In passing laws that require all other governmental officials to conduct their business in public, the Legislature exempted its own meetings. Thus such private sessions are legal.

The mystery town house became the subject of many jokes Thursday as legislators dodged questions from reporters about the circumstances that led to the tax agreement.

House Speaker Jon Mills, Lt. Gov. Bobby Brantley and others denied knowing who lived at the apartment and said they could not remember its exact address.

J. M. "Mac" Stipanovich, chief of staff for Gov. Bob Martinez, even suggested that the apartment might be a "CIA safe house."

Although none of the legislators could remember where the apartment was, they all remembered eating pepperoni pizza with extra cheese and drinking cold beer as they reached agreement. Later, the group adjourned to Studebaker's, a '50s nightclub not far from the apartment.

Coker and Lee couldn't be reached for comment Friday. U.S. Sugar has been a frequent donor to House and Senate campaigns. In 1986, the corporation gave $19,250 to legislators and $4,500 to Martinez.

The sugar company apparently was not affected by the change in the sales tax law.

A Visit with Lucy Morgan

Sherry Ricchiardi: *How did you get into journalism?*

Lucy Morgan: It was a total accident. I was married to a high school football coach and living in Crystal River, Florida. I had three children by the age of 22, which was not too smart.

A local correspondent for the *Ocala Star Banner* was killed in a traffic accident, and they were looking for someone to replace her. An editor bumped into me one day and asked if I wanted the job. I said, "I've never done anything like that." The editor said, "Well, try it."

I needed the money, so I did.

Q. *You had no formal training?*

A. I have never had a journalism course. I signed up for one once, but the dean signed me out of the class. He said my experience exceeded that of the instructor. He was afraid the instructor, who had a master's degree but no experience, would be intimidated.

Q. *Tell me about your career.*

A. I worked as a reporter for the *Ocala Star Banner* from 1965–1968, covering general news and government in Citrus and Levy counties. I did some chicken-dinner-type stuff like civic clubs and womens' social groups, but I never did those kinds of stories exclusively.

I began working part-time for the *St. Petersburg Times* in mid-1967 while still at the *Star Banner.* I was in the middle of a divorce and needed both incomes. In early 1968 I became a full-time staff writer for the *Times.*

My children were 4, 5, and 7 years old when I divorced. I married Richard Morgan a year later. He was editor of the *Times* regional edition for Pasco County.

Q. *Who served as your mentors along the way?*

A. My husband has been the dominant mentor in my life. I worked for him during my early years at the *Times.* He has a master's degree from Northwestern University. He had all the education I didn't have.

He was a very meticulous editor; a nut on accuracy. I've seen him make 10 phone calls to confirm the spelling of the name Brown. He helped me learn to write a cleaner story. He retired after 30 years with the *Times.*

Q. *Did you have any female mentors?*

A. There were very few women doing hard news when I came into this business and most of them were stringers rather than full-time. They worked for weeklies or small editions of bigger newspapers. At least, that's what I saw in Florida around 1965.

There were no women news editors back then. From time to time we'd have females in the second or third tier of editing positions, but I can't remember any women in those years who directly supervised me.

Q. *Did that bother you?*

A. Not really. The men never treated me badly. The *Times* has a good record in dealing with women. They were good about putting women in positions like I was in. I never felt discriminated against at the *Times*.

On many occasions I've been the only female in the room. There were times when the public officials, reporters, editors, law enforcement officers—which was everyone I dealt with—would all be male. That hasn't been nearly as true in recent years.

Q. *Have you ever experienced sexism on the job?*

A. In my younger years women were likely to get propositioned, particularly by law enforcement officers. Oddly enough, I remember an incident back in 1966 when I was covering a story in a small Florida town where a 7-year-old had disappeared into a wooded area.

I rode out with the search party into the swamp only to return and be chewed out by their wives. They felt it was dreadful that I disappeared into the woods with six men. I was in rural Florida in an era when women didn't do those things.

Q. *Has being a female reporter ever worked to your advantage?*

A. Yes, it has. When I worked on the drug stories in Dixie and Taylor counties, I spent a lot of time in rural areas. These counties all are chauvinistic and racist; people there tend not to view a woman as a threat.

I was able to do a tremendous amount of research before anybody realized what I was about. They assumed I was somebody's secretary when I first started looking through courthouse records.

They underestimated me because I was female. That almost always works to my advantage. I would rather have them underestimate the impact of what I might write than be afraid of me.

Being female has kept me from being slugged on several occasions.

Q. *Are there any other advantages?*

A. A lot of people are more willing to talk to women; I'm not sure why. Women are less suspicious of questions posed by another woman. They are more likely to let me in the door. I believe we are less threatening. A lot of men, particularly southern men, would rather talk to a woman.

Q. *Are there disadvantages to being a woman in this business?*

A. Well, for one thing, it's hard to duck into a men's room in pursuit of a public official. One state legislator held a press conference in a men's bathroom to be cute. He thought the female reporters wouldn't come in. At first, I was the only one who walked though the door, then the other women followed. It became quite an event.

I don't play golf with the guys; I don't go hunting with them. My male counterparts have more access to the go-out-in-the-woods-and-get-dirty type of affairs. It's harder for me to do man talk. It may be harder in the South than in other areas of the country. That built-in male chauvinism has hung on longer here.

Q. *Have you made any personal sacrifices for your career?*

A. Just the same kinds of things that most working women have to deal with. I remember being called to cover a fire at 3 A.M. and taking three children with me when I was a single parent. The only other choice was not to go.

I've worked hard news all of my career, which means I'm subject to be thrown into whatever wind is blowing by at the time. I think women reporters sacrifice more than men do in the quality of time they spend with their children, friends, and other family members.

Q. *When you talk to other women reporters do you notice any common threads?*

A. Almost every one of them is struggling with something outside of the job. That's more common to women because more falls to them, such as child care and care of elderly parents. I'm responsible for a mother in a nursing home. A lot of men don't seem to have those responsibilities. I've often said, "What I really need is a wife."

Q. *How do you handle that?*

A. My husband contributes dramatically. Since he retired from the *Times* and took a job with the state, he has regular hours, so he has assumed most of the household work. He's the neat freak in our home anyway.

Q. *Any other common concerns you hear from female reporters?*

A. A lot of them are torn about how to establish relationships, particularly with men, in an arena where they are trying to do hard-hitting reporting. This is a phenomenon I see more now than I used to.

Some female reporters are hung up on the ethical question of whether they should date someone they might come in contact with for a story, such as a legislator or a lobbyist. I see a lot of women anguishing over that. That's why a lot of us marry within the news industry.

Q. *Do you have any regrets about giving so much of yourself to a career?*

A. Absolutely not. I can't envision myself doing anything else. I've had offers from political types to do public relations or to work as an aide, but that really never interested me.

There might come a time when I want to get out of the daily grind and back into long-range projects.

Q. *Do you ever use feminine wiles to gain information?*

A. Over the years I have flattered people shamelessly and gotten information out of them. I call up a high-ranking official and flippantly say, "How's the best looking law enforcement officer in Florida today?" He knows I'm kidding, but he's flattered by it anyway.

At times, I'm pretty frank with these people. I say, "Look, you don't have to be a horse's ass. You can be straight with me." I don't think I could get away with that if I wasn't female.

Q. *Do you feel women bring a special dimension to reporting or to the newsroom in general?*

A. Most of us have dealt with some form of discrimination. That helps us to be more sensitive than men to discrimination blacks or members of ethnic groups might experience.

Women seem more sensitive to the nuances of things; we are more intuitive. We pick up quicker on what's going on in peoples' lives.

Q. *Don Fry of the Poynter Institute coined a term "phallic journalism" to describe the macho nature of newsrooms—tough-talking editors bossing people around. Have you experienced that type of an editor?*

A. I've seen only one female I would put in that category, but I've seen a number of males. They are not sensitive to what's going on around them. If their secretary's husband just died, they wouldn't know it.

I can think of one editor in particular who fits that category. He has temper tantrums and screams at people. He never speaks to his secretaries when he comes in in the morning. He simply lacks consideration and an appreciation for the ordinary niceties of life.

Q. *How are women editors different?*

A. Most of the women editors I know are aware of their employees and their families. They know whether they have problems or not.

If I'm going to ask my secretary to stay late, I consider whether she has to pick up her child at day care.

A lot of men never think of things like that. They get caught up in getting where they're going and damn what they step on along the way.

Q. *Have you had to work harder than your male counterparts to get ahead?*

A. Some of us joke that we have to be smarter and work harder than any man to reach the same point. Fortunately being smarter is not that difficult.

Women my age may have felt it more than the women behind me. If we have gotten somewhere in a male-dominated world, we have done it because we were willing to work harder.

Q. *Do you see any differences in young female reporters today?*

A. Alot of them simply take it for granted that they are as good as any man. Younger women often come up after they hear me speak on a panel — and the panels usually are all male except for me — and say they don't want to do the kind of journalism I do. That's a sad commentary. Many younger women are shying away from hard-edged news.

Q. *Do you have any insight as to why?*

A. After I was sentenced to jail for not revealing confidential sources, a lot of women told me they couldn't do that kind of reporting. They admitted they were afraid of jail. Women often are squeamish about going up against authority. In my job, I do that all the time.

Q. *Have you ever felt your life was in danger because of the kinds of stories you worked on?*

A. Oddly enough, my editors worried about me a lot. After the first drug-smuggling series ran, they insisted on sending somebody with me each time I went to Dixie County, which I thought was pure bullshit. Hell, the person with me wound up being scared, I wasn't.

I've taken refuge in the fact that: (A) I am female and I think people will be less likely to hurt me; (B) I am going to be prudent about what I do.

Q. *What do you mean by prudent?*

A. During the drug series, for instance, sources asked me to meet them at midnight in remote locations. One guy wanted me to meet him at midnight on the Steinhatchee River bridge in Dixie County. I said, "Look buddy, I'll meet you at noon on the courthouse steps any day." That's sort of the way we ended up meeting.

I've met a lot of strange people in strange places, but I've always tried to keep it in public, in broad daylight, and on my turf.

Once as I came out of a restaurant, a group of good old boys lined up in a circle and twirled the barrels of their guns for a little display as I walked by. I guess it was meant to intimidate me.

Most of the threats came during the Pasco sheriff's series and a lot were secondhand. Deputies would call and say, "We understand somebody's going to put a bomb in your car."

At times, my daughter-in-law and grandchild were the subject of threats. That pissed me off. This was going on during 1983 and 1984.

Q. *And that's the series that lead to the Pulitzer in 1985?*

A. Yes, it was.

Q. *Can we talk about the obstacles you had to overcome with the investigation of the Pasco County Sheriff's Department?*

A. Sheriff Short and his supporters tried to stop people from talking to me. They called other sheriffs and state agencies and urged them not to cooperate. In most instances it backfired and made people more willing to talk.

I walked into the sheriff's department in Key West to do some background checks on Short's employees and one of the top officers came up and said, "Are you Lucy?" I said, "Yea, why?" He said, "Well, I just want to meet the lady who is terrorizing sheriffs."

He explained that some guy named Short called and suggested they not let me see any records. The deputy said, "What would you like. We'll give it all to you."

Q. *How did you find out about the murder contract on your life?*

A. I knew for a fact that one group of drug smugglers discussed killing me because one of them later told me about it. He said a member of the group argued against it saying, "Look, if you kill her they're just going to bring in 15 more reporters like her."

In Charlotte County, police arrested a guy they believe had just taken a contract to murder me and make it look like suicide.

Q. *Tell me about the story you wrote headlined "Tax Deal Cut Over Pizza and Beer at Mystery Townhouse" and the follow-up.*

A. The real story we were after was, "What is the deal you've cut. How much are we going to be taxed? Tell us the elements of it." Along the way to getting that, we asked, "Where did you meet?" Each legislator was reluctant to answer that question.

If I'm not present when something is happening, I like to get enough facts in my head to be able to picture it. That's all I was trying to do when I began asking, "Where were you? What time of night did this take place? What were the circumstances?"

When they left the capitol that night they didn't have a deal. When they came back at 9 A.M. the next day, they had a deal. We knew it had developed after hours.

Q. *When did you realize that the location itself was a story?*

A. Everybody kept being so terribly vague. They would say, "Well, we were at somebody's town house."

"Whose town house?"

"I don't know."

"What did it look like?"

"Well, I don't remember, but it had two stories."

Q. *How did you go about finding it?*

A. I interviewed each of the 30 people I thought might have been at the meeting the night before and by pulling a shard out of each one, I was able to piece together the name of the street.

Then, by taking the city directory and calling people who lived on that street I was able to determine that only one set of town houses had two stories. I was able to narrow it to within 10 apartments.

I went to City Hall and pulled the water accounts. A lot of people up here rent during the legislative session but they pay their own water and electricity deposits. I pulled the city accounts to see who was actually paying the utility bills in each of those apartments. I found two lobbyists in the group.

During an interview with one of the participants, I asked which apartment he was in and he replied, "I can't tell you." But he held up the number of fingers to match the number of the apartment. That helped narrow it down.

I then confronted the president of the senate. I said, "All right. I know you were in the U.S. Sugar town house."

Q. *Did you do all this in one day?*

A. I started around 8 A.M. and by noon I realized that we had a good story. Anytime somebody is evasive in answering my questions, it raises a flag. The sugar company, in this case, was not affected by the new tax law. They were just doing it as a favor. Lobbyists like to do anything they can to get in good with the leadership.

Q. *Did your stories bring any response?*

A. Oddly enough the tax was later repealed. A lot of people believe that some of the public pressure stemmed from the manner in which it was adopted—late at night in a town house owned by a lobbyist, over pizza and beer.

Q. *What advice do you have for young investigative reporters?*

A. Learn the system. Learn what public records are. I teach a seminar that I call Public Records 101, simply pulling together examples of public records and showing what's out there.

When I did the investigation on the Pasco County sheriff's department, for instance, I made a list of about 15 people I knew had some important relationship to the sheriff and his top men.

I did a complete record sweep in the counties they lived in, pulling records on what they owned and copies of their driving records. If they had any traffic accidents, I pulled those. I looked at their voter registration records.

Q. *Is that always part of your investigations?*

A. I do that with legislators, cabinet members, and the governor here. Florida has a pretty good financial disclosure law. I pull a copy of everybody's financial disclosure and put it in a file in the office, so if at 5 P.M. we have a legislator with a possible conflict of interest, we know what he owns, his salary, everything he derives major income from, a list of gifts he declared in the preceding year, his corporate information, his campaign financial documents, and hopefully news clips of what he's done in the past.

Florida has a computerized corporate records system. If a person is an officer or director of a corporation, you can pull it through the state's computers. In addition, I have a computerized campaign election project.

Q. *Tell me more about that.*

A. I have a research assistant who during an election takes the major contributors, $100 or more, to every legislator and inputs that into a computer system so that at anytime during the year I can take a name, place it into that system and tell if that person donated money to anybody.

I can pull out the names of everybody who donated to a particular candidate. I can do it by interest group. If I want to know who doctors were donating to, I can pull that out. I try to amass that kind of information and teach reporters what's there.

Q. *How about process of writing. How would you describe your style?*

A. Once I have the lead, I have very little problem with the rest of it. There have been times when I have gone back later and totally altered a lead, but that's rare. Usually whatever step I first take to get into a story stays the same. I may go back and change a few words.

Q. *Do you work from an outline?*

A. Rarely. If, for instance, I'm covering a trial where I'm sitting all day through testimony, I often do what I call out takes. When a witness says something that is particularly succinct, I write "good quote; good thought." I'll write the quote on a separate piece of paper or a yellow legal pad, and by the end of the day I'll have a collection of those to look through.

I started doing that when I was working for an edition that had very early deadlines. Often I had to have the story written at the moment court adjourned.

If I'm working on a complex project, I might be more inclined to use an outline.

Q. *Do you have any special method for organizing material during a major project?*

A. I'm very quick to create files with headings. I did a series on Gerald Hemp, a man who masterminded what was then the largest cocaine smuggling operation in Tennessee. He wound up escaping from a Florida prison.

I developed a general Hemp file, a Hemp Florida prison escape file, a Hemp in Tennessee file that related his drug smuggling adventures. I had a file for Hemp's family members I interviewed. There were around eight separate files when it was over.

Q. *Tell me about how you write leads. Do you have any methods that always work?*

A. I tend to take a more direct route into a story than a lot of reporters perhaps because I'm a direct person. I don't like to beat around the bush; I like to get to the point and go on. In these times, everybody is trying to write shorter and tighter.

There are times when I try to catch the humor of a situation and build it into the lead. You see that in the pizza and beer story. I seldom begin a story with a quote although I have been known to. It's rare to get one quote that explains enough to suit me in a lead.

Q. *Tell me about the Pulitzer Prize. What effect has it had on your career?*

A. It has made it harder for me to go into a courthouse and pull together research without drawing attention. I have a higher profile and my presence triggers alarms. When I go into a courthouse, they immediately recognize my name and say, "Why are you here?" Now I often send a research assistant in to look at records.

Q. *What's the hardest thing about being a reporter?*

A. I'm often there at the worst moment in people's lives. We are there when somebody's child is killed, when somebody is thrown in jail, when somebody loses an election, when somebody is seriously injured. A lot of reporters simply can't take that kind of emotion day after day.

There are other avenues to travel in this business, but I feel reporters have to learn to deal with all of these emotions. Life experience helps.

For instance, since my own son was killed in a traffic accident, I have absolutely no qualms about walking up to someone who has lost a child and attempting to interview them. But I'm going to be sensitive. I'm going to say, "Look, I have been where you are. I have lost a child."

Q. *Do you network with other women journalists?*

A. Not as much as I probably should. At times in my life I have joined groups, but I was too busy to go to meetings. Years when I had children at home, I funnelled any spare time to them. Now I spend all of my spare time with my grandchildren.

2 Jacqui Banaszynski

PUBLIC AFFAIRS ■ *St. Paul Pioneer Press Dispatch*

JACQUI BANASZYNSKI is a risk taker. The reporter for the *St. Paul Pioneer Press Dispatch* is willing to get emotionally involved in a story. The result is writing that makes the reader care.

Banaszynski won the 1988 Pulitzer Prize for her series entitled, "AIDS in the Heartland." The stories chronicled the last months of a Minnesota farmer who died of AIDS. "The kind of journalism I try to do opens doors for people so they can walk in someone else's moccasins for awhile," Banaszynski says.

A Wisconsin native, Banaszynski, 37, graduated from Marquette University in Milwaukee and completed internships at the *Wall Street Journal* and the *Indianapolis Star.* Before joining the *Pioneer Press* in 1984, she worked at the *Minneapolis Star and Tribune,* the *Eugene* (Oregon) *Register-Guard,* the *Duluth News-Tribune & Herald,* and the *Janesville* (Wisconsin) *Gazette.*

She was a finalist for a 1986 Pulitzer Prize in international reporting for her account of African famine. Her AIDS series also won a Distinguished Service Award from the Society of Professional Journalists, Sigma Delta Chi.

AIDS IN THE HEARTLAND
Ill Activist Struggles to Carry On

Death is no stranger to the Heartland. It is as natural as the seasons, as inevitable as farm machinery breaking down and farmers' bodies giving out after too many years of too much work.

But when death comes in the guise of AIDS, it is a disturbingly unfamiliar visitor, one better known in the gay districts and drug houses of the big cities, one that shows no respect for the usual order of life in the country.

The visitor has come to rural Glenwood, Minn.

Dick Hanson, a well-known liberal political activist who homesteads his family's century-old farm south of Glenwood, was diagnosed last summer with acquired immune deficiency syndrome.

23

His partner of five years, Bert Henningson, carries the AIDS virus.

In the year that Hanson has been living — and dying — with AIDS, he has hosted some cruel companions: blinding headaches and failing vision, relentless nausea and deep fatigue, falling blood counts and worrisome coughs and sleepless, sweat-soaked nights.

He has watched as his strong body, toughened by 37 years on the farm, shrinks and stoops like that of an old man. He has weathered the family shame and community fear, the prejudice and whispered condemnations. He has read the reality in his partner's eyes, heard the death sentence from the doctors and seen the hopelessness confirmed by the statistics.

But the statistics tell only half the story — the half about dying.

Statistics fail to tell much about the people they represent. About people like Hanson — a farmer who has nourished life in the fields, a peace activist who has marched for a safer planet, an idealist and gay activist who has campaigned for social justice, and now an AIDS patient who refuses to abandon his own future, however long it lasts.

The statistics say nothing of the joys of a carefully tended vegetable garden and new kittens under the shed, of tender teasing and magic hugs. Of flowers that bloom brighter and birds that sing sweeter and simple pleasures grown profound against the backdrop of a terminal illness. Of the powerful bond between two people who pledged for better or worse and meant it.

"Who is to judge the value of life, whether it's one day or one week or one year?" Hanson said. "I find the quality of life a lot more important than the length of life."

Much has been written about the death that comes with AIDS, but little has been said about the living. Hanson and Henningson want to change that. They have opened their homes and their hearts to tell the whole story — beginning to end.

This is the first chapter.

The tiny snapshot is fuzzy and stained with ink. Two men in white T-shirts and corduroys stand at the edge of a barnyard, their muscled arms around each other's shoulders, a puzzled bull watching them from a field. The picture is overexposed, but the effect is pleasing, as if that summer day in 1982 was washed with a bit too much sun.

A summer later, the same men — one bearded and one not, one tall and one short — pose on the farmhouse porch in a mock American

Gothic. Their pitchforks are mean looking and caked with manure. But their attempted severity fails; dimples betray their humor.

They are pictured together often through the years, draped with ribbons and buttons at political rallies, playing with their golden retriever, Nels, and, most frequently, working in their lavish vegetable garden.

The pictures drop off abruptly after 1985. One of the few shows the taller man, picking petunias from his mother's grave. He is startlingly thin by now; as a friend said, "like Gandhi after a long fast." His sunbleached hair has turned dark, his bronze skin pallid. His body seems slack, as if it's caving in on itself.

The stark evidence of Dick Hanson's deterioration mars the otherwise rich memories captured in the photo album. But Hanson said only this:

"When you lose your body, you become so much closer to your spirit. It gives you more emphasis of what the spirit is, that we are more important than withering skin and bone."

Hanson sat with his partner, Bert Henningson, in the small room at Minneapolis' Red Door Clinic on April 8, 1986, waiting for the results of Hanson's AIDS screening test.

He wouldn't think about how tired he had been lately. He had spent his life hefting hay bales with ease, but now was having trouble hauling potato sacks at the Glenwood factory where he worked part time. He had lost 10 pounds, had chronic diarrhea and slept all afternoon. The dishes stayed dirty in the sink, the dinner uncooked, until Henningson got home from teaching at the University of Minnesota-Morris.

It must be the stress. His parents had been forced off the farm and now he and his brothers faced foreclosure. Two favorite uncles were ill. He and Henningson were bickering a lot, about the housework and farm chores and Hanson's dark mood.

He had put off having the AIDS test for months, and Henningson hadn't pushed too hard. Neither was eager to know.

Now, as the nurse entered the room with his test results, Hanson convinced himself the news would be good. It had been four years since he had indulged in casual weekend sex at the gay bathhouse in Minneapolis, since he and Henningson committed to each other. Sex outside their relationship had been limited and "safe," with no exchange of semen or blood. He had taken care of himself, eating homegrown food and working outdoors, and his farmer's body always had responded with energy and strength. Until now.

"I put my positive thinking mind on and thought I'd be negative," Hanson said. "Until I saw that red circle."

The reality hit him like a physical punch. As he slumped forward in shock, Henningson — typically pragmatic — asked the nurse to prepare another needle. He, too, must be tested.

Then Henningson gathered Hanson in his arms and said, "I will never leave you, Dick."

Hanson is one of 210 Minnesotans and 36,000 Americans who have been diagnosed with AIDS since the disease was identified in 1981. More than half of those patients already have died, and doctors say it is only a matter of time for the rest. The statistics show that 80 to 90 percent of AIDS sufferers die within two years of diagnosis; the average time of survival is 14 months after the first bout of pneumocystis — a form of pneumonia that brought Hanson to the brink of death last August and again in December.

"For a long time, I was just one of those statistics," Hanson said. "I was a very depressing person to be around. I wanted to get away from me."

He lost 20 more pounds in the two weeks after receiving his test results. One of his uncles died and, on the morning of the funeral, Hanson's mother died unexpectedly. Genevieve Hanson was 75 years old, a gentle but sturdy woman who was especially close to Dick, the third of her six children. He handled the arrangements, picking gospel hymns for the service and naming eight of her women friends as honorary pallbearers — a first in the history of their tiny country church.

But Hanson never made it to his mother's funeral. The day she was buried, he collapsed of exhaustion and fever. That night, Henningson drove him to Glenwood for the first of three hospitalizations — 42 days worth — in 1986.

"Dick was real morbid last summer," Henningson said. "He led people to believe it was curtains, and was being very vague and dramatic. We all said to be hopeful, but it was as if something had gripped his psyche and was pulling him steadily downward week after week."

Hanson had given up, but Henningson refused to. He worked frantically to rekindle that spark of hope — and life. He read Hanson news articles about promising new AIDS drugs and stories of terminal cancer patients defying the odds. He brought home tapes about the power of positive thinking and fed Hanson healthy food. He talked to him steadily of politics and all the work that remained to be done.

He forced himself, and sometimes Hanson, to work in the garden, making it bigger than ever. They planted 58 varieties of vegetables in an organic, high-yield plot and christened it the Hope Garden.

But Hanson returned to the hospital in August, dangerously ill with the dreaded pneumonia. His weight had dropped to 112 from his usual 160. He looked and walked like an old-man version of himself.

"I had an out-of-body type experience there, and even thought I had died for a time," he said. "It was completely quiet and very calm and I thought, 'This is really nice.' I expected some contact with the next world. Then I had this conversation with God that it wasn't my time yet, and he sent me back."

Hanson was home in time to harvest the garden, and to freeze and can its bounty. He had regained some of his former spunk, and was taking an interest again in the world around him.

"I'd be sitting next to him on the couch, holding his hand, and once in a while he'd get that little smile on his face and nod like there was something to hold on to," Henningson said. "And a small beam of life would emerge."

A month later, Hanson's spirits received another boost when he was honored at a massive fund-raising dinner. Its sponsors included DFL (Democratic-Farmer-Labor Party) notables — among them Gov. Rudy Perpich, Lt. Gov. Marlene Johnson, St. Paul Mayor George Latimer, Minneapolis Mayor Don Fraser and Congressmen Bruce Vento and Martin Sabo — and radical political activists Hanson had worked with over the years, farmers who had stood with him to fight farm foreclosures and the West Coast power line, women who remembered his support during the early years of the women's movement, members of the gay and lesbian community and other AIDS sufferers.

What started as a farewell party, a eulogy of sorts, turned into a celebration of Hanson's life. Folk singer Larry Long played songs on an Indian medicine man's healing flute. Friends gathered in a faith circle to will their strength to Hanson. Dozens of people lined up to embrace Hanson and Henningson. For most, it was the first time they had touched an AIDS patient.

"People are coming through on this thing and people are decent," Hanson said. "We find people in all walks of life who are with us on this struggle. . . . It's that kind of thing that makes it all worth it."

So when the pneumonia came back in December, this time with more force, Hanson was ready to fight.

"The doctor didn't give him any odds," Henningson said. Hanson was put on a respirator, funeral arrangements were discussed, estranged relatives were called to his bedside.

"He wrote me a note," Henningson said. " 'When can I get out of here?' He and I had never lied to each other, and I wasn't about to start. I said, 'You might be getting out of here in two or three days, but it might be God you're going to see. But there is a slim chance, so if you'll just fight. . . . ' "

People from Hanson's AIDS support group stayed at the hospital round the clock, in shifts, talking to him and holding his hand as he drifted in and out of a coma. Friends brought Christmas to the stark hospital room: cards papered the walls and a giant photograph of Hanson's Christmas tree, the one left back at the farmhouse, was hung.

The rest was up to Hanson.

"I put myself in God's healing cocoon of love and had my miracle," he said. "I call it my Christmas miracle."

He was released from intensive care on Christmas Eve day and since has devoted his life to carrying a seldom-heard message of hope to other AIDS patients, to give them—and himself—a reason to live as science races to find a cure.

"I'd like to think that God has a special purpose for my life," he said. His smile under the thinning beard is sheepish; faith is personal, and easily misunderstood.

"I don't want to come across like Oral Roberts, but . . . I believe that God can grant miracles. He has in the past and does now and will in the future. And maybe I can be one of those miracles, the one who proves the experts wrong."

Hanson has spent his life on the front line of underdog causes— always liberal, often revolutionary and sometimes unpopular.

"Somewhere along the line Dick was exposed to social issues and taught that we can make a difference," said Mary Stackpool, a neighbor and fellow political activist. "That's what Dick has been all about—showing that one person can make a difference."

Hanson put it in terms less grand: "You kind of have to be an eternal optimist to be a farmer. There's something that grows more each year than what you put into the farm. . . . I've always been involved in trying to change things for the better."

He was born into the national prosperity of 1950 and grew up through the social turmoil of the 1960s. A fifth-grade teacher sparked his enthusiasm in John F. Kennedy's presidential campaign. He was 13 when his father joined the radical National Farmers Organization, took the family to picket at the Land O'Lakes plant in nearby Alexandria and participated in a notorious milk-dumping action.

He later led rural campaigns for Eugene McCarthy, George McGovern, Mark Dayton (a Minnesota businessman who ran for the U.S. Senate), and his current hero, Jesse Jackson. He led protests against the Vietnam War, and was a conscientious objector. He organized rival factions to try to stop construction of the high-voltage power line that snakes through western Minnesota.

He was an early member of the farm activist group Growndswell, fighting to stop a neighbor's foreclosure one day, his own family's the next. The 473-acre Hanson farm has been whittled to 40 by bankruptcy; Hanson and Henningson are struggling to salvage the farmhouse and some surrounding wetlands.

He has been arrested five times, staged a fast to draw attention to the power line protest and stood at the podium of the 1980 DFL district convention to announce—for the first time publicly—that he was gay. That same year, he was elected one of the first openly gay members of the Democratic National Committee and, in 1984, made an unsuccessful bid for the party's nomination for Congress from the Second District. In 1983, he and Henningson were photographed in their fields for a 1983 Newsweek magazine story about gays responding to the AIDS crisis; neither knew at the time they carried the virus.

"He just throws himself into a cause and will spare nothing," Stackpool said. "He will expose himself totally to bring out the desired good."

Now the cause is AIDS. The struggle is more personal, the threat more direct. But for Hanson, it has become yet another opportunity to make a difference.

"He's handling this just as he would anything else—with strength and lots of courage and hope," said Amy Lee, another longtime friend and fellow activist. "And with that pioneering spirit. If there's anything he can do, any way he can help other victims, any time he can speak—he'll go for it."

Hanson has become one of the state's most visible AIDS patients. He and Henningson are frequently interviewed for news stories, were the subject of a recent four-part series on KCMT-TV in Alexandria and speak at AIDS education seminars in churches and schools throughout the state. Last month, Hanson addressed the state Senate's special informational meeting on AIDS.

"I want to take the mask off the statistics and say we are human beings and we have feelings," he said. "I want to say there is life after AIDS."

Rather than retreat to the anonymity of the big city, as many AIDS sufferers do, Hanson has maintained a high political profile in Pope County. He is chairman of the DFL Party in Senate District 15. He and Henningson continue to do business with area merchants and worship weekly at the country church of Hanson's childhood, Barsness Lutheran.

"I've always been a very public person and I've had no regrets," Hanson said. "One thing my dad always emphasized was the principle that honesty was the most important thing in life."

Hanson and Henningson use their story to personalize the AIDS epidemic and to debunk some of the stereotypes and myths about AIDS and its victims. They are farmers who have milked cows, slopped hogs and baled hay like everyone else. Their politics and sexual orientation may disturb some. But their voices and values are more familiar, and perhaps better understood, than those of some of their urban counterparts.

"It makes people aware that it can happen here," said Sharon Larson, director of nursing at Glacial Ridge Hospital in Glenwood.

That honesty has carried a price. A conservative Baptist minister from Glenwood criticized their life-style at a community forum and again in a column in the *Pope County Tribune*. Some of Hanson's relatives were upset by the Alexandria television show and demanded he keep his troubling news to himself. There have been rumblings in his church from people concerned about taking communion with him, and a minor disturbance erupted in a Glenwood school when his niece was teased about him.

But his connections also carry clout.

"It brings it a little closer to home to the guys in the Capitol who control the purse strings," a fellow AIDS patient said.

When they speak, Hanson and Henningson touch on a variety of topics: the need for national health insurance to guarantee equitable care, the cruelty of policies that force AIDS patients into poverty before they are eligible for medical assistance, the need for flex-time jobs so AIDS sufferers can continue to be productive, the imperative of safe sex.

They also stress the personal aspects of the disease: the need for patients to be touched rather than shunned, the importance of support from family and friends and, most dear to Hanson, the healing powers of hope.

"I know there are some who die because they give up," he said. "They have no hope, no reason to fight. Everything they're faced with is so desperate and dismal. . . . I believe the biggest obstacle for us who have AIDS or AIDS-related complex is fighting the fear and anxiety we have over the whole thing. Every positive thing, every bit of hope is something to hold on to."

Next month, Hanson and Henningson will celebrate five years together, perhaps with a gathering of friends and an exchange of rings. They exchanged vows privately that first summer while sitting in their car under the prairie night.

"We asked the blessing of the spirit above," Hanson said. "It was a pretty final thing."

At first blush, they seem an unlikely couple.

"Bert the scholar and Dick the activist. . . . In some ways they're just worlds apart," Stackpool said. "But politics brought them together, and now they take delight in those differences and in their special traits. They've figured out things many married couples never come close to figuring out."

Henningson is bookish and intense, a Ph.D. in international trade, a professor and essayist. He is a doer and organizer. He charts the monthly household budget on his Apple computer, itemizing everything from mortgage payments to medicine to cat food. He sets a hearty dinner table, which is cleared and washed as soon as the last bit of food is gone. He buries himself in his work during the week, becomes reclusive when he retreats to the farm on weekends and has worked hard over the years to control an explosive temper.

Hanson is more social, an easygoing, non-stop talker with a starburst of interests. He spent 12 years detouring through social activism before finally earning a bachelor's degree in political science at the university's Morris campus.

He has a political junkie's memory for names, dates and events, thrills in company and is quick to offer refreshments, having inherited his mother's belief in friendship through food.

But they also have much in common.

Henningson, 40, grew up on a farm near Graceville, in neighboring Big Stone County. His life paralleled Hanson's in many respects: the radical farm movement, anti-war protests, involvement in liberal political campaigns.

Both suppressed their homosexuality until they were almost 30. Hanson kept so active with politics and the farm that he didn't have time for a social life. After acknowledging his homosexuality, his sexual life involved weekend excursions to the Twin Cities for anonymous encounters at the gay bathhouse. "I had to taste all the fruit in the orchard," he said. "I had some real special relationships, but if they suggested it just be us I felt trapped, like they were closing in on me."

Henningson threw himself into graduate school, tried marriage and took on a demanding career in Washington D.C., as an aide to former U.S. Rep. Richard Nolan. He divorced and returned to Minnesota, where he enrolled in a human sexuality program at the University of Minnesota. He had three homosexual involvements before meeting Hanson at a political convention.

"There were some major forces working in the universe that were compelling us together," Henningson said. "I don't know that we ever had much to say about it. I've always believed in serendipity, but I also feel you have to give serendipity a little help. So I didn't sit back and wait for Dick to call—I called him."

Any doubts Hanson had about their relationship were squelched by his mother. She visited the farmhouse one Sunday morning with freshly baked caramel rolls, which she served Hanson and Henningson in bed. Henningson was accepted as part of the family, moved to the farm and eventually assumed financial responsibility for the family's farm operations.

"It was so good to work together, to sweat together, to farrow those sows and help the sows have those little piglets," Henningson said. "We literally worked dawn to dusk."

That hard but somewhat idyllic life has been altered drastically by AIDS. Hanson does what he can, when he can, perhaps baking cookies or doing the laundry. But the burden of earning an income, running the house and caring for Hanson has fallen heavily on Henningson's shoulders.

Hanson's medical bills—totalling more than $50,000 so far—are covered by welfare. Henningson's temporary job at the state Department of Agriculture, where he writes farm policy proposals, pays their personal bills, helps pay their apartment rent in the Twin Cities so Hanson can be near medical care during the week and allows them to keep the farmhouse.

"Dick's optimism is fine," Henningson said. "But you have to help optimism along now and then with a little spade work. I ended up doing all of the work with no help. What could have happened is that I could have grown resentful and blamed the victim.

"But I tried to put myself in his shoes—having pneumonia

twice — and with all my anger and short temper, could I live with that? Could I even get through that? I'd probably have the strength to go to a field and dig a hole and when the time came crawl in and bury myself. But I don't know if I'd have the strength to do what he did."

So, their commitment to each other remains absolute, perhaps strengthened by facing a crisis together.

"When you know that somebody's going to stand by you, and when they prove that they will, when they go through what Bert's gone through this past year in putting up with me . . . you just know it's very, very special what you have," Hanson said.

Each week, Hanson checks in at the AIDS clinic at Hennepin County Medical Center. He and Henningson make the three-hour drive to Minneapolis every Monday and spend their week in the Twin Cities. Henningson has work through June at the Agriculture Department. Hanson's full-time job is AIDS.

He has his blood tested to determine his white blood cell count — his body's natural defense system. It often is below 1,000; a healthy person's count would be closer to 5,000.

He has a physical exam, chats with two or three doctors, gives encouragement to fellow patients and collects hugs from the nursing staff. He is a favorite with the social workers, who tease him about his lack of interest in the women who flock to his examination room each week for a visit.

He does weekly inhalation therapy, breathing an antibiotic into his lungs to ward off the dreaded pneumonia. Then he buses to St. Paul for a long, healing massage from one of several local massage therapists who donate time to AIDS patients.

Thursday mornings find him at the University of Minnesota Hospital and Clinic for eye treatments. Doctors inject medicine directly into his eyeball to thwart a virus that is attacking his vision. Sometimes the needle punctures a blood vessel, leaving Hanson with bright red patches in his eyes.

On Thursday nights, he and Henningson attend an AIDS support group meeting, where as many as 30 patients, relatives and friends gather to share comfort and information.

For eight months, Hanson has taken AZT, or azidothymidine, an experimental drug believed to prolong life for AIDS sufferers. He takes other drugs to counter the nausea caused by AZT's high toxicity, and he is watched closely for bone marrow suppression. He uses various underground treatments, all with his doctor's knowledge. He

rubs solvent on his skin to try to stimulate a response from his immune system, and spreads a home-brewed cholesterol agent on his
toast, hoping it will help render the virus inert.

He watches his diet to prevent diarrhea and takes various pre-
scription drugs for depression and anxiety.

His spare time, what there is of it, is devoured by long waits for
the bus or slow walks to his various appointments. He naps often to
keep his energy level up and spends evenings watching the Twins on
TV. Reading has become painful for him, straining his eyes and making him dizzy.

"It comes back and back and back many times," he said. "Is this
my total life? Has the illness become such an all-encompassing thing
that my life will never be judged by anything but this brand of
AIDS?"

Weekends are spent on the farm, where Hanson often can be
found kneeling in his flower beds. The impatiens, moss roses and
sweet Williams are planted especially thick this summer; Hanson was
eager to see their cheerful pinks and reds cover the crumbling stone
foundation of the old farmhouse. He insists on having fresh flowers
in the house every day, even dandelions and thistles. Once, after
pranksters broke the peony bushes in the church cemetery, Hanson
gathered up the broken blossoms and took them home, placing them
around the house in shallow bowls of water.

Or he can be found singing in the empty silo, practicing hymns
for Sunday's church service. His voice is sweet and natural, with a
good range. It is inherited, he says, from his mother, who sang to him
when he was in the womb and tuned in opera on the radio in the farm
kitchen when he was a youngster. He has sung for his brothers' wed-
dings but is better, he says, at funerals.

On hot summer nights, he and Henningson sleep in twin beds in a
screened porch upstairs. The room is kept cool by towering shade
trees and constant breezes blowing off the marsh that winds in front
of the house. From there, the men note the comings and goings of
their neighbors: egrets and blue herons, Canada geese that feed on
what Henningson calls Green Scum Pond, a doe and her buff-colored
fawn. There is an owl in the nearby woods, a peregrine falcon nesting
in the farmhouse eaves and an unseen loon that sings to them at dusk.

If the weekend is slow, the weather is mild and his energy is high,
Hanson can be found in a dinghy somewhere on Lake Minnewaska,
the sparkling centerpiece of Pope County. He's a skilled fisherman,
and remembers weekends when he would haul home a catch of 200

pan fish for one of his mother's famous fries.

"I find that going out in the garden is a good way to get away from things, or going fishing, or just visiting with people and talking," he said. "I don't want my whole life to be branded by AIDS."

Hanson awakes in the Minneapolis apartment on a recent morning to the sound of his mother's voice.

"It wasn't part of any dream," he said. "Just her voice, crystal clear, calling."

He has been running a fever for several days, and suffering headaches. His white blood cell count has dropped precipitously. His chatter, usually cheerful, is tinged with fear.

"I got pretty emotional about it," he said. "But Bert held me and said, 'Don't be afraid. Don't fight it.' And I remember a year ago when I was so sick, and she was reaching to me, and I was so scared I was almost pushing her away. And Bert said not to fight it, to let her comfort me even if she's reaching to me on a level we don't understand. . . .

"There are days I think I'm just going to get out of this, put this whole thing behind me and get a job and go on with my life again. Then I have a rough day like this and I have to look at things much more realistically."

Hanson seldom talks of death. When his health is stable, there seems little point. He has beaten the odds before and will, he says, again.

"Intermittently, there has been some denial," said his physician, Dr. Margaret Simpson, director of the sexually transmitted disease clinic at Hennepin County Medical Center. "That's not too surprising. When you're feeling good, it's easy to think this isn't true.

"But he's deteriorating again, and it's worrisome. I don't make predictions, but I think now in terms of weeks and months rather than months and years."

Hanson senses that urgency. But he remains a fighter. His attitude, he says, is not one of delusion but of defiance.

"I think I'll know when the time is right and it's coming," he said. "Should it be, I'm ready to meet my maker. But I'm not ready to give up and say there's nothing that will turn around so I can live."

A week later, Hanson is in the hospital. The headaches are worse, and doctors do a painful spinal tap to determine if the AIDS virus has entered his brain. His white blood cell count is dangerously low, but a transfusion is risky.

It is the first hospitalization in six months, and only an overnight stay for tests, but it evokes painful memories of the past and fears for the future.

Henningson telephones Hanson's sister.

"I told Mary it may be only three or four months and we have to respond to him accordingly," he said. "Not treat him as someone who's going to die, but accord him the time and attention you want. We can't just say, 'See you next week.' It's not a matter of dealing with certitude anymore, but a great deal of uncertainty about where it's going to lead."

Hanson is quiet this evening and seems distracted. The Twins game plays silently on the hospital room TV, but relief pitcher Jeff Reardon is losing and Hanson pays only passing interest. He gets up once during the evening to vomit and occasionally presses his hand to his temple. But he never mentions the nausea, the throbbing headache or the pain from the spinal tap.

Henningson sits next to him on the bed and thumbs through their photo album, recalling lighter times.

Suddenly, Hanson waves his hand vaguely, at the room, at his life. "I'll miss all this," he confided. "I'll just miss all these wonderful people."

Then he and Henningson discuss—gently—the logistics of his death. Should he be placed in a nursing home if he becomes invalid? Should life-sustaining measures be used if he falls into a coma again? Should he donate his body to research?

The morbid conversation is held in matter-of-fact tones and seems to soothe Hanson. It is Henningson's way of pulling out the emotions, the soft rage and futility that Hanson otherwise would keep tucked inside.

"Talking about things like that helps you understand your mortality, that it may not be much longer," Henningson said. "And that helps relieve your fears. Dick's fears are not so much for himself as for me. Will I live out here all by myself? Will I find someone else? I say don't worry about that, it's out of your control."

But Henningson, too, is shaken. He sits at the window next to Hanson's hospital bed, and holds his hand. Finally, he abandons the diversionary talk and cries. He is worried about losing the farm, about the political hassles involved in getting housing assistance, about getting a job after his contract with the state expires, about not having enough time left with Hanson.

And he can't help but worry about the AIDS virus in his body and his own health prospects. Although he guards his health carefully and is optimistic about medical progress on the AIDS front, he fears that the stress of caring for Hanson is taking its toll. He watches Hanson, and wonders if he is watching his own future.

Then he comforts himself with a wish.

"I want to be cremated and have my ashes thrown in Big Stone Lake. And from there I would flow to the Minnesota River, down to the Mississippi River, all the way to the Gulf. And I'll hit the Gulf Stream and travel the world.

"And I told Dick if he'd like to be cremated, they could put him in Lake Minnewaska, and he would flow to the Chippewa River and then into the Minnesota and the Mississippi and to the Gulf and around the world. And at some point we would merge and we'd be together forever."

He stops, perhaps embarrassed.

"You can't control what happens to people after they're dead," he said. "But even if it doesn't happen, it's a lovely, consoling thought."

A Visit with Jacqui Banaszynski

Virginia Young: *Tell me about your career. When did you decide to become a reporter?*

Jacqui Banaszynski: I've been doing this since I was 14. I'm from a small farm town in northeastern Wisconsin and my high school had a phenomenal journalism program. It's the only high school in the country that puts out the community newspaper. It was a big deal to work on the newspaper and I was into being a big deal. I was bored, I was restless, I was in a small town, and I needed challenges.

And I fell in love with it. It was incredibly difficult, very challenging, and also enormously satisfying. It gave me access to things I normally wouldn't have access to. It opened up my life.

I wanted to go into broadcasting. But when I got to college two things happened: one is a bunch of professors steered me away from that, saying, "What you need to do is write." The other is my mother told me in no uncertain terms that I had a face made for radio.

Q. *What happened after you graduated from college?*

A. I went to a real dinky paper. And I worked my way up—
clawed and scraped and scrambled. That was hard. It wasn't a lot of
fun. My first full-time job was at the *Janesville* (Wisconsin) *Gazette,*
27,000 circ., no Sunday paper. I stayed there for 16 months. Each
move I made I learned more.

   Q. *Did you start out covering zoning boards and sewer commis-
sions?*

   A. Yes. Ten years of hard news beats. My first job was covering
county government and I did the cop run every morning and the fire
station and the courthouse.

   I tended to splinter off and do projects, human interest–related
stories. The irony in that is, when I started in the business, I refused
to do features.

   I'd go onto papers and I'd say, "Look, I'm not cute and I don't
write cute. I don't do cute." Part of the reason was there were still
women's pages back then. And I was astute enough to realize that the
women were librarians, feature writers, society writers and religion
writers, and the boys were having all the fun. I wanted to have some
fun.

   Q. *Did anyone ever try to pigeonhole you into a women's page
job?*

   A. No. I was too big. They were afraid of me (laughing). I would
do features but usually they had a news edge to them. I had an
attraction to tragedy and people who were fighting injustice or struggling to survive or had been through some really cataclysmic event
and were coping with it. They make fascinating stories.

   Q. *Why did you move to the* St. Paul Pioneer Press Dispatch
from the Minneapolis Star and Tribune?

   A. I needed more hand-holding than the *Star-Tribune* could give
me, more nurturing. I needed more attention. If you walk by my desk
once a week and pat me on the head and say, "Gosh, we're glad you're
here," I'll do anything for you. I will stand out by the bomb at ground
zero and write about it.

   But if you don't tell me that, I start getting real squirrelly. The
Star-Tribune was not a place where there was a lot of positive reinforcement. It was a very male culture.

   I have a history and a reputation of being intense, passionate and
flamboyant, of challenging and questioning things, and demanding
that when an editor gives me an assignment they justify the assignment. I push the limits of an institution. And sometimes I do it loudly.

   We were a bad fit. I always felt like a trapezoid. They were trying to cut off so many of my edges nothing would have been left when they got done.

Q. *Does working for an institution run by a woman differ from working at a male-run newspaper?*

A. I find working in a newsroom run by a woman, especially a woman as strong and forceful as Deborah Howell, that we tend to look at things a little differently than the more traditional male mainstream newsroom. I think "AIDS in the Heartland" is a perfect example.

Q. *Could you explain what you mean?*

A. I think most men would have been less comfortable with the approach. The conflict was apparent while we were doing it. I'd come back from the farm after interviewing Dick and Bert and I'd write about — in addition to their illness, their family struggles, their financial problems, and their political and legal battles — the bread they were baking, the kittens under the porch, and the flowers they were raising.

And the managing editor would go nuts. He'd say, "What is this stuff? What is this kittens-under-the-porch drivel? This is too flowery, too fancy, too mushy." Deborah would see the story and it was exactly that stuff that she liked the most.

By using that stuff we were able to keep readers who could make a connection to these two men because maybe they too planted flowers or had a cat. We gave them some real human, homey qualities that made people understand who they were other than these two political activists who happened to be gay.

That was a very feminine approach. What our newspaper does is feminist journalism. Not exclusively, but we have a talent for going after stories that enlighten the human condition. Deborah has to be given a lot of the credit. Most people wouldn't even be aware that those stories are there. She thinks of them.

Q. *Do you have freedom to choose your stories?*

A. Yes. I have an enormous amount of freedom now, almost too much. My job is in transition because of the Pulitzer — they don't quite know what to do with me.

I'm the special projects reporter who does the people stories as opposed to the investigative paper-trails stories. I essentially have first right of refusal. They'll come up with stories and say, "Are you interested?" And if I want it, I've got first dibs and if I don't, I just say, "No, not really." And conversely, I come up with my own ideas and there's no one who'll say, "No, you can't do that."

Q. *Do you ever work at home?*

A. No. I don't have a computer. I don't want to bring my work home if I can avoid it. I also get a lot out of the stimulation of the newsroom. I like having people around and I need to get up and talk and get reactions. I'm not very good at that lone ranger–type writing. I need distractions or I get real crazy.

Q. *Do you ever worry about becoming too involved in your stories?*

A. One of my advantages as a reporter is I'm not afraid to get involved.

Jean (Pieri, the photographer) and I both got very involved in Dick and Bert's lives. And the way we handled it was to be very honest with them, very honest with ourselves, and very honest with the editors.

Q. *How did you do that?*

A. I came back early in the interviewing process and said, "You all have to know that we care about these guys and we're going to care about them more as time goes on. We're going to have to take special care with my copy to make sure I don't go too far. I can't paint these people as heroes. I need you to backstop me."

We were able to get the kind of story we did because we got so involved. I don't believe in objectivity anyway. I think it's a myth and a crock and a dangerous concept. I don't think we should teach it. I think what we should teach is fairness—how to be fair and professional as opposed to how to be objective. If you're objective about something it means you don't care.

The professionalism comes in when you make sure you let the other person know, "I'm doing a job here." When you sit down to write, you remember that you're not writing for the subject, you're writing for the reader. So you give the reader the information the reader needs, even if it's painful for the subject.

Q. *Have you made personal sacrifices to get where you are?*

A. Sure, I've made personal sacrifices. I'm not married and I don't have children. At 37 staring at 38, that's tough. I can't blame all that on my career but it's a major factor.

I can't tell you the number of dinner dates I've missed, the number of theatre tickets I've let go of, the number of family visits I've cancelled at the last minute, the number of vacations I've cancelled at the last minute or just never scheduled, the number of people I've disappointed because I've made them a promise and then said, "Oops, can't make it, got a story." Yea, those are too numerous to talk about.

Q. *Any regrets?*

A. No major regrets. I did what I did and I am who I am and that's how it played out.

Everything led up to me doing the kinds of stories I do now, especially "AIDS in the Heartland." And that story meant an enormous amount to me, not because of the Pulitzer but because I really wanted to tell that story. So, if I would have had a kid when I was 25, maybe I wouldn't have gotten to do those things.

If somebody asks me when I'm 65 am I going to regret it, I don't know. If I'm going to crawl into bed with a piece of paper from the Pulitzer committee and a pair of wool socks on my feet instead of a warm body, maybe I will. But I'm not 65 yet.

Q. *Do you think you have had to work harder than your male counterparts to get where you are?*

A. In general, women have to work harder to be taken seriously. This is a tricky question for me because I've never wanted to go into management or get that big promotion or do classic traditional journalism. I long ago abandoned any hope to go to Washington or work for the *New York Times* or be a big-deal investigative reporter and therefore, I haven't been bumping up against a lot of guys along the way. Most men don't want to do what I'm doing.

But yea, I spent 10, 12 years working diligently in the trenches, proving myself, to get to the point where I am now and I see men doing it when they're 26 and 27. I think it's very hard for a woman's voice to be heard.

Q. *Because those doing the listening are men?*

A. Uh-huh. And even when they're women, we're just cultured in this society to not hear women's voices. So you have to either talk a little louder or be a little better.

I always tried to look at every story as a potential Page 1 story — sometimes to the great frustration of editors, who would say, "Jacqui, this is a simple 8-inch inside story. Why are you making a project out of it?" But I felt it was important to show that I could constantly and consistently produce.

A lot of men who are highly valued in the business are inconsistent. They can be brilliant one day and unpublishable the next. I never felt that I had that luxury. I never felt I had the freedom to go into a major slump or kiss something off.

Q. *What do you want from an editor? You mentioned the nurturing, positive reinforcement.*

A. What I want from an editor has changed a lot. When I was

younger, I used to walk around the country looking for the editor who
was going to make me great, the one who was going to give me good
story ideas, put me on the fast track and make me the best I could be.
I don't look for that anymore because I think that's unrealistic.

Now I want an editor who gives me the freedom and tools to do
my best work, doesn't get in my way, listens to me when I want to
talk, and serves as a sounding board. I expect occasional handhold-
ing, and I expect to be told when I've done well and when I haven't.

Sometimes I expect a swift kick in the ass. If I'm slumped or I'm
feeling down, I like an editor to know when it's time to say, "You need
a story, go get one. Your only problem is you haven't written anything
lately."

Q. *Some writers say they experience a sense of fear when they
finish a good story and have to go on to the next one. Do you experience that?*

A. I don't know if it's that tangible, but I often have this sense —
when I write something I really like — that that's the last time I'll write
anything really good.

I'll read a story I wrote and I'll be amazed. I'll go, "Wow, where
did I get those words?" Like it comes out of some Muse that exists
within me but I'm not consciously in touch with. It's a real frightening
thing.

I don't know how to consciously tap into that Muse. I've come up
with techniques that have never failed me. But I'm never sure. And
I'm always afraid that one of these days the Muse is going to fail me.

Q. *What do you mean by techniques that never fail you?*

A. If I'm real blocked when I'm doing a story, I'll talk to people
who know nothing about it, and I'll tell them the story so I can get it
out.

Some of my best stories have been written essentially as long
letters to my best friend. I'll be real blocked and I'll start writing a
letter to my friend Becky. And it'll start coming out.

Sometimes, when I've been sitting at the keyboard and gotten
nowhere, I've been laboring with two paragraphs for eight hours, I'll
just start typing, just to get my fingers moving. I'll let go of whether
it's journalistic, whether it's clear, whether the grammar's right, and
I'll just write it. I call it vomiting on the keyboard. That loosens me
up and lets me start writing.

I eat a lot of chocolate, which has some kind of drug in it that
does amazing things to me.

Deadline is an incredible motivator for me and if I really get stuck, the closer deadline gets the more sure I am I'll come up with something.

Q. *Who is your reader?*

A. I constantly keep in mind what I call benchmark readers. There are four or five specific people in my life who I think about when I'm writing a story. For me they represent the great wash of newspaper readership.

One's my mother, a very intelligent, unsophisticated, non-college-educated woman. She's lived in a small town all her life, she's extremely bright, but she's not worldly. And if I can write a story that appeals to her and teaches her something then I've reached my goal.

Q. *How do you know when you've hit that level of readability?*

A. It's got a few components. One is not writing above their level of understanding, not assuming they know certain things, which keeps me plugged into being basic, simple, and clear. If I'm going to write about AIDS, I have to explain how you get AIDS and what it is. If I'm going to write about tax-increment financing, I've got to tell people about that in some way they can relate to.

I don't write down to people, don't condescend and insult their intelligence. I try to find something in my story, a person or a happening or a way of looking at life that they can relate to. The common denominator. That's why it was so important for me to write about kittens and flowers in the garden when I was writing about Dick and Bert.

Another way to describe that is looking for the drama of the mundane, things in everyday life that we're all familiar with, but looking at them in a way that's fairly dramatic and seeing them for the first time.

Q. *Are women more prone to look for the drama of the mundane?*

A. I know some men who do it but I don't know if it comes as naturally to them. Men tend to not see a pair of shoes on the steps when they walk up the steps. The woman will see them and pick them up.

Women notice more. The way I was raised, the expectation was that I was going to be tuned to everything and everyone around me, because I was going to make sure everyone was taken care of. Make sure Dad had sugar for his coffee, the baby was fed, and the boys got their cheeseburger before they went to basketball practice. That was the female role.

Q. *Is it legitimate to use feminine wiles to get a story and have you done that?*

A. I don't know that I have because I've never felt like a very flirtatious, coy person. There are times when you get into a conversation with someone, like you're interviewing a legislator, and you starting teasing on a more human level. I try to stay away from that, in part because I've had a few nasty experiences with people coming on to me. If you're going to tease, you better be willing to deal with it afterward.

I think it is okay, though, to use your femininity in a way that puts people at ease. People are more comfortable talking to women. We grew up talking to our moms. The men all talk to their wives and big sisters. We are less intimidating people. People expect us to be softer, more understanding, and less demanding than men. I don't think there's anything wrong with using that expectation and then living up to it. Being a compassionate listener, someone who empathizes and can say, "Gosh, it sounds like this is real hard for you."

I interned at the *Wall Street Journal* for a summer and I noticed that if people don't take you seriously, one of two things happens: they either dismiss you and you get nowhere or they figure you're totally harmless because you're not going to figure out a damn thing they said anyway. So they'll tell you stuff.

Q. *Are women more empathetic interviewers?*

A. I know some men who are real good, warm conversationalists. Maybe the ones who are successful are men who can draw on their feminine side — slow down, be an active listener, be less directed and less goal oriented.

When I do an interview it goes all over the place. It's like canoeing the white water. I'm in the canoe and I have to read the rocks and read the river and stay off the shoals but the river's going to take me where it wants to go. The person I'm interviewing has to take the interview where they want to go because it's their story.

Q. *Don Fry of the Poynter Institute coined a term, "phallic journalism" to describe the macho nature of newsrooms, people yelling at each other, tough-talking editors bossing people around. Have you found that and how have you coped with it?*

A. I can be as tough-talking, kick-people-around as the next guy. Not that that's something to be proud of. I don't like doing it. Maybe that's where men have it over women. Psychologically, evidence shows that women are into compromise and resolution as opposed to conflict and victory. I see that played out in the newsroom all the time.

Q. *What advice would you give women coming into the business?*

A. It's absolutely essential that women at all times act as consummate professionals so they don't give anybody a chance not to take them seriously. They have to produce what they promise. They don't have the freedom to fail yet. That may sound harsh but I see too many women getting pegged as flaky and inconsistent or emotional. It's dangerous to be emotional in an office when you're just starting out. I can get away with it now but I've worked for people where I wouldn't advise it.

I see too many people coming into the business because they want to be writers. They forget that first they have to be reporters. They're bored with the county board meeting and they want to do great social justice journalism. Well fine. Pay your dues, honey. Work at it for 10 years, 15 years. Don't cry on my shoulder because you're 22 and you're not doing groundbreaking stuff on crack babies. You've got to prove that you can handle any story.

Q. *Are there aspects about being a woman in this business that we haven't talked about?*

A. The profession is harder on women personally. I see men given foreign assignments or sent out of town on a moment's notice, who automatically get considered for promotions without anybody considering what their home situation is.

Women in that situation, there's this automatic instinct to say, "Well, but she just had a baby." Or "Do you think her husband would be willing to go with her? What would Joe say?" I don't see anyone saying, "What would Susie say?" if Joe went out of town.

It's harder for women to have a personal life and a professional life. Men seem to be looked at just as reporters and whatever's happening at home will be taken care of. Women, probably for the better, aren't. They're looked at as more complete human beings. But that takes away from their role as reporters.

I see a lot of women in my peer group having babies and coming back to work. It puts an enormous amount of pressure on them because they want to get home to those kids. They're torn as hell. Meanwhile, the bosses are saying, "We can't rely on so and so any longer 'cause she's always off worrying about this damn kid. So we're going to rely on Joe." It's a terrible, terrible conflict. Women have to make more compromises in their career because of that.

Q. *Let's talk about your working methods. Whose idea was "AIDS in the Heartland?"*

A. I call it spontaneous combustion in the newsroom. In 1985 the medical reporter, myself, and our editor got together and plotted

AIDS strategy. We came up with dozens of story ideas. One of them was a diagnosis-to-death story.

Jean Pieri, the photographer, came to me and said, "When you do this, would you keep me in mind?" And I said, "Sure." But I was off doing other things. Jean wouldn't let it go, and she kept bugging me about it.

Jean and I went out one evening with someone from the Minnesota AIDS Project. He told us about Dick. And Jean got very excited. But I said, "I don't think so, he's too well known."

Jean wouldn't let it go. She went out to the farm and met Dick and Bert. She got all caught up in the fact that not only are they dealing with AIDS, they're losing the farm to foreclosure. She put the pictures in front of me and the message was, "You tell me there's no story here." And I looked at her and said, "I'll be ready to leave in 10 minutes. Go get the car."

Q. *When did you decide to make it into a series?*

A. One night Dick, Bert, Jean, and I went to dinner. My notebook was put away and Jean's cameras were down. We were just four people out to dinner. They started talking much more freely about relationships, about family issues, about the conscious decisions they had made as a couple about staying together once they knew Dick had AIDS.

The editors had me budgeted for 50 inches on a Sunday, but I was frustrated because I had all this stuff. Finally a feature writer said, "Why don't you make it an intermittent series?" So then I had to ask Dick if I could watch him die. He and Bert said yes without much hesitation.

Q. *Did you have any ground rules?*

A. We discussed what was on the record, what was off the record. If I wasn't taking notes, then we were just talking as friends. But I could go back and ask them about it. We made clear that every time Jean or I came to see them, we would let them know whether we were working or whether it was a social call.

Q. *Weren't you always working?*

A. Yes, in a way, but I felt they needed some freedom to talk about certain things openly and not worry that they'd show up in print. So if I was just visiting with them socially, I wouldn't use it unless I brought it up later and got their permission.

I was getting to know them, establishing that relationship and trust. Dick could talk for maybe half an hour, then he'd have to lay down. I'd say, "Let's take a break," and we'd make dinner, bake bread or take a walk. I didn't want them to think they had to be on during those times.

Q. *Did they ask you to leave anything out?*

A. We made an agreement with Bert. He was already showing signs of the early stages of AIDS. That was one of the most poignant parts of the story—that the partner had been given the virus by his lover and had chosen to stay and nurse his lover until death. He didn't want me to write about it. He was trying to get a loan to save the farm. He said, "Jacqui, they don't give a loan to a dying man." So I said, "I won't write about it until you get the loan or until it gets to the point in the story where I have to—by the last chapter I gotta write about it."

Q. *Had you ever negotiated with a subject like that before?*

A. On a much more limited basis. For example, I did a story on a man who lost his wife and daughter in a pipeline explosion. I said, "I know this is tough. I'm going to ask what I want to ask you. But you have the right to say no. If you say no I may try to convince you why I need that information."

Some people think that's stupid because I'm talking myself out of stuff, but I've found it works because it gives them a feeling that they're in control. They're being given some respect. It's never failed me.

Q. *How did you get such rich detail of scenes that happened before you met Dick and Bert and other scenes that you didn't observe?*

A. That was Bert. Dick was sick so much and sleeping so much and Bert and I would just have this dead time. We'd just talk and talk and talk. He was a historian. His strength was his thoroughness. He told me wonderful little anecdotes. He'd describe things and he'd remember the colors, the way things smelled and tasted. I was able to help him bring that out.

Q. *How do you do that?*

A. If he's starting to tell me a story—"Back when Dick used to come home from his congressional campaigns, I'd wait up here on the porch for him"—I'd say, "Really, tell me about that. What would you do? What time of year was it?"

One of the things I've learned to do is just keep my mouth shut. If he starts a story and stops, the tendency is to rush in and fill that gap. If you keep your mouth shut the other person will fill the gap and pretty soon they're telling you all this wonderful detail. I say over and over and over, "Give me a for instance. Tell me what it was like."

Q. *How often did you visit them?*

A. We went to the farm on weekends. Jean and I traded off because it got to be too much for them to have both of us there at once. During the week, I'd often meet them at the clinic on Wednesday mornings. Usually once or twice a week I'd meet Dick for lunch or take him and Bert out for dinner. When Dick was in the hospital I'd stop in once or twice a day.

Q. *Did you use a tape recorder?*

A. No. I don't use a tape recorder. I've found I didn't listen as carefully if I had a tape recorder going because I knew I could go back to it. When I do an interview without a tape recorder, I know that's my one opportunity so I listen and it's an exhausting process. I come out of interviews feeling like I've run a marathon. But I hear so much and remember alot and I can feel myself editing and writing in my head. I can hear my leads happening. That doesn't happen when I've got a tape recorder turned on.

Q. *How do you take notes?*

A. I have my own bastardized version of shorthand where unemployment is an "n" and woman is the little symbol and money is a dollar and things like that. Some words are just the letter. I tend to leave out articles. I write very very fast. I edit while I'm listening. I only write down the things I need. Often the person will be three or four sentences ahead and I'll be writing the sentence I really want.

If I've missed something, nobody seems offended if I say, "I'm really sorry, could you go over that again?"

Q. *So you're cleaning up the quotes as you're taking them down?*

A. I tend to write through people's vernacular and colloquialisms and make them more understandable. I don't clean up quotes once they're in my notebook. But I'm sure I'm cleaning them up while they're talking to me. If somebody uses an improper subject/verb agreement, I don't write it that way. It's just going to confuse the reader. I don't know if that's unethical. I do know it has been a long, long time since anyone accused me of misquoting or even taking something out of context.

Q. *How did you get control of such a massive amount of information? How do you organize your notes?*

A. I number the notebooks. And on the cover of the notebooks, I write a word or two about what's in there. For instance, if I had done an interview with Dick about his sexual history, I'd write, "sexual history." Or "interview with father." Most of it I just have in my head, though.

Q. *How many notebooks did you have at that point, when you were writing Chapter 1?*

A. Probably about seven or eight.

Q. *What's your writing process like?*

A. Normally, I read through my notes the night before, right before I go to bed, circle everything and then sleep on it. And when I wake up in the morning, I start writing. Usually I don't even look at my notebooks until I'm ready to start plugging in quotes.

Once I've written my lead and the first three to ten inches of a story, my nut graph or nut graph section, then I just start writing. I write as fast as I can and often I'll remember that I have a quote that says exactly what I need to illustrate this point, but I won't take the time to look in my notebook. Instead I'll put ". . .". And I'll leave blanks for times and places. Then I'll come back and fill in the blanks.

Q. *Do you use an outline?*

A. I don't outline on paper but I outline in my head. Once I write my lead and my nut graph, the outline is this grocery list of the issues, the subject areas I want to hit on. It's just these vague, general categories.

Q. *How long did it take you to write the first chapter?*

A. I dinked around on the first chapter for almost two weeks. I spent a week writing the first italic section. I threw out more attempts than I care to think about.

Q. *Do you revise in blocks or when you've blasted through it?*

A. I do both. Sometimes I'm in a mood to get something exactly right; other times I'll just blast through it. I prefer to do it the first way. I'd rather fix while I work. I do an enormous amount of rewriting.

Q. *What was the editing process like?*

A. This was Deborah's and my story. The managing editor and the metro editor were not to touch it. They could read it, they could make suggestions, but it wasn't their call. That's one of the things I like about the *Pioneer Press*. They don't do gang-bang editing. They let you have a voice.

I write in sections which range from 6 to 25 inches long. Deborah took a scissors and cut the sections apart. Then we went into a conference room and she taped each section up around the room and walked around and read them. Then she'd take a piece and move it, take another piece and move it. I had to go back and fix the transitions and make sure everything fit and flowed. It's a frightening, jarring process but it's also a brilliant one.

Q. *Did she cut the story?*

A. Not much. Deborah does what she calls taking the tinsel out of my copy. She says I hang too much tinsel on my copy, and she's probably right. She was good at appreciating the picture I was painting but taking away extraneous detail and therefore leaving the picture more spare and more powerful.

Where it would get a little too maudlin, a little too sweet, she pulled me back. But to her credit she encourages me to go that far and she says, "My job is to pull you back."

Q. *You've said the biggest challenge was to use your emotional involvement to breathe passion into the story while staying true to the facts. How did you achieve that?*

A. I relied heavily on other people around me, especially the cynical ones. I would give it to them and say, "Tell me if you want to barf. Tell me if I've basically made these people out to be too squooshy mooshy." That was how I kept my emotional involvement in check.

Q. *How did you decide how much to use about their sex lives? How did you ask them about their sex lives?*

A. They were very open about it. I wasn't asking stupid questions. I wasn't acting shocked. So they told me everything. In writing, the rule of thumb I tried to use was to give as much explicit information as I could to make people understand where they got the virus, how it was passed on, what they would have done in their lives to put them at risk, without going so far as to be kind of lurid and pandering. I didn't want to appear sensational nor did I want to turn people off. But I felt I had to say Dick had hundreds of sex partners.

Q. *You didn't say hundreds.*

A. I had it in there. Deborah took it out. She said, "I don't believe it."

Q. *No matter how irrational it might be, did you ever have any fears yourself about being with them?*

A. I don't think I did. At the end when Dick was real sick and I'd hold his hand or his arm, give him a kiss on the forehead or the cheek, sometimes he'd be real sweaty, and there were times when I'd wonder, God, is this being foolish? And I'd think, no. If the doctors and nurses are touching them, why should I worry? If they're safe and comfortable so am I.

Q. *It certainly would've destroyed some of that trust you were building if you'd been hesitant to touch him.*

A. When I met Dick, the first thing I did was shake his hand very firmly. I wanted a very visible way to display the fact that I wasn't turned off by him, I wasn't repulsed.

Q. *How do you see your mission as a journalist?*

A. I used to want to save the world; now I just want to change it. I hope to enlighten people, not just reflect society, not just react to it, but take a look at situations and issues and use those to enlighten people about the human condition. Give them enough information so they can not only think about an issue but care about it, respond to it emotionally as well as intellectually.

The kind of journalism I try to do opens doors for people so they can walk in someone else's moccasins for a while.

Q. *Is there enough of that kind of journalism going on and what makes it possible?*

A. There's more of it all the time. I like to think, this again is pretty superior and sexist, there's more of it going on because there are more women. It may be that this is just the next wave of New Journalism and it doesn't have anything to do with gender. But I tend to see that kind of journalism being done initially by women.

There's not enough of it going on because we're a profession that still has to do the meat and potatoes and this stuff tends to be gravy. A lot of people would perceive it as luxury journalism. You're not going to get beat on a story like this.

You have to be in a special place working for special people. And I think you have to be a special person to want to do it.

3 Alice Steinbach

FEATURES ■ *Baltimore Sun*

ALICE STEINBACH didn't get into journalism the conventional way. Art, not writing, was her first love. While public information director at the Baltimore Museum of Art, Steinbach began free-lancing stories about artists and their work to magazines and newspapers around the country. She calls that period an apprenticeship.

By 1981 she had worked her way into a full-time job in the features department of the *Baltimore Sun.* Four years later, Steinbach won a Pulitzer Prize.

A Baltimore native, she studied for one year at the University of London, then married and dropped out of college. Steinbach talks of the "damned hard work" it took to become a self-taught reporter whose prose leads readers down the dark halls of psychiatric wards and into the nightmares of neglected children.

Her story headlined "A Boy of Unusual Vision" won the 1985 Pulitzer Prize for feature writing. Among other honors: a 1987 United Press International Award for quality of writing; the Chesapeake Associated Press Award for best feature story 1985 and 1987. She now writes a column for the Sun.

A BOY OF UNUSUAL VISION

First, the eyes: They are large and blue, a light, opaque blue, the color of a robin's egg. And if, on a sunny spring day, you look straight into those eyes—eyes that cannot look back at you—the sharp, April light turns them pale, like the thin blue of a high, cloudless sky.

Ten-year-old Calvin Stanley, the owner of these eyes and a boy who has been blind since birth, likes this description and asks to hear it twice. He listens as only he can listen, then: "Orange used to be my favorite color but now it's blue," he announces. Pause. The eyes flutter between the short, thick lashes, "I know there's light blue and there's dark blue, but what does sky-blue look like?" he wants to know. And if you watch his face as he listens to your description, you get a sense of a picture being clicked firmly into place behind the pale eyes.

53

He is a boy who has a lot of pictures stored in his head, retrievable images which have been fashioned for him by the people who love him, by family and friends and teachers who have painstakingly and patiently gone about creating a special world for Calvin's inner eyes to inhabit.

Picture of a rainbow: "It's a lot of beautiful colors, one next to the other. Shaped like a bow. In the sky. Right across."

Picture of lightening, which frightens Calvin: "My mother says lightening looks like a Christmas tree—the way it blinks on and off across the sky," he says, offering a comforting description that would make a poet proud.

"Child," his mother once told him, "one day I won't be here and I won't be around to pick you up when you fall—nobody will be around all the time to pick you up—so you have to try to be something on your own. You have to learn how to deal with this. And to do that, you have to learn how to think."

There was never a moment when Ethel Stanley said to herself, "My son is blind and this is how I'm going to handle it."

Calvin's mother:

"When Calvin was little, he was so inquisitive. He wanted to see everything, he wanted to touch everything. I had to show him every little thing there is. A spoon, a fork. I let him play with them. The pots, the pans. Everything. I showed him the sharp edges of the table. 'You cannot touch this; it will hurt you.' He still bumped into it anyway, but he knew what he wasn't supposed to do and what he could do. And he knew that nothing in his room—nothing—could hurt him.

"And when he started walking and we went out together—I guess he was about 2—I never said anything to him about what to do. When we got to the curbs, Calvin knew that when I stopped, he should step down and when I stopped again, he should step up. I never said anything, that's just the way we did it. And it became a pattern."

Calvin remembers when he began to realize that something about him was "different": "I just figured it out myself. I think I was about 4. I would pick things up and I couldn't see them. Other people would say they could see things and I couldn't."

And his mother remembers the day her son asked her why he was blind and other people weren't.

"He must have been about 4 or 5. I explained to him what happened, that he was born that way and that it was nobody's fault and he didn't have to blame himself. He asked, 'Why me?' And I said, 'I don't know why, Calvin. Maybe there's a special plan for you in your life and there's a reason for this. But this is the way you're going to be and you can deal with it.' "

Then she sat her son down and told him this: "You're seeing, Calvin. You're just using your hands instead of your eyes. But you're seeing. And, remember, there is nothing you can't do."

It's spring vacation and Calvin is out in the alley behind his house riding his bike, a serious looking, black and silver two-wheeler. "Stay behind me," he shouts to his friend Kellie Bass, who's furiously pedaling her bike down the one-block stretch of alley where Calvin is allowed to bicycle.

Now: Try to imagine riding a bike without being able to see where you're going. Without even knowing what an "alley" looks like. Try to imagine how you navigate a space that has no visual boundaries, that exists only in your head. And then try to imagine what Calvin is feeling as he pedals his bike in that space, whooping for joy as the air rushes past him on either side.

And although Calvin can't see the signs of spring sprouting all around him in the neighboring backyards—the porch furniture and barbecue equipment being brought out of storage, the grass growing emerald green from the April rain, the forsythia exploding yellow over the fences—still, there are signs of another sort which guide him along his route:

Past the German shepherd who always barks at him, telling Calvin that he's three houses away from his home; then past the purple hyacinths, five gardens away, throwing out their fragrance (later it will be the scent of the lilacs which guide him); past the large diagonal crack which lifts the front wheel of his bike up and then down, telling him he's reached his boundary and should turn back—past all these familiar signs Calvin rides his bike on a warm spring day.

Ethel Stanley: "At 6, one of his cousins got a new bike and Calvin said, 'I want to learn how to ride a two-wheeler bike.' So we got him one. His father let him help put it together. You know, whatever Calvin gets he's going to go all over it with those hands and he knows every part of that bike and what it's called. He learned to ride it the first day, but I couldn't watch. His father stayed outside with him."

Calvin: "I just got mad. I got tired of riding a little bike. At first I used to zig-zag, go all over. My cousin would hold on to the bike and then let me go. I fell a lot in the beginning. But a lot of people fall when they first start."

There's a baseball game about to start in Calvin's backyard and Mrs. Stanley is pitching to her son. Nine-year-old Kellie, on first base, has taken off her fake fur coat so she can get a little more steam into her game and the other team member, Monet Clark, 6, is catching. It is also Monet's job to alert Calvin, who's at bat, when to swing. "Hit it, Calvin," she yells. "Swing."

He does and the sound of the ball making solid contact with the bat sends Calvin running off to first base, his hands groping in front of his body. His mother walks over to stand next to him at first base and unconsciously her hands go to his head, stroking his hair in a soft, protective movement.

"Remember," the mother had said to her son six years earlier, "there's nothing you can't do."

Calvin's father, 37-year-old Calvin Stanley, Jr., a Baltimore city policeman, has taught his son how to ride a bike and how to shift gears in the family's Volkswagen and how to put toys together. They go to the movies together and they tell each other they're handsome.

The father: "You know, there's nothing much I've missed with him. Because he does everything. Except see. He goes swimming out in the pool in the backyard. Some of the other kids are afraid of the water but he jumps right in, puts his head under. If it were me I wouldn't be as brave as he is. I probably wouldn't go anywhere. If it were me I'd probably stay in this house most of the time. But he's always ready to go, always on the telephone, ready to do something.

"But he gets sad, too: You can just look at him sometimes and tell he's real sad."

The son: "You know what makes me sad? 'Charlotte's Web.' That's my favorite story. I listen to the record at night. I like Charlotte, the spider. The way she talks. And, you know, she really loved Wilbur, the pig. He was her best friend." Calvin's voice is full of warmth and wonder as he talks about E.B. White's tale of the spider who befriended a pig and later sacrificed herself for him.

"It's a story about friendship. It's telling us how good friends are supposed to be. Like Charlotte and Wilbur," he says, turning away from you suddenly to wipe his eyes. "And when Charlotte dies, it makes me real sad. I always feel like I've lost a friend. That's why I try not to listen to that part. I just move the needle forward."

Something else makes Calvin sad: "I'd like to see what my mother looks like," he says, looking up quickly and swallowing hard. "What does she look like? People tell me she's pretty."

The mother: "One day Calvin wanted me to tell him how I

looked. He was about 6. They were doing something in school for Mother's Day and the kids were drawing pictures of their mothers. He wanted to know what I looked like and that upset me because I didn't know how to tell him. I thought, 'How am I going to explain this to him so he will really know what I look like?' So I tried to explain to him about facial features, noses and I just used touch. I took his hands and I tried to explain about skin, let him touch his, and then mine.

"And I think that was the moment when Calvin really knew he was blind, because he said, 'I won't ever be able to see your face . . . or Daddy's face,' " she says softly, covering her eyes with her hands, but not in time to stop the tears. "That's the only time I've ever let it bother me that much."

But Mrs. Stanley knew what to tell her only child: "I said, 'Calvin, you can see my face. You can see it with your hand and by listening to my voice and you can tell more about me that way than somebody who can use his eyes.' "

Provident Hospital, November 15, 1973: That's where Calvin Stanley III was born, and his father remembers it this way: "I saw him in the hospital before my wife did, and I knew immediately that something was wrong with his eyes. But I didn't know what."

The mother remembers it this way: "When I woke up after the caesarean I had a temperature and I couldn't see Calvin except through the window of the nursery. The next day a doctor came around to see me and said that he had cataracts and asked me if I had a pediatrician. From what I knew, cataracts could be removed so I thought, 'Well, he'll be fine.' I wasn't too worried. Then when this pediatrician came and examined him he told me he thought it was congenital glaucoma."

Only once did Mrs. Stanley give in to despair. "When they knew for certain it was glaucoma and told me that the cure rate was very poor because they so seldom have infants born with glaucoma, I felt awful. I blamed myself. I knew I must have done something wrong when I was pregnant. Then I blamed my husband," she says, looking up from her hands which are folded in her lap, "but I never told him that." Pause. "And he probably blamed me."

No, says her husband. "I never really blamed her: I blamed myself. I felt it was a payback. That if you do something wrong to somebody else in some way you get paid back for it. I figured maybe I did something wrong, but I couldn't figure out what I did that was that bad and why Calvin had to pay for it."

Mrs. Stanley remembers that the doctors explained to them that the glaucoma was not because of anything either of them had done before or during the pregnancy and that 'congenital' simply means 'at birth.'

They took Calvin to a New York surgeon who specialized in congenital glaucoma. There were seven operations and the doctors held out some hope for some vision, but by age 3 there was no improvement and the Stanleys were told that everything that could be done for Calvin had been done.

"You know, in the back of my mind, I think I always knew he would never see," Mrs. Stanley says, "and that I had to reach out to him in different ways. The toys I bought him were always toys that made a noise, had sound, something that Calvin could enjoy. But it didn't dawn on me until after he was in school that I had been doing that—buying toys that would stimulate him."

Thirty-three year old Ethel Stanley, a handsome, strong-looking woman with a radiant smile, is the oldest of seven children and grew up looking after her younger brothers and sisters while her mother worked. "She was a wonderful mother," Mrs. Stanley recalls. "Yes, she had to work, but when she was there, she was with you every minute and those minutes were worth a whole day. She always had time to listen to you."

Somewhere—perhaps from her own childhood experiences— Mrs. Stanley, who has not worked since Calvin was born, acquired the ability to nurture and teach and poured her mothering love into Calvin. And it shows. He moves in the sighted world with trust and faith and the unshakable confidence of a child whose mother has always been there for him. "If you don't understand something, ask," she tells Calvin again and again, in her open, forthright way. "Just ask."

When it was time to explain to Calvin the sexual differences between boys and girls, this is what Mrs. Stanley said: "When he was about 7, I told him that when you're conceived you have both sexes. It's not decided right away whether you're going to be a boy or a girl. And he couldn't believe it. He said, 'Golly, suppose somebody got stuck?' I thought, 'Please, just let me get this out of the way first.'

"And I tried to explain to him what a woman's sexual organs look like. I tried to track it on a table with his fingers. I said, well you know what yours look like, don't you? And I told him what they're called, the medical names. 'Don't use names if you don't know what they mean. Ask. Ask.'"

"When he was little he wanted to be Stevie Wonder," says Calvin's father, laughing. "He started playing the piano and he got pretty good at it. Now he wants to be a computer programmer and design programs for the blind."

Calvin's neatly ordered bedroom is outfitted with all the comforts you would find in the room of many 10-year-old, middle-class boys: a television set (black and white, he tells you), an Atari game with a box of cartridges (his favorite is "Phoenix"), a braille Monopoly set, records, tapes and programmed talking robots. "I watch wrestling on TV with my friends. It's fun."

He moves around his room confidently and easily. "I know this house like a book." Still, some things are hard for him to remember since, in his case, much of what he remembers has to be imagined visually first. Like the size and color of his room. "I think it's kind of big," he says of the small room. "And, it's green," he says of the deep rose-colored walls.

And while Calvin doesn't need to turn the light on in his room he does like to have some kind of sound going constantly. Loud sound.

"It's 3 o'clock," he says, as the theme music from a TV show blares out into his room.

"Turn that TV down," says his mother, evenly. "You're not deaf, you know."

From the beginning, Ethel and Calvin Stanley were determined their blind son would go to public school. "We were living in Baltimore county when it was time for Calvin to start school and they told me I would have to pay a tuition for him to go to the public school, and that really upset me," Mrs. Stanley says. "I had words with some of the big honchos out there. I knew they had programs in schools for children with vision problems and I thought public education should be free.

"We decided we would move to Baltimore city if we had to, and I got hold of a woman in the mayor's office. And that woman was the one who opened all the doors for us. She was getting ready to retire but she said she wasn't going to retire until she got this straight for Calvin. I don't know how she did it. But she did."

Now in the fourth grade, Calvin has been attending the Cross County Elementary School since kindergarten. He is one of six blind students in Baltimore city who are fully main-streamed which, in this context, means they attend public school with sighted students in a regular classroom. Four of these students are at Cross Country Elementary School. If Calvin stays in public school through the 12th grade, he will be the first blind student to be completely educated within the regular public school system.

Two p.m., Vivian Jackson's class, Room 207.

What Calvin can't see: He can't see the small, pretty girl sitting opposite him, the one who is wearing little rows of red, yellow and blue barrettes shaped like airplanes in her braided hair. He can't see the line of small, green plants growing in yellow pots all along the sunny window sill. And he can't see Mrs. Jackson in her rose-pink suit and pink enameled earrings shaped like little swans.

("Were they really shaped like little swans?" he will ask later.)

But Calvin can feel the warm spring breeze — invisible to everyone's eyes, not just his — blowing in through the window and he can hear the tapping of a young oak tree's branches against the window. He can hear Mrs. Jackson's pleasant, musical voice and, later, if you ask him what she looks like, he will say, "She's nice."

But best of all, Calvin can read and spell and do fractions and follow the classroom work in his specially prepared braille books. He is smart and he can do everything the rest of his class can do. Except see.

"What's the next word, Calvin?" Mrs. Jackson asks.

"Eleven," he says, reading from his braille textbook.

"Now tell us how to spell it — without looking back at the book!" she says quickly, causing Calvin's fingers to fly away from the forbidden word.

"E-l-e-v-e-n," he spells out easily.

It all seems so simple, the ease with which Calvin follows along, the manner in which his blindness has been accommodated. But it's deceptively simple. The amount of work that has gone into getting Calvin to this point — the number of teachers, vision specialists and mobility instructors, and the array of special equipment is staggering.

Patience and empathy from his teachers have played a large role, too.

For instance, there's Dorothy Lloyd, the specialist who is teaching Calvin the slow and very difficult method of using an Optacon, a device which allows a blind person to read a printed page by touch by converting printed letters into a tactile representation.

And there's Charleye Dyer, who's teaching Calvin things like "mobility" and "independent travel skills," which include such tasks as using a cane and getting on and off buses. Of course, what Miss Dyer is really teaching Calvin is freedom: the ability to move about independently and without fear in the larger world.

There's also Lois Sivits, who, among other things, teaches Calvin braille and is his favorite teacher. And, to add to a list which is endless, there's the music teacher who comes in 30 minutes early each Tuesday to give him a piano lesson, and his home room teacher, Mrs. Jackson, who is as finely tuned to Calvin's cues as a player in a musical duet would be to her partner.

An important part of Calvin's school experience has been his contact with sighted children.

"When he first started school," his mother recalls, "some of the kids would tease him about his eyes. 'Oh, they're so big and you can't see.' But I just told him, 'Not any time in your life will everybody around you like you—whether you can see or not. They're just children and they don't know they're being cruel. And I'm sure it's not the last time someone will be cruel to you. But it's all up to you because you have to go to school and you'll have to deal with it.' "

Calvin's teachers say he's well liked, and watching him on the playground and in class you get the impression that the only thing that singles him out from the other kids is that someone in his class is always there to take his hand if he needs help.

"I'd say he's really well accepted," says his mobility teacher, Miss Dyer, "and that he's got a couple of very special friends."

Eight-year-old Brian Butler is one of these special friends. "My best friend," says Calvin proudly, introducing you to a studious-looking boy whose eyes are alert and serious behind his glasses. The two boys are not in the same class, but they ride home together on the bus every day.

Here's Brian explaining why he likes Calvin so much: "He's funny and he makes me laugh. And I like him because he always makes me feel better when I don't feel good." And, he says, his friendship with Calvin is no different from any other good friendship. Except for one thing: "If Calvin's going to bump into a wall or something, I tell him, 'Look out,' " says Brian, sounding as though it were the most natural thing in the world to do when walking with a friend.

"Charlotte would have done it for Wilbur," is the way Calvin sizes up Brian's help, evoking once more that story about "how friendship ought to be."

A certain moment:

Calvin is working one-on-one with Lois Sivits, a teacher who is responsible for the braille skills which the four blind children at Cross Country must have in order to do all the work necessary in their regular classes. He is very relaxed with Miss Sivits, who is gentle, patient, smart and, like Calvin, blind. Unlike Calvin, she was not able to go to public school but was sent away at age 6, after many operations on her eyes, to a residential school — the Western Pennsylvania School for the Blind.

And although it was 48 years ago that Lois Sivits was sent away from her family to attend the school for the blind, she remembers — as though it were 48 minutes ago — how that blind 6-year-old girl felt about the experience: "Oh, I was so very homesick. I had a very hard time being separated from my family. It took me three years before I began getting used to it. But I knew I had to stay there. I would have given anything to be able to stay at home and go to a public school like Calvin," says the small, kind-looking woman with very still hands.

Now, the moment: Calvin is standing in front of the window, the light pouring in from behind him. He is listening to a talking clock which tells him, "It's 11:52 a.m." Miss Sivits stands about 3 feet away from him, also in front of the window holding a huge braille dictionary in her hands, fingers flying across the page as she silently reads from it. And for a few moments, there they are as if frozen in a tableau, the two of them standing in darkness against the light, each lost for a moment in a private world that is composed only of sound and touch.

There was another moment, years ago, when Calvin's mother and father knew that the operations had not helped, that their son was probably never going to see. "Well," said the father, trying to comfort the mother, "we'll do what we have to do and Calvin will be fine."

He is. And so are they.

A Visit with Alice Steinbach

Sherry Ricchiardi: *How did you get into journalism?*

Alice Steinbach: My background actually is in art history. I was doing public information work and writing a monthly newspaper for the Baltimore Museum of Art. I began to free-lance for *Art in America* and other national art publications.

I had absolutely no trouble selling my stories. From the first moment I submitted my stuff to newspapers and magazines, they bought it. I have no idea why. I really didn't know anything about journalism.

Q. *How did you learn to market your stories?*

A. If you're smart, you figure these things out. I guess it's great to go to journalism school, but I don't think you have to go to journalism school. You go to the library; you check out books that tell you who is the editor of what. You report. You research.

Being a reporter wasn't mysterious to me. I went about it as though it were a business.

Q. *What lessons did free-lancing teach you?*

A. I always laugh when a beginning writer says, "I don't want to put all this time into an article if I don't know somebody's going to buy it." I saw free-lancing as my apprenticeship.

I would get $75 for an article that I had traveled to Washington, D.C., or New York City to do on my own money. Then I'd spend a week researching, interviewing, writing. That was not an unusual fee. For magazine pieces, I got more.

I took vacation days to do interviews and spent nights and weekends writing. It was a great investment of time. I free-lanced from about 1976 to 1981 and also worked full time at the art museum.

Q. *Who served as your mentors along the way?*

A. Good writers. I always loved writing; I always loved reading. The two are inextricable. James Agee and E. B. White are two of my absolute favorites, and in my opinion, two more diametrically opposed writers you will never find. They are a curious hybrid of journalist and creative writer.

Both of those writers stray from strict journalistic stance by interjecting little pieces of themselves. I also tend to do that. I guess I could be faulted for it. People could say this is not pure reporting.

Q. *Could you elaborate?*

A. If you're going to write a very long piece about someone like Calvin Stanley or about a universal issue, why would anyone wade through it if it was strictly who, what, when, where, why, and how?

To me, feature writing at it's best is a combination of style and substance. And, there's a third thing, which is perilous and very tricky, and that is a vantage point. To be utterly successful at these kinds of stories, you have to be standing somewhere. You have to be looking at your subject from a vantage point.

Some stories lend themselves better to this approach than others. There are some stories in which you couldn't do it. It would be arrogant and wrong; it wouldn't work.

I believe whatever success I've had has come because I walk a line between journalism in the traditional sense and literary journalism.

Q. *How did your job at the* Baltimore Sun *come about?*

A. I wasn't really aiming for a full-time position on a newspaper. But I had sold many articles to the *Baltimore Sun* and I got a lot of encouragement from the feature editors. Eventually there was an opening and I was asked to apply. That was 1981.

Q. *Does being a woman affect the subject matter you write about?*

A. The person I am affects the subject matter I write about. Part of what I am is a woman, but there are many other parts and they all form the whole.

I have no strong sense that being a woman dominates what I do or that it plays a negative role. In some cases, it may have played a positive role. Sometimes during an interview a woman is less threatening. She's not perceived to be as tough as a man and that can work for me.

I'm never afraid to say, "I don't understand." Culturally, that may be more difficult for men.

I haven't felt sexual discrimination of any kind at this newspaper. Of course, I have never worked in any other newsroom.

Q. *Were there major obstacles along the way?*

A. I was a single parent and my two sons were young enough to need supervision when I started this. They now are 21 and 24. I had a good support system from family and friends. I was lucky, but I can't say it was a piece of cake.

It was damned hard work without a guarantee of any kind of return. It's important for young people in any field to realize they get out of it what they put into it.

Q. *Is networking with other female journalists important to you?*

A. I have a network of friends — some in the business and some not. It's a rather large network in that I have lived in this city on and off all of my life. I would call it a rather informal networking. I don't belong to any groups.

Q. *Tell me about the Pulitzer Prize.*

A. My mother had died a month before the Pulitzer was announced. I had taken a month off. Quite frankly, reporting and newspapers were far from my experience at that time.

When I came back to work, somebody in the newsroom told me I was a finalist. I couldn't believe it. I was in a period of reassessment. It was unreal.

Q. *How has it affected your career?*

A. It changed it in interesting ways. I had to make a decision about whether to move on. I got job offers from larger newspapers; one offered me a wonderful job. They said I could do anything I wanted, even write a column. I had to decide if I wanted to leave Baltimore and a life I had fashioned for myself.

Was I really in this to move from newspaper to newspaper? Or was I in it to do what I wanted to do which this paper was letting me do? The Pulitzer opened quite a few doors.

Q. *Where did the idea for the Calvin Stanley piece come from?*

A. The idea came from a very concrete incident. I was driving to work one day and stopped at a red light downtown. Out of the corner of my eye, I saw this young girl, about 15 years old, walking down the street. She was so cute and dressed in the latest fashion. When I looked back, I saw a white cane flash out. I was startled that she was blind.

That told me that I needed to revise my impressions of the blind. Why should I be so startled that a very contemporary-looking teenager was blind? I decided to write about it. I started calling sources to find a teenager like the one I had seen.

I didn't know what the story was going to be. I trust my instincts. I trust that if it interests me, it will interest the reader.

Q. *But, Calvin wasn't a teenager. How did you decide on him?*

A. Everybody I called said, "I don't know anybody like that, but there's this boy named Calvin." I said, "No, no. I don't want a 9-year-old. I want a teenager."

People kept raving about this boy they had met in one way or another. So I finally decided to interview him.

Q *How did you go about gaining the family's trust?*

A. I called the school and asked them to see if Calvin's mother and father would come for an interview. I wanted the parents to know what I was attempting to do.

I talked with the Stanleys at some length and knew immediately that I had a good story. There were 100 good quotes in that first interview. But, I didn't take notes. I just wanted to find out who they were. I explained what an article like this could mean, particularly to Calvin.

I was very honest with them about the intimacy. I would be hanging around. I would want to be in their home on weekends; I would want to go out with them. I told them that the photographer — a great photographer named David Harp — would want to be with me, too. I told them we would want to be in Calvin's classroom.

This was a 9-year-old boy and I didn't want to compromise him in any way. They immediately said they would do it. I told them to think about it for a week. I then talked to each of them separately and to Calvin and told him all of the same things.

I said, "Calvin, this could change how your classmates and your teachers feel about you. You might be embarrassed." I also gave the family some of my articles to read—some very intimate articles.

They were private citizens; they didn't know the rules of the game. I called at the end of the week and they said yes. I went into the story with no holds barred.

Q. *When did you know it would work?*

A. When Calvin told me his favorite book was "Charlotte's Webb," by E. B. White, I knew it was meant to be. That's also one of my favorite books. He and I cried together as we sat in the dark in his room and listened to the record one night.

I knew immediately that I had a kid here who was everything I could have wanted in a subject.

Q. *How long did you work on the story?*

A. One month. Three weeks of reporting; one week of writing. It was one of the easiest things I have ever written in my life. I went in on Monday, wrote some and put it away. I did that every day through Friday. It just came out.

Q. *Was it really that easy?*

A. Actually, it wasn't as easy as it sounds. I do a lot of unconscious groundwork, looking for a narrative, a way to tell the story. To me that is the key, to find the backbone on which you're going to lay all the musculature. It's like building a sculpture in a way.

I once read a book called *Listening with a Third Ear.* That's what you have to do to get detail into a story, which is a key element.

You have to be like a psychoanalyst, making free associations: "Tell me more about that." You're listening for certain things. You know instinctively what needs to be elaborated on because it speaks volumes about something.

I always overinterview and overresearch. I will use one-tenth or one-fiftieth of it, but it pays off because I really know the subject. I know the person or the situation well enough to recognize the outstanding detail.

Q. *How did you go about organizing the story?*

A. If there is a rule of thumb for how I organize a story, it's that there is no rule of thumb. There probably are 100 different ways to organize a story, which is why I say there is no such thing as objective reporting.

People will tell you there are rules for organizing, but I don't believe there are. I remember going to a lecture once and hearing a distinguished reporter give a talk on how he writes. He had a 26-point list of how he organizes.

A writer's sensibility ultimately is what organizes the story. It can be pretty frightening when I sit down with stacks of notes.

Q. *Do you work from an outline?*

A. Never. When an editor says, "Make an outline on that," I never do. I pretend I didn't hear and I never bring it back.

Q. *So, how do you organize?*

A. With big stories, I get a spiral-bound notebook and write down the names of the people I interview on separate pages. I go through my notes and pull out all the best quotes and write them on their page with a cross-reference to where the quote came from.

I number all the pages of my notes. I go through and do this for each person who is important to the story, otherwise I would be doing nothing but looking through hundreds of pages of notes. Unconsciously, with every step, I do more organizing than I think.

Q. *Do you write from the lead down?*

A. I'm a person who thinks a lead is extremely important and I cannot begin a story without one. Until I get it right, I'm not comfortable. At that point, the lead is for me, not the reader.

Until I know I have a good handle on the lead, and it doesn't have to be letter perfect, I can't go on. I have to know I'm in the ball park.

Q. *How did you decide on the lead for the Calvin story?*

A. The Calvin lead just came. I remember thinking, it has to be first the eyes. You don't meet Calvin without noticing his eyes. They were the most unusual eyes I'd ever seen; I had never seen that color blue before.

I said, "Listen to this, Calvin." I read the lead to him. He loved the description. I wanted the readers to see him as I saw him. There were probably 100 other leads I could have used. Now, that's not objectivity. That's me.

Q. *How much time did you spend with the family?*

A. Some days I didn't go over at all. I felt it was important to take a day off in between and type up my notes. I debriefed myself to see what I had and what I needed. An advantage to doing a long story is being able to go back and ask more questions.

One weekend the photographer and I went over and watched a baseball game in Calvin's backyard. It was a rag-tag group of kids;

they were adorable. Dave was standing on top of the garage taking pictures. By the end of the day, Dave was pitching and I was playing third base.

You get your best stuff then and you're not even taking notes. I write it down after it happens. In any story that's successful, 50 percent of the credit goes to the people you write about—maybe more.

Q. *How did you get the rich detail, such as the smell of hyacinths when Calvin was riding his bike or the barking dog?*

A. I went into his classroom; I rode the school bus with him. When he went out with the mobility teacher, I walked behind them. I spent time with Calvin alone in his room when he watched TV; I listened to records with him. I rode a bicycle in the alley alongside of him.

Each time I would notice a different detail. It was a middle-class neighborhood. I noticed the barbecue equipment and that a dog leaped out and barked every time Calvin rode by. We rode back and forth 12 to 15 times together.

I thought, this is what Calvin can't see. I wrote it down and put it in the story. I was trying to determine what kind of signals this boy was getting. A pattern began to emerge. If I hadn't done it with him, I wouldn't have known.

Some reporters pride themselves on being distant. To me, that's not even desirable.

Q. *What was your goal with this story?*

A. I have had people say, "I read that story and I felt I could see it—I felt I was standing right there." That's what motivates me. I want readers to have the sense they are experiencing it.

When Calvin was riding the bike, I wanted them to smell the hyacinths, to feel the crack in the sidewalk.

My ultimate goal was to place the reader in the Stanleys' lives. One of my strategies is always to open up a little piece—a tiny piece— of other worlds so we can look into them.

Q. *What was the Calvin story really about?*

A. I don't think I knew as I was writing it, but unconsciously toward the end, I realized that it was about Ethel Stanley. About the kind of mothering love that can prepare a person for a place in the world, no matter what. That seemed universal to me.

It was not a story about conflict and resolution; it was about people, about how they affect one another. I never saw it as a story about a handicapped child, not after I met the three of them.

Q. *What about the content and form?*

A. This story didn't require a lot of research, not in the traditional sense. In the beginning, I had to report, which to me means listening, looking, hearing, asking questions to understand people.

If you have the time, you immerse yourself in their world as much as they'll let you. After you get all of that, you think about form. The content is what determines the form.

Q. *Tell me more about that.*

A. I love putting together words that are beautiful. It's always thrilling for me to find the right words and think, without being arrogant or conceited, "That's rather nice. Those words sound rather beautiful together."

I think of writing very much like music. I think of punctuation as the rhythm. A semicolon is a semistop; a colon is a stop. There is a rhythm to my writing. I can hear a dissonant word a mile away—it's too hard, too soft, too pretty, not pretty enough. It's alliterative, not alliterative enough.

I want to grab people with the writing, with the descriptions I create.

Q. *What kind of stories do you look for?*

A. I look for a story that I have some empathy with. I say there is no such thing as a totally objective reporter. If you were, I wouldn't want to read you. If you are a feature writer—and that's all I've ever wanted to be—the stories you're drawn to show a certain amount of subjectivity.

When I feel I have a story that demonstrates a universal principle, I'm in heaven.

Q. *Tell me about the interviewing process with the Stanleys.*

A. I started out interviewing them one at a time. I began with the mother. I spent about two and one-half hours with her one afternoon in her dining room. We had about 85 cups of coffee.

I always interview people separately first because the group dynamic tends to take over and you have the dominant person talking. Besides, I didn't want each parent to hear what the other was saying. Frankly, I didn't want them influenced by one another.

I interviewed Calvin alone many times. I interviewed the parents together and with Calvin. It was a combination of many things. I instantly knew that Mrs. Stanley was the key figure and I was going to get the outline of the story from her.

Q. *Do you imagine the shape of a story during the interviewing?*

A. Not really, but parts of it will float out at me. I am organizing in my mind when I'm preparing to write. It's a little like being an athlete. Until the gun goes off and you start to run, it's a little scary and makes you feel anxious.

Q. *Do deadlines help?*

A. Oh yes, absolutely.

Q. *Do you wait until the last minute to write?*

A. Usually, but with Calvin, I didn't have a fixed deadline. It would have been better in some ways if I had. I give myself deadlines. I say, "Today I have to do an interview, get records, transcribe a tape. If I get all that done, I'll have put in a good day's work."

I set little goals but the start of writing is the horrendous part.

Q. *Do you experience a sense of fear in the beginning?*

A. It's horrible. Once I get 15 to 25 inches into the computer, I'm all right. I sometimes try to start a big story at home because I need room to spread my notes out. Starting is the hardest part for me.

Q. *Do you transcribe tapes yourself?*

A. Always. Although it's the biggest drag in the world, you hear things when you're transcribing that you didn't hear in the interview. It's amazing. You hear inflections in voice; you hear hesitations.

I usually use a tape recorder for long one-on-one interviews. I carry a notebook all the time. I record observations. I'm a very accurate note-taker.

I very seldom do phone interviews. There's nothing like a face-to-face interview to get that special quote. There is no substitute.

Q. *Do you clean up quotations?*

A. Never. I don't tamper with quotes. I don't use them if they need to be tampered with.

Q. *Do you have any magic tricks for reporting or writing?*

A. One thing I learned that is very important as an interviewing technique is to give your interviewees their due. So many reporters ask questions and don't give people a chance to say what they'd like.

Also, reporters should learn to front-load their questions. You never start with the one that is going to get you thrown out, that's common sense. But, I do prioritize questions in my mind that I absolutely must have answers to.

Q. *Do you rewrite much?*

A. I rewrite a tremendous amount, but on these wonderful word processors, you don't feel like you're rewriting so much.

Q. *How did you decide on the ending for Calvin's story?*

A. I made a value judgment; that's another thing reporters aren't supposed to do. But I thought, what the hell, I was there. Readers have to trust that I am telling the truth as I saw it.

So, I decided to cross the line and come right out and say the Stanleys were a fine family. It felt right to end the story that way.

4 Bella Stumbo

FEATURES ■ *Los Angeles Times*

BELLA STUMBO'S start in journalism was inauspicious. Of her days at UPI in 1967, she says:

"I mostly fetched coffee and donuts for the fellas, did rewrites, and once got to write about Muriel Humphrey. I wasn't liberated enough to get angry about it. I felt bad and didn't know why."

As the women's movement built, Stumbo found out why she felt bad. She also found a better job: reporting for the *Los Angeles Times,* where she has been since 1972. She is a national correspondent.

Born in eastern Kentucky, Stumbo, 46, was raised in southeastern Colorado. She received her bachelor's degree in political science and journalism from the University of Denver. She has a master's degree in political science from the University of California, Santa Barbara, and a master's in journalism from Northwestern University in Evanston, Illinois.

She has won the Paul Myhre Award, J.C. Penney-University of Missouri award, and the Los Angeles Press Club award. In January 1990, she was the subject of a *Newsweek* magazine article titled, "People Say the Darndest Things to Bella Stumbo." It was sparked by her interview with Washington, D.C., Mayor Marion Barry and the revealing story that followed in the *Los Angeles Times.* According to *Newsweek,* Barry was another in a long line of prominent politicians to be *"Stumboed."*

SIAMESE TWINS, 32
A Single-Minded Dream for Separate Identities

Siamese twin girls, they were of the rarest kind, the type that occurs, the experts estimate, only once in every 2.5 million births.

They were born on May 14, 1949, at Los Angeles County General Hospital. Described in medical terminology as craniopagus twins, they were joined at the tops of their heads.

For nearly two years they remained at the hospital, while teams of doctors monitored their every movement, whimper and smile.

In the end, all the doctors agreed: Here was a natural tragedy that man could not reverse. Little Yvonne and Yvette Jones had separate brains, normal bodies and different personalities. But their blood

71

stream was irrevocably shared. They could not be separated.

The mother was summoned to hear the final news.

Her name was Willa Jones, ("Willie" to her friends) and she was then 38. A black woman, she was divorced, had five other, normal children at home and worked as a presser in the garment district. Her health was poor because the birth of the twins had been hard. But her attitude was good.

"God gave them to me," she said, dispatching a nightmare, "so I guess he'll show me the way to raise them."

The doctors regarded her with sad smiles. They suggested that she give the babies up, that they be turned over to the courts. Institutionalized.

Willie Jones regarded the doctors with horror.

They tried in vain to make her see what was in store. Just to keep the twins alive, they explained, a full-time nurse would be required to watch them constantly. For example, they pointed out, one twin might easily break the neck of the other, merely by jerking her head abruptly.

In addition, the doctors said, the twins would need special exercise machinery to prevent muscle atrophy since they would probably never accomplish more than an awkward crawl.

Certainly, they told Willie Jones, who had quit listening, the twins would never walk.

Yvonne and Yvette Jones, 32, were having dinner with a couple of friends in a midtown Italian restaurant.

The young waiter was so shocked that he could barely serve.

First, he didn't bring them menus. Then he returned with only one, blushed, rushed off again and returned with two. He dropped his order pad, spilled a glass of wine and tried three times before he managed to get Yvette's cigarette lit. He didn't know where to fix his eyes, what to do with his face.

Yvonne watched for a while in silence, her bright, lively eyes following his every fumbling move. "What's your name, hon?" she finally asked, a slight smile playing on her face.

"Steve," he said, looking at the bread basket.

"I'm Yvonne," she said, then introduced her two friends across the table. There was a small pause.

"And I'm Yvette," Yvette finally said in a small voice.

"Oh, yeah," exclaimed Yvonne in apparent surprise. "I forgot about her."

For a split second, the young waiter looked like a man trapped in a madhouse. His jaw dropped, his eyes rolled.

Then he realized it was a joke. He grinned uncertainly, then giggled, then, in an explosion of tension, he laughed out loud. For the first time all evening, his attention found a natural focus. Still chuckling, he looked directly into the laughing brown eyes of the young woman with the sense of humor. Yvonne winked at him.

Yvette, quiet and shy compared to her vivacious sister, offered a bashful smile and told him the spaghetti was good. She loves to eat, and the spirit showed. Before long, the young waiter had heard all about her ongoing battle against fat, how she once jumped from her present size 7 to a 22, and Yvonne had ballooned, too, from a 5 to a 20.

"It was so bad, you could hardly see my eyes," Yvette confessed.

By the end of the meal, he was nagging the twins about their eating habits.

They always eat and drink exactly the same things, in precisely the same amounts, and always at the same time. He wanted them to try two different desserts, both house specialties.

Grumbling good-naturedly, they did. By the time they left the restaurant, the beaming young waiter was treating them both like old friends.

The pattern rarely varies. Wherever they go, the Jones twins are a measure of human nature. They are unrelentingly friendly, always smiling, joking and reaching out. They know that it is up to them to try to set people at ease. Given the opportunity, they generally succeed.

Siamese, or conjoined, twins—infants physically joined at birth in some fashion—occur once in about every 50,000 births, according to most medical authorities. Few survive more than a few days.

The defect occurs when the single fertilized ovum that produces identical twins fails to separate properly. Why this improper separation occurs remains a matter of medical conjecture.

Medical history is filled with references to conjoined twins and efforts to separate them. The earliest pair on record were sisters, born in England in 1100. With a single set of arms and legs, they lived to be 34.

The first recorded effort to separate conjoined twins occurred in Germany in 1505, when doctors attempted unsuccessfully to save a 10-year-old craniopagus twin whose sister had died.

It was not until 1902 that a pair of twins, joined at the chest (thoracopagus twins, the most common kind), were separated, with one twin surviving. Since then, countless sets of twins have been successfully separated the world over. Parents nowadays almost always opt for surgery, even when it means risking the life of one or both babies.

Separating totally joined craniopagus twins remains the most hazardous operation. Not until 1952 did at least one twin survive surgery. At present, the only total craniopagus twins who have been separated, with both still surviving, are Lisa and Elisa Hansen of Ogden, Utah. Now almost 4, the twins underwent the first in a series of complicated operations in May, 1979, at the University of Utah Medical Center.

Conjoined twins became popularly known as Siamese twins in the nineteenth century, when the world discovered Chang and Eng, a pair of twins born in 1811 in rural Siam (now Thailand).

Joined at the chest by a thick, five-inch-long ligature, Chang and Eng were bright, nice-looking boys whose deformity was just grotesque enough to fascinate, without being monstrous enough to sicken. They first captured the fancy of their king, Rama III, who wined and dined them at his Bangkok palace when they were 14.

From there, the pair went on to achieve international fame, exhibiting themselves profitably for many years to eager throngs throughout Europe and America. High society fawned over them, the press reported their every move, even Mark Twain sought an audience. With the possible exception of Tom Thumb, P. T. Barnum's great 28-inch-high find, they were everybody's favorite human novelty.

Eventually, the twins retired from show business and became prosperous farmers and slave owners in North Carolina, where they married two sisters and produced 21 children between them.

When Chang fell ill and died in 1874, at age 63, the healthy Eng immediately sickened. Within two hours, he was dead, too, before doctors had an opportunity to sever the ligature that bound them.

The medical consensus was that Eng died of shock and sheer terror. (Born today, doctors say, they could have been separated at birth, or later.)

Chang and Eng were the first and the last Siamese twins to achieve great fame, perhaps because no others since have been so actively promoted.

Yvonne and Yvette Jones, for example, are the only adult

Siamese twins, still joined, who survive, according to available records. Yet, they are almost unknown outside limited church circles in the black communities of Los Angeles, where they have lived most of their lives, and Augusta, Ga., where they lived from 1972 to 1977 and became gospel singers.

Almost nothing has been written about them, apart from articles in medical journals and a handful of stories in black publications. They appeared once a few years ago on a television talk show about abnormal people. Even the producers of TV's "That's Incredible" have not approached them.

The *Los Angeles Times* stopped writing about the twins in 1951, the year they were released from the hospital. The final flurry of stories concerned Willie Jones' struggle to keep her children out of a circus.

According to the *Times,* when Jones went to retrieve her children after their two-year stay at the hospital, she was presented not only with a list of expensive special requirements for rearing Siamese twins but also with a $14,000 hospital bill. This stunned her because she had thought all the attention being lavished upon her babies was free. Also, she didn't have any money.

"The only suggestion yet made for providing such a sum is by exhibiting them for money, probably in a circus sideshow," the *Times* reported on Feb. 5, 1951.

"They're worth more than money," Jones protested to reporters when the first circus offers began to pour in. "I love them just as dearly as I do my other children." She vowed to find another way.

In the end, however, a saddened Willie Jones capitulated, according to the *Times*, and signed a contract with the Clyde Beatty circus. A superior Court judge approved the document, which stipulated that 30 percent of the twins' earnings would go toward their county hospital bill.

And so, in the tradition of Chang and Eng more than 100 years earlier, the twins went on exhibit. They were transported by ambulance, the *Times* said, to the glassed-in mobile unit that became their home.

By all accounts, they were a huge success, the premiere attraction among other, less breathtaking human examples of nature's caprice. They subsequently worked carnivals, too.

But it didn't last long. Within two years, Willie Jones was back in Los Angeles, her pride damaged but her will evidently intact.

She had married a factory worker named Charles McCarther,

who promised to help. From money she had saved, she made a small down payment on a house, satisfying her lifetime dream of owning "a home of my own." And soon after, before they were 4, the twins were walking.

They were standing in front of a mirror in their bedroom, intently combing their hair. They constantly fiddle with their hair, which rarely seems to please them.

They were dressed in matching jeans and striped, scoopneck T-shirts, which they step into. They always dress identically because, said Yvonne, "Otherwise we'd look awkward."

"My hair's too short," grumped Yvette, who had been to the hairdresser the day before. "I went to some new place, and I shouldn't have," she explained. The twins always speak in the singular, never the plural. It can be disconcerting at first.

"Mine's too curly," said Yvonne. "I think I'll get it straightened some."

"I just hope mine'll grow out fast," sighed Yvette, glaring at her reflection in the mirror.

A BOUNDARY LINE FOR HAIR CARE

They combed in silence for a time, two combs, four hands, four elbows busily churning in the air.

Asked finally how they determine whose hair is whose, Yvonne's hands hardly skipped a lick.

"It's simple. Here, I'll show you," she said, still peering at herself in the mirror. With a practiced flick of the wrist, she drew an arbitrary part across the long, continuous crown that connects her to her sister.

"That hair," she said solemnly, pointing to the far side of the line, "is her hair, and this hair," she said, pointing to the near side of the line, "is my hair."

Her lips twitched as she fought back a grin, laughter welling in her eyes.

Sometimes, it seems that the Jones twins never stop laughing, that, inwardly, life is to them just one continual put-on, a long private joke. Yvonne, in particular, is hard to read, the expression in her eyes almost sly.

What is clear, however, is that they generally enjoy life.

They say they are happy, that they don't feel self-conscious about their condition, and that they regard themselves not as handicapped or deformed but merely different. And it all appears to be true. A better-natured, more well-adjusted pair of people would be hard to find.

IN PRIVATE, NO SELF-PITY

In private, they are consistently without a trace of self-pity, complaint or despair. In public, they seem to accept equally the cruelty as well as the occasional grace of others.

"People can't help themselves," said Yvette, brushing the self-evident aside. "They're just so . . . surprised when they see us. But once they get over that, people are usually nice. And curious. They always want to ask us a bunch of questions."

There is almost no question the twins won't answer, although, they say, they've heard some pretty crazy ones in their time, and a few they resent, too.

"One of my favorites," said Yvette, exasperated, "is, 'How do you take a bath?' Now, how do people think I take a bath? I climb into a tub, just like everybody else."

Finished worrying their hair, the twins sat down on their king-sized bed.

Among questions they most resent are those that insult their intelligence. Most people, they say, immediately assume they must be mental defectives because they are Siamese twins.

"The question that bugs me the most," said Yvonne, mimicking a solicitous, high-pitched squeak, "is, 'Can you read, dears?' "

The twins can read, although their education is only rudimentary. During their childhood, the school system sent volunteer tutors to their home for a few hours each week, and in 1967 they were given high school equivalency certificates.

They did not attend public school, although they were both physically and mentally able, "because nobody ever suggested it," said Yvonne.

They would still like to go to college someday, she added, turning suddenly shy. "We'd probably do pretty good working with handicapped kids," she murmured.

The twins also say they would like to get married someday. They say this so naturally, it's clear they think it might happen. They point to the example of Chang and Eng. With a minimum of girlish flutter, they say they would like to have children, too. Six or more each.

Their relationships with men, mostly members of their church circle, have so far been platonic. "They kiss both of us goodnight," said Yvonne, grinning. Neither twin has felt jealous yet, she added.

Yvonne and Yvette Jones see nothing remarkable about their attitudes. This, they say, is the way they were raised.

Willie Jones McCarther taught them at an early age that they had no cause to cry in life, that they were the work of God, a condition to be accepted, not rejected.

TOO POOR TO BE PAMPERED

They were raised, too, to do for themselves whenever they could. Part of a large family of children, always too poor to be pampered, they especially remember the lessons taught by an older brother: When one cried for a toy out of reach, he would say, "Get it yourself, nigger, you got feet." And soon they did.

They were also raised to think of themselves as separate people, not one, but two.

And, to the best of their ability, they try.

They underscore their separateness mainly in small ways. Most notable is their almost constant use of singular pronouns, even when they are clearly referring to two. ("I went to the movie last night," or "I got up early today.")

Wherever they go, both twins also carry large, identical handbags, which must weigh 15 pounds each, stuffed with two complete identical sets of everything, from cosmetics and family photos to giant jars of multivitamins, enough to supply one twin for a year.

Though they both smoke the same cigarette brand, Benson & Hedges menthol, each carries her own pack, her own lighter.

Both wear wristwatches. "I wouldn't want her always grabbing at my arm to see what time it is," sniffed Yvette disdainfully.

NEVER A FIGHT OR CROSS WORD

"I speak for myself, she speaks for herself," said Yvonne firmly.

Even so, the twins admit they agree on everything. As far as they can remember, they always have. They have never had a fight (although their mother says they used to hit each other as babies), and they can't recall the last time they had even a minor spat.

Temperamentally and intellectually, they are a far cry from Chang and Eng, whose regular quarrels sometimes exploded into bizarre, bloody fistfights.

"Poor guys, I'd hate to have been them," Yvonne said with a nervous laugh. Her eyes were distant, as if she were trying to comprehend what it might be like to be joined for life with someone you didn't always like.

From the time they wake up until they go to sleep, the twins say, they make their communal daily decisions in perfect harmony. They are so naturally attuned, they say, that they never even discuss such basics as getting up, sitting down or going to the bathroom.

"I just . . . know when she's ready to move. It's just . . . natural," explained Yvette, shrugging, helpless to explain. Finding words to describe a world no one else shares is a constant problem for the twins.

They never argue about when to get up in the morning or when to go to bed at night, they say. Usually, they wake up and go to sleep simultaneously. In case one can't sleep, however, they keep a jar of sleeping pills handy. When one takes a sleeping pill, it affects them both.

LEADING A NIGHT-OWL LIFE

Night owls, they usually stay awake until 3 or 4 a.m., then sleep till noon.

Standing in front of the closet, deciding what to wear, they often reach for the same clothes at once, without saying a word. In restaurants, there is never any debate over the menu. They eat at the same pace, and lay their forks down simultaneously.

They smoke the same number of cigarettes each day, always lighting up at the same time. "I guess we just get the urge for nicotine at the same time," said Yvonne, looking as if she had never thought about it before. Heavy smokers, the twins say they are trying to "slack off" without much success.

Both are also hooked on coffee and Cokes. Light drinkers, both get high at the same time on a glass of wine.

Among their minor physical differences, Yvette's eyesight is worse, their menstrual cycles differ, and occasionally, one catches a cold but the other doesn't.

Rarely is either one sick. "And we never have headaches," said Yvonne, grinning at the single question they are most often asked. In fact, she said, there is no sensation at all at the juncture of their heads.

Nor, they say, does it hurt their necks, bent to angles of nearly 90 degrees, when they walk. The twins walk with an agility verging on grace, sometimes even bursting into an exuberant run. They never fumble, jerk or bump into each other. In motion, whether they are walking, sitting down or rising, they are a perfect partnership of give and take.

And, in their world, this is a source of great pride. One night, shyly showing off, they managed, somehow, to climb into the front bucket seats of a Mazda RX-7.

"Think small, Bonnie," Yvette shouted, giggling, to her sister who had to climb in first. Their nicknames for each other are Bonnie and Betty.

Only once, the twins say, have they had any serious problems navigating themselves. They got stuck in a toilet on an airplane.

"I thought that stewardess would never get her wits together enough to let me out," said Yvette, smiling at the ignominious memory. The twins have tried to avoid small toilets ever since.

"Where was I going on that trip, anyway?" Yvonne asked her sister. "I can't remember," said Yvette, frowning. Both twins have poor memories and they are continually consulting each other.

They are attached at such an angle that neither twin can ever see her sister's face. When they talk to each other, they both turn their faces toward the ground. Sometimes when they talk, their lips move busily, but, even at a distance of three feet, they seem to be making no sounds.

Their mother says she has wondered for years if they're reading each other's minds.

Asked about it, the twins only laugh and say they have learned to speak especially low.

"I don't know what Betty's thinking till she says it—and I can't feel her aches and pains, either," said Yvonne.

Whatever the twins do, wherever they go, whatever opinions they express, it's almost always Yvonne, the twin on the right, who takes the lead, perhaps because she has a better, more direct view of the world. The twins are attached at such an angle that Yvette's face is permanently turned slightly down. Sometimes she emulates her sister's gestures, and frequently echoes her words.

Both twins tend to finish the other's sentences.

And rarely does either twin ask a question beyond the most superficial kind. It is perhaps their most striking personality trait. Lively as they are, clearly interested in the world around them, neither twin ever attempts to probe beneath the surface. They never ask personal questions of others, they never question conditions or events. They simply react to whatever is.

It is a characteristic that obviously extends to their own condition—or perhaps derives from it. Either way, it has spared them pain and maybe saved their sanity. Even as adolescents, they say, they never lay awake at night wondering why.

Likewise, they do not waste time worrying about the future. When one dies, the other obviously will too, but, to the twins, that is only another fact of life.

"Everybody's gotta go sometime," said Yvette, sounding almost bored. "I'll worry about it when the time comes," said Yvonne, shrugging.

SEPARATION WOULD BE "SO STRANGE"

They say they wouldn't want to be separated now, even if they could be. They say this with level gazes and helpless expressions, knowing they will never be able to fully explain.

"It (separation) would just seem . . . so strange," said Yvonne, looking strained. "We've been . . . this way for so long . . . "

"We're too old now . . . maybe if we were babies," Yvette said, falteringly. "But now, I don't know. I guess I'd probably miss her." She laughed, softly, embarrassed, and reached over to turn on the TV, changing the subject.

"Boy, I'd love to be on 'The Price Is Right.' I just know we could win," she declared enthusiastically as a game show came into focus.

The twins watch a lot of TV. That is, in fact, mainly how they spend their days, lying on a bed at home in front of their small black-and-white screen. Sometimes they read or work word puzzles.

They live with their mother in a small, rented room at the back of a rundown, four-room house in Central Los Angeles. All three share the same bed. Their belongings are stored in boxes on the floor. A curtain divides their room from an adjacent bedroom occupied by a disabled black woman, formerly a domestic, and her 15-year-old, who has leukemia. The kitchen is communal.

Now, as the twins chatted and watched TV, their mother was lying behind them, on the far edge of the bed, trying to sleep. She tossed restlessly. The room was not only noisy, it was hot and dim, without a fan, the shades pulled down against a 100-degree day. Her nylons were rolled down, below badly swollen knees and without her wig, she looked very much like the tired gray-haired woman of 67 that she is.

Willie McCarther never did get a home of her own. The one she bought after she returned from the circus she soon lost. Her husband lost his job, and they couldn't make the payments. For the next 20 years, he worked at odd jobs but always made ends meet.

When he died, almost 10 years ago, Mrs. McCarther and the twins moved to Georgia, where they earned a living for almost five years singing on the gospel circuits. The twins are poor singers, but, in black church circles of the South, it didn't matter; they were inspirational in other, more stirring ways.

She and the twins returned to Los Angeles, once again, more than four years ago, when she was no longer able to drive from town to town, church to church. Her legs are almost crippled with arthritis and varicose veins, and the pressures of the last 32 years have also ravaged her nerves.

Since then, they have lived on Social Security and welfare.

The daughter of a Texas sharecropper, Mrs. McCarther was taught as a child that welfare is a disgrace, if not an outright sin, and she has never understood any element of the government bureaucracy. Vaguely, she understands that there is no shame, that public assistance was meant specifically for people like her. But Willie McCarther's will appears to be gone.

She has not learned how to take advantage of what she might get, much less exploit her unusual position.

She is so disorganized and uninformed that she is only barely aware of the difference between Social Security and SSI (Supplemental Security Income), she does not know from one month to the next how much she should receive in assistance from either.

But however confused and unstable her life may be, however sick and tired she has become, a couple of traces of the old Willie McCarther remain. She still talks of "owning my own home" and she dotes on her two daughters as much as ever.

Some days, sounding almost like a woman in a dream, she talks of leaving California soon, going to some state where real estate is cheaper, becoming a foster parent for several "little children with no one to love them" and, from the income, saving the down payment on a home. She talks, too, "of finding some kind of program" that would send the twins to school.

"They have keen minds, and if they had educations, they could work, be productive," she said. She worries incessantly about the twins' current life-style, their obvious boredom, the fact that "there's nothing in their environment to stimulate their minds."

She still receives an occasional money-making proposition from people interested in the twins. She turns them down, partly because she is afraid any outside income might threaten her Social Security income, but mainly because of the same reason she gave when the twins were born.

"My babies aren't freaks! Somebody from a state fair in Puerto Rico just offered to pay me $600 a week—if I'd let them show my girls in a tent! A tent!" She spat it out like a dirty word.

Mrs. McCarther takes the twins' sunny natures for granted. "They've always been that way . . . I guess it's because they grew up surrounded by so much love," she said simply.

Willie McCarther does not think her daughters are without fault, however. Among other aggravations, they smoke. Beyond the health hazard, smoking is, in her eyes, an unseemly thing for women to do.

"Girls," she begs, mortified, every time they go out, "don't smoke in public."

Whenever she feels able, she takes them out, usually to church or to visit friends. And, just as she has for 32 years, she watches over them like babies. She may not be able to protect them from crude comments and stares, but she sees that they never bear it alone. They are not allowed to go anywhere by themselves and she won't leave them in the house alone.

"There are a lot of mixed-up people in the world," she observed sadly. But, like her daughters, she prefers to dwell on the positive side of human nature.

"The world is full of truly beautiful people, good Christian people," she said, letting warm memories and faith wash the tension away. "And wherever the twins go, they are greeted with love, nothing but love, once people get to know how sweet and good they are."

When the twins occasionally go somewhere with a friend, she waits up until they come home.

As they walked down Hollywood Boulevard, crowds parted, traffic screeched to a halt, and a few people covered their eyes.

"Oh, gross! How gross!" a giggling teenager shrieked into their faces.

"Why would they come out in public?" a tight-lipped woman snapped as they passed, sounding personally offended.

Three youths stopped directly in their path, staring.

"Hi, guys, how ya doing?" Yvonne said, offering her brightest smile, sounding as friendly as she could. None of the three answered her and they made no move to step aside. Patiently, the twins backed up and went around.

They had never been to Mann's Chinese Theater before. When they saw the famous patio, they were thrilled. They darted excitedly about, sometimes dropping to their hands and knees, discovering in cement the hand- and footprints of their favorite stars. A hush fell over the crowd. Tourists with cameras snapped their picture.

A big black man walked over, kissed each smiling twin on the hand, said "God Bless, sisters," and walked off with tears in his eyes.

Inside, they declared the theater to be one of the most beautiful places they had ever been. So that her sister might turn her face upward enough to see the high, ornate walls, Yvonne spent several boring minutes staring at the ceiling.

They loved the movie, "Raiders of the Lost Ark." Along with the rest of the audience, they hissed, cheered, booed and gasped with lusty enthusiasm.

Mrs. McCarther, true to her rigidly Southern Baptist roots, never has approved of movies, so the twins don't often get the opportunity to go.

"Did you understand it, girls?" an elderly woman asked them on the way out, meaning to be kind. A flash of irritation passed simultaneously over both their faces. Politely, they told her they did.

The evening ended with a walk along the Santa Monica Pier, which was a mistake. The twins hadn't gone 50 feet before a crowd began to collect. The crowd promptly turned into an excited, noisy mob, and the mob kept moving closer and closer. Breathlessly, people were pushing and shoving to get a better look.

"It's OK," said Yvonne, trying to sound nonchalant. "You should have seen it when we went to Knott's Berry Farm." Both twins tried to laugh but Yvette looked afraid.

"Sometimes," she quietly confessed, "people do scare me a little."

Soon there must have been 200 of them, a few beachfront bums, a handful of dull-eyed dopers, but mostly, just ordinary-looking people, old and young, all trotting behind the twins, alongside them, darting forward, eyes glittering, to catch a glimpse from the front. Like a pack of animals, they seemed ready to break to fall upon the twins snatching souvenirs.

Some of them trailed the twins nearly to the car.

"It's a joke, isn't it?" shrilled one woman. "Tell me," she persisted, almost begging. "Isn't it a joke?"

"Sorry, lady, no joke," murmured Yvonne who looked too tired to smile.

When they got home, their mother was lying in bed, reading her Bible. She kissed them both, wearing a wide anxious grin.

"Oh Ma, we had a great time," exclaimed Yvonne, her energy abruptly revived, her smile almost extravagantly gay. "We went to a movie, and then out to the ocean, and we had a lot of fun. Everybody was real nice to us!"

"Real nice to us," Yvette agreed.

Fingering her tattered Bible, Willie McCarther beamed with relief, another night of worry lifted from her tired mind.

A Visit with Bella Stumbo

Virginia Young: *Why did you become a newspaper reporter?*

Bella Stumbo: I grew up in this tiny town in Colorado, and summertimes I worked at the local newspaper. I graduated from high school in 1961. In those days, women did not go to law school. Most of them were nurses or teachers and I didn't want to be either. One of the comic strips I read a lot was Brenda Starr and it gave me the idea. I had an English teacher who said, "Gee, you're a gifted person, you should write."

Q. *Your first job after graduate school was at the UPI office in Hartford, Connecticut. What did you do for the wire?*

A. All we did was rewrite stuff out of the Hartford newspapers. Then I went to Boston and it was a bigger office and I was the only woman there. There were probably 10 or 15 men. I don't remember doing much reporting. Muriel Humphrey was the apex of my career. She came to the airport and gave a speech. I got to do that.

But mostly, I would go get coffee for the fellas. They would ask me and I wasn't liberated enough to get angry about it. Betty Friedan's *Feminine Mystique* hadn't hit the airwaves yet. It was about the last year before the women's movement hit in full force and started to build. So I had no tools, no peer group, no sense of anything except trying to please people, who were always male.

There were the usual jokes about the cute little reporter. It was one of the coldest winters in history; they had snow that covered cars and I remember wearing miniskirts and boots. It never occurred to me not to do those things.

Q. *Were there men your age who got good assignments?*

A. I can't give you an intelligent answer because I wasn't even conscious of that. I do not remember questioning or challenging anything. Unconscious resentments were building, but I was too naive to even question. I felt bad and didn't know why. That's why, when the women's movement started, nobody identified with it more quickly than I did.

Q. *Where did you go after you left UPI?*

A. I took a job at the Atomic Energy Commission in New York. The job again was sort of a mindless thing and I was bored to death. After a year I started looking for a job in journalism. I had no clips; all I had was a terrific academic record. Meanwhile, this man was proposing and I went to Bangkok, because that's where he was working. I was as much motivated by a desire to see the world as I was to carve out a career in journalism.

We got married in Hong Kong in 1969. I didn't use my husband's name, which was a shock to everybody, including my parents. I didn't see why I should not be Bella Stumbo. I worked for the *Bangkok World,* an English paper. But it wasn't reporting because none of us could speak Thai. So the Thai translator gave us a mishmash and we rewrote it.

Q. *How did you get from there to the* Los Angeles Times?

A. We came back to the United States and I got a job at the *Hollywood Citizen News.* That's the first place I got to do any writing. The editor of the paper was about my age and a free spirit. The 60s were in full flower. I wrote stories on the gay movement before it was fashionable, Vietnam War stories. I loved it there.

Betty Friedan came to town. She was promoting *The Feminine Mystique* and I got to do the interview. It was true love. I was an enlisted person in an army. The women's army. Crazy people feel that way when they hit a shrink's couch; there's finally somebody who's willing to listen.

The *Citizen News* lasted five months before it went bankrupt. Everything I had written was flailing left wing. These stories were so intellectually one-sided as to be laughable, but they were well-written. These were the clips with which I impressed Jean Taylor, who was the editor of the View section of the *Los Angeles Times.*

Q. *Where did you develop your writing technique?*

A. I was writing stuff when I was a kid; I remember reading

Shakespeare when I was 13. I was one of those kids who was in the library three times a week, checking out every book.

I was given a forum in which I could experiment at the *Citizen News,* and I did. But it didn't come from any prior training. I don't think writing can be taught. With feature writing, you've either got the instinct or you don't.

Q. *Was the* View *section the* Times's *women's section?*

A. It had been traditional women's pages — society and nothing else. Jean Taylor took over and she wanted to make it an overall features section. She was a great editor. She taught me more about writing and journalism than anyone. We sat around and talked about writing. It was the seminars that I never had in graduate school.

Q. *What kind of features did you do there?*

A. I did a long piece on rape. I followed the trial of this woman who was the classic victim. She was real plain. So the implication at the trial was, why would this guy rape a girl as ugly as you? That was the sort of thing we started doing.

That piece became a TV series and a state law got passed to protect the rights of a victim. Jean told us these things were possible. I stayed there two and one-half years, moved to the metro staff in 1975, then the national staff in 1984.

Q. *How has being a woman affected your career?*

A. It enabled me to get the job I got, but it hasn't helped me as a human being. If I'd been a man, Jean Taylor might not have hired me, because she wanted to hire a woman. Later, I think I was brought into metro from *View* because they needed women and I was talented. I benefitted from that period in which people were looking for women. They had to. It was the law.

But I don't think the attitudes toward women have changed. Women are still being included actively, not naturally. It's still a man's world. We're always going to be the guests.

Q. *What kind of sexism have you encountered in your career?*

A. So much of it is subtle and unspoken. Women are judged on everything from how they look to how they dress. You can't come in here in the same dress every day. You can't come in in jeans. Men glide along in their grey suits and their red ties and they can wear the same thing every day.

I don't have any horror stories. If somebody wants to call me dolly or baby or explain something elemental to me, that's fine. I feel patronized in a lot of situations.

Q. *Does that ever work to your advantage?*

A. I've always found being female an advantage in interviewing situations. If the man's over 40, he's going to think you're less intelligent than you are and you're going to find out more because it's so easy to sit there and look dumb. You don't even have to look dumb. They don't feel threatened. I've been insulted more times by people who don't even know it. It's a great character builder.

Q. *Have you had to work harder than your male counterparts to get where you are?*

A. I can't separate what's female and what's me. I worked like hell. I'm a workaholic, a perfectionist. I'll take a sentence and work it over 20 times, 40 if I have the time.

Q. *Do you think women have to work harder to be taken seriously?*

A. Absolutely. And I'm still not sure they are.

Q. *What personal sacrifices have you made for your career?*

A. I'm not a maternal person, so I don't have a problem with not having children. My two marriages have both gone. I don't regret that; they were both good while I had them.

But I think if I'd grown up as a journalist 20 years earlier or 20 years later, I'd have a different life-style. I'd have made a more serious commitment to trying to be married. I spent 15 years wanting to establish myself in a good job with a good salary. I spent so long with those kinds of goals that I sacrificed the other side of life, the family. It's just now that I'm thinking about, do I want to get married for real? And should I have had kids?

Go up in the City Room and you'll find about 10 women in the same situation, unmarried women who are career minded and yet we find ourselves with our careers, period. Some have gone out at the last minute and adopted kids or gotten pregnant. You don't find it in any other generation of women.

Q. *How are women coming into the newsroom today different?*

A. I want to strangle some of them. Women between the ages of 25 and 30, maybe even 35, they take it all for granted. They think, "Of course you have a career, of course you have two or three children, a husband." It hasn't been long since you were lucky to get your job back if you had a baby. Women have forgotten that so fast. That battle's far from won; instead of making progress we're losing it.

Q. *What common obstacles do women reporters face?*

A. Overcoming sexism and having to work within a male-dominated, operated, and controlled media establishment.

Ongoing battles about promotions. Women editors got together here a couple years ago and wrote a detailed memo about promotions. We don't stack up very well against a lot of other papers. Nothing much happened.

We have one woman in our foreign bureaus, Marjorie Miller. She started here as a copy girl. She was ambitious. She got a job in our San Diego edition. Then she went to Mexico City. By virtue of talent and hustle and diligence, she became invaluable to the bureau there. She is now our foreign correspondent. I think she got it because she wouldn't go away.

Another woman here has just applied for our Manila bureau. She's a former Vietnam combat expert for the AP. She's a woman they can't say is too innocent. She's like a bulldog. We're talking to everybody about it so they can't pretend she didn't apply. The last woman who applied for a foreign bureau, she didn't tell anybody. Besides not getting the job, she was personally humiliated.

Q. *Do you network with other women journalists, share common problems, give each other advice on stories?*

A. I don't do much of it. I have a couple female friends in this building that I talk to. There was a time when I was uncomfortable with women. You achieve in a man's world. Your goal is always to charm the men, impress the men. Your grade school principal is a man; your employers are men.

Q. *Do you ever use feminine wiles to get a story?*

A. Everyone does, whether it's conscious or unconscious, blatant or minor, even if it's only playing innocent or more gullible than you are. You take the role that's presented to you.

Q. *Some women say they worry about failing because it would reflect badly on women. Have you ever felt that way?*

A. No. I'm too selfish to think in terms of that. If I fail, I'm going to fail me. That's why I rewrite sentences 29 times.

Q. *How did you happen to do the Siamese twins story?*

A. A photographer had run into them and he tried several sections of the paper but nobody wanted to do the story. An editor suggested he talk to me and I was in a goofy frame of mind and I agreed to do it. Two minutes later, I thought, "What have I done?"

Everyone was laughing and making jokes about it, saying, "How can you make a reasonable story out of it?" I was getting two-headed chicken jokes on my desk. I had doubts and was real nervous.

Q. *How did the twins react to your request for an interview?*

A. They were happy for the company. They're just friendly people. What surprised me was that more people hadn't done stories on them, like the National Enquirer. After ours appeared people did try to get their number and it was a real deluge. We tried to protect them from the real scuzzes.

Q. *How long did you spend with them?*

A. Off and on, a couple weeks. But I still see them. So does the photographer.

Q. *Is this one of your favorite pieces?*

A. Yea. I'm proud of the writing because I had doubts about whether you could turn something that bizarre into a serious and touching piece and most people thought I succeeded.

Q. *How did you do that?*

A. The secret is, I was around them enough that they became real people to me. We went to movies. We went to restaurants. So it was easy for me to write about them as two people who had a problem. When I sat down to write it, I wasn't thinking that I've got Siamese twin freaks here. I was thinking, I've got to write about Yvonne and Yvette. They weren't freaks to me.

Q. *How do you organize your material?*

A. I've never learned to outline. I look through my notes and try to categorize them. On the computer, I have three columns of notes. One says issues; one says scenes; one says miscellaneous. As I'm going through the notebook, if something stands out I'll stick it in one of those groups and I'll make a note, Notebook 1, Notebook 2. The scenes are the thing I end up going to. They are the things I can shut my eyes and remember the best.

Then I go out and drive around a lot. I do my best thinking on the freeway. It's the physical act of motion and speed. My brain works with it. I come back and know what I'm trying to say. I get so familiar with my material that I don't need these notebooks. Once I get the first two or three pages down the rest is easy.

Q. *What do you do if you have writer's block?*

A. Sometimes I've been so desperate that I will try to write a letter. I'll write to my sister. I say to myself, "All you're doing is telling a story. What is it that you saw?"

When I come back from an assignment, I'll tell somebody what excited me, what the story was. Then I'll forget. So I always call back that person and say, "What did I say the story was?" One of my husbands used to serve that function for me.

Q. *Who is your reader?*

A. I don't think of a reader out there. I write for me.

Q. *Do you use a tape recorder?*

A. I try not to. I don't like to transcribe them. Also, they inhibit people. I take notes even if I've got a tape on. My notes have the high points, the things that impress me the most. The tape always makes me forget them.

Q. *How do you get such rich detail?*

A. I'm a watcher. It's totally invaded my private life. I can walk in a room and scope everything out: what's on the walls, what's on their clothes, and what's in the mail. I interrogate the hell out of people. I can't meet a stranger without getting a resume before we sit down. It's like a button that kicks in.

Q. *How do you take notes?*

A. I use my own version of shorthand. I go to the bathroom and fill out my sentences. I used to come back and two days later I couldn't read my stuff.

Q. *Do you work at home?*

A. When I get real serious and get down to writing, I'll usually go home. I don't want to be disturbed. In the office I'll spend the day socializing. I'm a procrastinator. At home I'll feed the cat and water the plants and scrub the floors.

Q. *How much of your material do you end up using?*

A. I throw out 99 percent of it. I'll spend six times longer with a person than what it requires. That's one of the things I want to stop doing.

Q. *Does your stuff get edited much?*

A. Too little. I am a true believer that you need a good editor. Otherwise you're going to make a fool of yourself.

Q. *Do you ever feel, after you've done a good story, that you'll never do anything that good again?*

A. Constantly. This is the most masochistic job in the world because you're only as good as your last byline. Sixteen years ago, it was easier for me because there was always black and white. Now, I no longer feel qualified to make these imperial judgments. I'm double-checking myself more.

Writing is such an arrogant process, especially profiles. So much of this business is armchair psychology. There is no such thing as objective journalism. The burden is monstrous.

Q. *What advice would you give women coming into the field today?*

A. They're taking way too much for granted. They're going to find the party's over and they're going to gradually slip back where they were. I would advise them to get with the women's thinking.

5 Cynthia Gorney

PUBLIC AFFAIRS ■ *Washington Post*

CYNTHIA GORNEY figures she was "right on the cutting edge of generational change for women in the newsroom."

She wasn't barred from doing exciting or important stories; as a 21-year-old intern at the *Washington Post* in 1975, she covered presidential press conferences and drug murders.

Moving back to her native California, she became the *Washington Post's* West Coast correspondent for the Style section. Her fresh approach to stories brought her honors early in her career. She won the American Society of Newspaper Editors contest for nondeadline writing in 1980. She is one of only seven women ever to win the contest.

After a stint as South America bureau chief in 1980–1982, Gorney, 36, resumed writing for Style from her Oakland, California, home. She was a fellow at the Aspen Institute's Seminar on Justice and Society in 1987. Gorney also taught at her alma mater, the School of Journalism at the University of California-Berkeley, in 1983 and 1986.

Since 1988 she has been writing chiefly about issues involving family, society, and the law. She says her goal is to "start arguments, stimulate thinking." An article and an essay follow.

WHOSE BODY IS IT, ANYWAY?
The Legal Maelstrom That Rages When the Rights of Mother and Fetus Collide

Case History, D.C. General Hospital. A 19-year-old woman named Ayesha Madyun is in labor with her first child. Her waters broke before she arrived at the hospital; 70 hours have passed since the breaking of waters, and she is three-quarters dilated, but making no further progress. The hospital's obstetrical residents have been taught that infection, which without warning can kill the baby or cause severe brain damage, threatens any woman who has not de-

93

livered within 24 hours of breaking her waters. The obstetricians say
Madyun must have a cesarean section to pull the baby out quickly;
Madyun, convinced that if they leave her alone she will deliver natu-
rally, refuses to let them operate.

This is her baby, she says, and her body; her religion teaches that
the decision must be hers.

Now what?

Should the obstetricians honor her instructions, and hope the
baby survives?

Should they call for a court order, and operate without her consent?

If she fights the procedure, should they hold her down?

What if she were refusing the cesarean because she was vain, and
wanted her abdomen free of scars? What if she were refusing the
cesarean because she was ill already, and knew that surgery would
seriously endanger her own life?

What if she gave no reason at all—simply sat up in her hospital
bed, a competent adult fully informed of the consequences, and
looked her obstetrician in the eye, and said no?

In the offices of the District of Columbia Court of Appeals, a
remarkable collection of friend of the court briefs has been distributed this fall to the chambers of all nine judges. The briefs are signed
by the American Medical Association, by the National Organization
for Women, by the American Jewish Congress and the Women's Legal
Defense Fund and the U.S. Catholic Conference—more than 120 separate organizations and individuals have joined their names to the fat,
stapled documents arguing the merits of a case whose formal name is
so small and plain that it looks at first glance as though some harried
typist neglected to fill in the rest.

The facts of "In re: A.C." have been well aired in public by now,
each account retelling an episode of nearly unrelenting grief. A 27-
year-old cancer patient named Angela Carder lay under heavy seda-
tion in the intensive care unit at George Washington University Hospital. Her doctors believed she would die within days, a condition that
AMA lawyers would later say enormously heightens the risk of any
surgery, but Carder was 26½ weeks pregnant. On June 16, 1987, after
listening to three hours of medical testimony and argument by attorneys called to the hospital to counsel for and against the surgery, D.C.
Superior Court Judge Emmet Sullivan ordered GW Hospital to pro-
ceed with a cesarean section to try to save the fetus, even though

Carder's parents and physicians believed she had clearly showed she did not want the surgery done.

Angela Carder's baby was named Lindsay Marie and died, shortly after birth, of what the death certificate described as "extreme immaturity"; the baby was not developed enough to survive outside the womb. Carder died two days later, having briefly regained consciousness long enough to know the baby had been taken and had not lived. "We well know that we may have shortened A.C.'s life span by a few hours," wrote now-retired D.C. Court of Appeals Judge Frank Nebeker in November 1987, explaining in the published opinion why a three-judge panel from the Court of Appeals had upheld Sullivan's order for the cesarean. "With a viable fetus, a balancing of interest must replace the single interest of the mother, and as in this case, time can be a critical factor."

That passage, and the reasoning that shaped it—the idea that the state can somehow view a pregnant woman as two people with competing rights, and that intrusive and possibly dangerous medical treatment can be forced on one to help the other—is what galvanized scores of organizations and individuals, nearly all of them opposed to the surgery order, when the full D.C. Court of Appeals agreed to rehear the case last September. The kinds of questions raised by Angela Carder's cesarean section had confronted American judges before; two physicians and a lawyer writing in the *New England Journal of Medicine* last year found 11 different states in which judges had in recent years ordered cesarean sections for women who had refused them. An unsettling new shorthand was finding its way into medical journals and law review articles and fliers for whole conferences aimed at professionals whose work compels them to think about the nature of pregnancy and individual rights: The shorthand, with implications that kept multiplying the longer the concept was considered, was "maternal-fetal conflict."

Pregnant women ordered into caesareans against their will could certainly be said to have encountered maternal-fetal conflict, but so could pregnant women jailed for drinking too much, or pregnant women locked up for flunking a drug test, or pregnant women confined by the courts for smoking or failing to control their diabetes or working in places where people thought toxins might poison the fetus. Some of these scenarios were theoretical, but a startling number were not; when a D.C. Superior Court judge last summer jailed a pregnant woman to protect her fetus because she had tested positive for cocaine use while awaiting sentencing on a check forgery charge, the judge seemed genuinely perplexed by the public clamor and said he and his colleagues had done this before with pregnant women and would probably do it again. The *New England Journal of Medicine* authors found that courts in Colorado and Illinois had ordered "hospital detentions" for pregnant women whose doctors believed they were risking fetal malformation by failing to control their diabetes, and nearly half the obstetricians surveyed in the article said women who endangered their fetuses by refusing medical advice should be legally detained "so that compliance could be ensured."

Since the nation has spent some years embracing the idea that competent adults may make their own choices about accepting or declining medical treatment, that makes this an argument of the most complicated proportions. What is a pregnant woman, in the eyes of society and the law? What is it that she carries inside her? Is her obstetrician treating one patient or two, and how much coercive power are we to grant to the obstetrician, to the hospital, to the judge awakened by a telephone call in the middle of the night?

"IN THE MATTER OF MADYUN FETUS"

The 19-year-old woman who refused a cesarean at D.C. General Hospital had read a good deal, she says, about pregnancy and natural childbirth. In the summer of 1986, Ayesha Madyun was married, enrolled at George Washington University, and pregnant; the notion that her delivery might go wrong, or that her own last name might someday be invoked in the legal turmoil over pregnant women and the American courts, seems unfathomable to her even now. "I knew I didn't want a cesarean, because I didn't feel like it was necessary for me to have one," she says. "There was nothing indicating I was to have a cesarean. I was fine."

Ayesha Madyun's waters broke during one of her classes, and she says she and her husband, Mustafaa Madyun, a theater director who at that time was unemployed, were turned away for lack of insurance from Greater Southeast Community Hospital. They went home, although they say the Greater Southeast staff had advised them to go by ambulance to D.C. General, and Ayesha Madyun lay in bed until her labor pains began.

By the time John Cumming took over the evening shift at D.C. General, Ayesha Madyun had checked into the hospital and lain in labor since early that morning. Cumming was the chief obstetrics and gynecology resident from Georgetown University, which shares with Howard University the residencies that serve D.C. General, and he says he was told when he checked in that a full-term laboring woman had gone more than 65 hours since the breaking of her waters, but was refusing a cesarean. A fetal monitor had been attached to Madyun's abdomen, and although it was showing no serious signs of distress in the baby, Cumming says Madyun was running a low-grade fever, which he says he had been taught is one possible sign of incipient infection.

"Ninety-nine," says Mustafaa Madyun. He says his wife's temperature never climbed above 99, and that the hospital staff would not allow her, because of the fetal monitor, to walk around or even sit up to help her labor along. "At one point the oxygen mask was gagging her so I told her to remove it so she could breathe," Mustafaa Madyun says. "One of the residents came down and said if I advised her to remove it again, he would call security, and I would be removed from the hospital."

Mustafaa Madyun had three children from a previous marriage, one delivered by cesarean section, and both he and his wife say now that they very much want to explain their feeling about natural childbirth. They knew that hospitals and doctors have been criticized in recent years for performing caesareans so readily and so often, but they say there were not unalterably opposed to the idea. Had they seen what they thought was any convincing evidence that the baby was in danger, they say, they would have agreed instantly to the surgery, even though they eventually wanted a large family and Ayesha Madyun was afraid that the uterine scarring and occasional medical complications of a cesarean might limit the number of children she would safely be able to deliver.

But they believe also that this decision was Ayesha Madyun's alone to make, and that their religion—both are Moslem—gives the mother the final decision, even if it turns out to be the wrong one, over what will and will not be done to her body and her fetus. "The decision, to me, it still lies with the mother," Mustafaa Madyun says. "As a male, if there's no circumstantial situation in which you can force surgery on me if I'm of sound mind, then I don't feel that a woman, just because she's a woman, should be in a situation where surgery can be forced on her."

Just because she's a woman: That is nearly the crux of the argument, but not quite. If Ayesha Madyun had been a man or a nonpregnant woman, competent and fully informed of the consequences, there is almost no circumstance under which American law could have forced her to undergo major surgery without her consent. Four years ago the Supreme Court took on the case of a Virginia armed robbery suspect who had a bullet lodged in his chest; police believed the suspect had been shot by the shopkeeper who was robbed, and the prosecutors wanted the courts to force the suspect into surgery under general anesthesia so the bullet could be recovered as evidence.

The Supreme Court refused to permit the surgery, citing Fourth Amendment protections of privacy against unreasonable government intrusion. It also seems widely accepted as American legal principle that a person cannot be forced to have surgery for another person's benefit; even the dead do not lose their organs to transplants unless the doctors have authorization to operate, and when a Pennsylvania court was asked 10 years ago to force a man into donating bone marrow that might have helped save his cousin's life, Judge John P. Flaherty wrote that he found the man's refusal morally repugnant but ruled that there was nothing the law could do about it. "For a society which respects the rights of one individual, to sink its teeth into the jugular vein or neck of one of its members and suck from it sustenance for another member, is revolting to our hard-wrought concepts of jurisprudence," Flaherty wrote.

So if Ayesha Madyun's baby had lain just outside her body, in mortal need of a kidney or bone marrow only she could provide, the state could not have forced her cut open to save the baby's life. But if Madyun had delivered her baby and then for some reason refused permission for other conventional medical treatments needed to keep it alive, the state could have swooped in and treated the baby without her consent. That was the reasoning the Georgia Supreme Court had used as its logical springboard five years earlier when it was asked to approve a forced cesarean order; a woman named Jessie Mae Jefferson, who was refusing a doctor-ordered cesarean because she believed the Lord would take care of her delivery, was found by the Georgia court to be depriving her fetus, a "viable human being," of "the proper parental care and subsistence necessary for his or her physical life and health."

The Georgia court gave temporary custody of the fetus to the state human resources department; those officials, said the court, could make whatever decision was best for the fetus, including cutting through Jessie Mae Jefferson to get it out. And that, *Jefferson v. Griffin Spalding County Hospital Authority,* was the only appellate-level forced cesarean decision on the books when D.C. Superior Court Judge Richard Levie was called down to D.C. General two years ago to determine whether a cesarean should be ordered for Ayesha Madyun.

Without the direction of a court, Cumming says, he envisioned trouble no matter what he did; he could imagine facing a lawsuit either for an infection-damaged baby or for an operation performed without the patient's consent. "Fear of liability is what's made these cases such an important issue—the doctors feel that they're in a double bind," says Veronika Kolder, the Chicago obstetrician who coauthored the *New England Journal of Medicine* article about court-ordered caesareans. "A release is essential, but it doesn't guarantee that there won't be a lawsuit."

The judge heard the case in the middle of the night, in a hospital conference room. Attorneys, each of them roused by late-night telephone calls and given less than an hour to prepare, argued for the District, the Madyuns, and for what the legal ruling would refer to as Madyun fetus. When the judge dictated his decision, signing off at 1:05 a.m., he made reference to the arguments he had heard: to the parents, who he said "impressed the court as sincere," and to Cumming, who had convinced Levie that the Madyun fetus was at much greater risk of dying from infection than Ayesha Madyun was of dying from a cesarean.

"It is one thing for an adult to gamble with nature regarding his or her own life; it is quite another when the gamble involves the life or death of an unborn infant," Levie wrote in the ruling published three months later. "All that stood between the Madyun fetus and its independent existence, separate from its mother, was put simply, a doctor's scalpel. In these circumstances, the life of the infant inside its mother's womb was entitled to be protected." On July 26, at 3:32 a.m., Ayesha Madyun delivered a 6½-pound baby boy who was born with excellent lungs and no sign of infection. He was delivered by cesarean section. The procedure was performed by John Cumming M.D., operating under the instructions and authority of a court of law.

Ayesha Madyun is still angry about it.

She knows, because she has read the newspaper accounts, that the trial judge who ordered Angela Carder's surgery relied in large part on In the Matter of Madyun Fetus, Civil Division, D.C. Superior Court.

And the idea that she set precedent—that she let people do this to her and declare that it was right—is difficult for Ayesha Madyun to bear. "I felt like I could have done something more to prevent what they did to her," she says. "I felt like it was my fault."

ONE PATIENT OR TWO

Point: If we live in a society that will not order one of its citizens to give up bone marrow so a dying man can live, then we have no business ordering a woman into surgery that carries with it a documented risk of death. "Fetal rights to what?" asks American Civil Liberties Union attorney Lynn Paltrow, who has led the effort to overturn the Angela Carder decision. "We're talking about endowing a fetus with more rights than a living person has."

Counterpoint: The courts have powers of persuasion that doctors do not, and in situations where all else has failed, society can use that persuasion to save the life of a fetus that in a matter of hours will be a newborn unless someone allows it to die. "The most important question is not whether courts have done it or haven't," says Norman Fost, a University of Wisconsin pediatrics professor who chairs the American Academy of Pediatrics Committee on Bioethics, "but whether they ought to—whether a woman who has a clear moral responsibility can and should be required to undergo certain modest deprivations to fulfill that obligation."

The physical ordeal of Angela Carder was so complicated that many pages of the legal briefs are filled with nothing more than the facts and what they can be said to have meant. She was so sick that there was argument about what she most wanted, about how long she would have lived had the surgery not been performed, about whether a cancer patient's 26-week-old fetus ever had respectable odds of being "viable" at all. The D.C. Court of Appeals could conceivably duck the broader issues in this case; the court could rule, for example, on whether the trial judge who ordered Carder's cesarean was trying to determine what Carder would have asked for if she had been more lucid.

But the nine judges' keen interest in this matter, and the sheer numbers of national organizations that signed on to the briefs the judges must examine to help them decide, suggest that the legal stakes are larger than that and some of the social implications broader still. Attorneys for the U.S. Catholic Conference and the Americans

United for Life Legal Defense Fund have argued that since certain doctors had predicted Carder was destined to die within days anyway, the cesarean would have been the right thing to do even if Carder had unquestionably refused it. "The life of a child hung in the balance," concludes the Catholic Conference's brief. "There really was no other choice."

A pregnant woman, the argument goes, does not have the right to be treated by law and society as though she is the only person inside her skin until the moment her baby emerges. "Who's going to be the advocate for the fetus?" demands John Cumming, who says that he has no regret about operating on Ayesha Madyun and would do the same thing if the decision ever confronted him again. "In extreme situations, I think we're dealing with two patients. And I have to deal with them as two distinct patients. I cannot let something happen to one patient because of what someone else wants to do."

Cumming is not troubled, either, by the fact that Ayesha Madyun's baby proved to have no infection at all. "You don't know that until it's done," he says. But that kind of uncertainty, given the current widely accepted figures suggesting that many caesareans need not have been performed at all, troubles the ACLU's Paltrow very deeply; a court order for surgery, she says, is a sledgehammer of a mandate for a physician who may in retrospect turn out to be wrong. The Jessie Mae Jefferson decision itself is a case in point: Jefferson's Georgia doctors ordered her cesarean because her placenta was blocking the birth canal, a condition the court was told kills 99 percent of babies in natural childbirth. When the court gave its order to operate on Jefferson if necessary, she went into hiding and delivered the baby vaginally. Apparently the placenta had shifted. The baby was fine.

Now suppose, Lynn Paltrow asks, that Jefferson had undergone her cesarean, and developed a severe allergic reaction to an anesthetic—this is rare but it happens—and died? "Why is it okay for the court to make a decision that results in a tragedy, but not okay for the woman on whom the surgery is going to be forced to make a decision that may result in a tragedy?" Paltrow asks. "It's worse. And the reason is that when she makes a bad decision, it's an isolated decision. And when the government makes a bad decision, it's not only that she dies, and the baby dies—they send a message to all women that you can't trust your doctors."

The ACLU joined the Angela Carder case as Carder's cesarean was first being contemplated, and Paltrow has argued from the beginning—with support now from groups as diverse as the American

Medical Association, the Center for Constitutional Rights and the National Council of Jewish Women—that a fetus' "rights" cannot be weighed against a woman's right to refuse major medical intervention. A fetus is not simply another patient to be attended to, Paltrow says; it is part of the woman who will bear it, and until the moment of its birth that woman must be granted the same rights as anybody else to keep a surgeon from cutting her open.

Even if the obstetrician has to stand there and watch the fetal monitor and know that a baby is dying when it might be saved?

"The doctors have a very deep obligation to convince her differently if they believe she's wrong," Paltrow says. "But that obligation does not extent to forcibly overriding her ultimate decision." The chief American obstetricians' organization agrees; a statement last year by an American College of Obstetricians and Gynecologists ethics committee concluded that resort to the courts is "almost never justified" to compel medical treatment of pregnant women.

And the very phrasing of the question—a baby is dying—tips it instantly, of course, into broader and more dangerous terrain. "Baby" is the word used almost always by those who want the state to forbid women from having abortions; what lies inside the mother's body is generally not spoken of as a "fetus," a word much cooler and more anatomically precise than "baby" or "unborn child."

If a sick child's father were blocking the house doorway to keep medical help away, pediatrician Fost once argued at an ethics conference, no one would hesitate before shoving the father away to get rescuers inside. The problem with this analogy, observes University of North Carolina law professor Nancy Rhoden, is that to carry it through the man would have to be impossibly wedged into the doorway, so that only by slicing through him could the rescue be managed.

There is in fact no really suitable analogy involving men, and that is what gives such passion and complexity to the arguments over pregnancy: Nothing else is like it. Nothing encloses inside the body of a man some growing arrangement of bones and flesh and beating heart that is part him and part someone else. Even if Fost did decide to chop through the obstructing father to get inside his house, he would still be rescuing a child, an individual, a person separate unto himself. Does that describe a human fetus, or not?

The U.S. Supreme Court's most famous abortion ruling spends many pages grappling with this, with the legal and medical nature of the fetus, and both sides in the cesarean debate now buttress their arguments with the language of *Roe* v. *Wade*. When Justice Harry

Blackmun wrote the majority opinion 16 years ago, he declared that the state does have an interest in a woman's fetus, and that when the fetus is viable that interest becomes strong enough to let the state move in to protect — by regulating or banning abortion — what Blackmun called "the potentiality of human life."

That means, reasoned the Georgia Supreme Court, that the state can tell doctors to take out Jessie Mae Jefferson's fetus. But Blackmun also said the "preservation of the life or health of the mother" had to come first, that the state could not prevent abortion even of a viable fetus if the pregnancy were endangering the mother's life or health. And that means, Lynn Paltrow says, that no judge can order potentially life-threatening surgery on any woman who clearly has refused it — whether the woman is dying of cancer or trying to deliver vaginally or waiting for assistance from the Lord.

CHOICE AND CONSEQUENCES

Ayesha Maydun had a second baby last summer, delivered vaginally, with the help of a midwife. She says her second pregnancy was much more difficult than the first, that she was hospitalized for bleeding and felt a great deal of pain, and that she believes the trouble was a legacy of her cesarean. She would like someday to go to medical school, but she has changed the specialty she has in mind; she thought at one time of becoming a gynecologist, but she thinks now that she will look to pediatrics instead. "I couldn't stand by being a doctor and watching my patients go through what I did, so I decided to stay away from it altogether," Madyun says.

John Cumming has not heard from the Madyuns in some time, but he says he is glad her babies are healthy; he believes he has something to do with that. "She was violated," he says. "She did have an operation. But she is alive and well. Her life was not lost. Isn't that a greater good than allowing somebody else to lose its life?"

Angela Carder's mother, Nettie Stoner, has not stopped believing that a trade was made: the last days of her daughter's life, Stoner says, for a fetus too small even to breathe. "I thought we had the right to choose what we were going to do with our bodies," Stoner says. "And Angela did not have the choice."

And women who do have the choice sometimes make it in ways that stay for a long time with the physicians and nurses who watch what happens next. Ten years ago a pregnant woman was brought to the University of California at San Francisco Medical Center; her waters had broken, signs of infection had set in, and it was clear to everyone watching her that without a cesarean her baby was going to die.

But the woman was a Jehovah's Witness and suffered already from a severe blood disease that had left her anemic and at risk for cerebral hemorrhage. A cesarean without blood transfusion would probably kill her, and she would not accept either the blood or the risk of a transfusion-free operation. The medical staff argued, consulted the family, examined the ethics of pursuing a court order to save the fetus—and decided, in the end, to let the woman's wishes stand.

The fetus, or baby, or unborn child, died before reaching the birth canal. The obstetrician in charge, UCSF obstetrics and gynecology professor Russell Laros, says he has no qualms about his decision, that he gave a great deal of thought to the depth of Jehovah's Witnesses' convictions, to a woman's right to refuse surgery, to the lifelong grief that might have followed a forced cesarean and transfusion of blood.

"Everybody turned out feeling very comfortable with the decision," Laros says. But he says this, too: The fetus might already have been damaged.

Infection had clearly set in. And Laros was thinking of the damage when he decided not to ask for a court order. Had he believed without question that a healthy baby was in mortal danger before him, Laros says, he thinks he would have gone to court and accepted the consequences.

ONE JAM THING AFTER ANOTHER
One Woman's Parable of Modern Life — and 92.5 Pounds of Apricots

OAKLAND — In the early part of summer, when the apricots come to the orchards up by the Sacramento River delta, I make jam. That is a nice plain way to say it, *I make jam,* but of course it is a larger business than that and began to sag with the trappings of parable even before the night of the awful thing. Working woman, circa 1987, two small children, edges frayed: My dining room chairs may collapse without warning and my son may wonder loudly in public about what an iron is used for, but once a year the weather warms and I get my canning kettle and I spend all weekend chopping and stirring and singing to very loud Huey Lewis tapes, and I make jam.

I started making jam because my friend Carol came over one day with some chutney she had made. It was incandescent chutney, and in fact had already won first prize at that year's county fair, but what really bowled me over was the fact that it came in little jars, and Carol had put it there. Someone I knew, another newspaper writer, a woman whose chairs had not in fact collapsed but looked as though they might someday — such a person was actually "putting up," as the more relentlessly domestic of the cookbooks described it.

I set the chutney jars on the shelf, and they gleamed. When sun hit the kitchen a kind of rich rose light filled the jars and you could see the curve of things inside, small pepper strips and chunks of peach. I began to covet these jars. I wanted rows of them. I wanted to look up when it was raining, one of those dead chilled February days, and see entire shelves filled end to end with fruit the color of stained glass, and I wanted also to know that I had put it there.

Groping, I suppose it was. We're trying to feel our way around here, make small decisions in the modern age. You hold your breath and leap into the grand ones — I will quit the job, I will place the baby in day care, I will petition for part-time status and thus remove myself from consideration for promotion — and then from the side come these sneak attacks full of loaded little messages about women and men.

Laundry figures heavily in all of this, and flower gardens, and drapery colors. Word is passed, grimly, about the public defender and mother of two whose entire freezer is stacked with labeled plastic canisters containing nutritionally balanced home-cooked meals. One year I baked whole-wheat bread every few weeks, which of course is the female equivalent of setting out after supper to dig eight-foot trenches across the back forty. I keep reading about people who have transcended this sort of thing without actually cross-dressing, but I haven't met any yet, and anyhow I like homemade jam.

You can put a ribbon on it and give it to your great-aunt for Christmas.

Right?

So I learned how to can. There wasn't a lot to it, especially if you stayed away from things like corned beef, which requires vigilance so as not to develop botulism and kill you. The first year I used a cooking pot, and the second year I went out and bought a black canning kettle with metal dividers to keep the jars apart while the water boiled around them. There were tongs involved and special funnels and Mason jars with flowers on the lids. One of my son's storybooks ends with a lyric picture of the mommy canning blueberries with her daughter; sometimes I felt like that, and sometimes I felt like a mad inventor waving hot tongs over the steam.

I was very happy. I made chutneys out of mangoes, and preserves out of apricots, and one month I got carried away and canned a lot of orange-tomato barbecue sauce. We began driving to the orchards in the summer, because the taste of the tree apricots was enough to make us weep, and we could spend most of a day scrambling up giant ladders in the heat and then driving home with dirt all over our clothes and great open boxes of apricots weighing down the back end of the car.

Thus it was that I pulled into our driveway two weeks ago in a van containing two adults, three children, seven sandy beach towels, six peanut butter sandwich crusts, eight empty Sprite cans and 185 pounds of apricots. Nobody was exactly sure how the apricots had come to weigh twice as much as all the children put together; the sky was blue and the trees were heavy with fruit and somehow we just kept climbing up those ladders and then climbing down when the apricots began to spill over the bucket edges.

It is probably worth noting that my husband, whose own sensible early-warning system might have saved us, had missed this apricot run. What we had instead was two women of the present era, each fixing one eye on the children and the other on the apricots that we were going to chop and cook and can and label before we were due at work Monday morning.

"I don't know," my friend said, looking dubious. We were standing at the apricot scale. The woman behind the scale kept merrily adding up figures in little columns, and when she was done we heaved the 185 pounds of apricots into the van and went home to divide it into 92.5 pounds each, which is still, I have to tell you, a very very large amount of apricots.

At 8 the next morning, the fruit and I were in full battle. Apricot boxes commanded crucial positions across the kitchen linoleum, which was already beginning to smack ominously underfoot, since my 15-month-old daughter had begun removing apricots one by one and then investigating how thoroughly they would squish after she had taken the first bite.

They squished pretty well, as it turned out, but I was unrattled. I sliced. I measured. Small piles of pits began to mount here and there, like spent shells. I have one principal preserves recipe, settled on after several seasons' experimentation; the recipe is printed in a cookbook that says in large alarming print, "DO NOT TRY TO DOUBLE BATCHES," and although it never says what will happen if you do, I had always figured it must be something fierce, involving genetic damage or the county fire department, so I didn't.

Instead I pulled out every pot we own, including the bent aluminum one that cost $3.99 and usually holds the sandbox toys, and I stood there stirring and sweating and timing boiling apricots until the entire kitchen had begun to look like a research facility at MIT. There were rows and rows of cooling apricots, all of them laid out in foil trays that ran the length of the kitchen counters, and I took it all in and wondered whether someone ought to come and photograph me, in the fashion of a sport fisherman posed beside his marlin.

I had to buy more Mason jars, but the momentum was unstoppable. Out came the canning kettle, the tongs, the sterilized lids. Children wandered in and were hustled away. Night was falling, my husband had settled into something swell on the television; I didn't care. I was canning. I was "putting up." Jar after jar slid into the kettle and came out again, each one shining in a kind of soft topaz, and as the line of bright small pots grew longer I could hardly wait to put them on the shelves, the very visible shelves, the shelves that were fixed to the wall to hold cookbooks and the kind of vases you only own because people gave them to you at your wedding so you would stop putting the daisies into apple juice bottles.

The jars were not even dry yet, but I wanted them up. I wanted it done.

There was so much jam that the shelf could hardly hold it all. I made a double row and stacked the jars, one on top of the other.

Then I stood back, and looked at the top shelf jam, and did a little dance.

Then I turned my back.

And then the shelves fell.

All of them. All the shelves. I once had to cover the eruption of Mount St. Helens, but this noise was worse; this was the noise of wooden shelves and ceramic salad bowls and 500-page cookbooks and the tortilla press and the porcelain jug and the vase with radishes painted on the sides, all crashing to the floor under the great and terrible weight of four dozen jars of homemade apricot preserves.

It was an amazing noise.

It went on for a very long time.

When the noise stopped, I looked at the kitchen floor. My husband, who had covered the entire distance from the living room sofa to the kitchen in one leap, looked at the kitchen floor and then looked at me. My 5-year-old son was looking at me too, since he had never before seen a grownup crying and kicking the walls, and my husband instantly steered both of us into the dining room. "I'll take care of it," he said.

After a time I came back to help, but I saw the broken radish vase and started to cry again. My husband had assumed the manner of a paramedic and suggested politely that I go somewhere else; late that night, after he had carted out the shards and mopped the floor with lemon-scented amonia, he told me some of the jam jars were still intact.

"If you hadn't been here," I said, "I would have taken the children and checked into a hotel."

"I know," he said. I looked out the window for a while, thinking about the fragility of some arrangements and the ferocious strength of others, and we slept.

A Visit with Cynthia Gorney

Virginia Young: *Why did you go into journalism?*

Cynthia Gorney: I always knew I was going to write. I remember feeling like an observer rather than a participant in the world. By the time I was 13 there was a constant stack of papers on my desk—typewritten snatches of short stories, descriptions. I also kept journals and diaries. Because I grew up in San Francisco, a town with awful newspapers, I thought I would become a magazine writer.

Q. *What changed your mind? How did you get a job at the* Washington Post *right after college?*

A. I did not go through the normal application process. My senior year I was a college stringer for the *New York Times*. Wally Turner, then the San Francisco bureau chief for the *New York Times,* had been a Nieman fellow with Howard Simons, who was then the managing editor of the *Washington Post*. Wally evidently called Howard and said, "I think you ought to give this person a job." So when I got to Washington it was wired. I just walked into the *Washington Post* to talk to Howard. And he said, "You want to work here this summer?" And I said, "Yea, I guess so." I was 21.

Q. *Did you have clips?*

A. I may have had two things published in the *New York Times,* without bylines. I had written some pieces for a weekly here called the *Bay Guardian*. And I had a great letter of reference from the guy who was heading the *New York Times* college stringers, who had written that I was the best college stringer that year. I had not graduated—I was three units short.

Q. *What did you do in Washington?*

A. The summer of 1975 I was an intern on the national staff. The White House reporter was retiring so I was thrown into what is supposed to be the sexiest job in Washington. I didn't know what a lead was. I sure didn't know what to do when you go to a White House press conference.

I went to one and Ron Nessen, Ford's press secretary, had decided to change his style. He decided to stroll around instead of being up at the podium. The reporters were a cynical bunch and everybody was wisecracking, nobody could see Nessen, there was just this disembodied voice. I found it hilarious. I wrote the story from the perspective of a 22-year-old Berkeley person who has just come from covering city council meetings where people talk about the great rat poison conspiracy that threatens to engulf us all. And I found the White House didn't look a lot different.

They gave it enormous play. Also, there had been some actual news, so my byline was on the story that led the paper that day. It isn't like I was this baby star. I was this baby weird thing. I was this peculiar Berkeley person.

Q. *What happened when your internship ended?*

A. I stayed on as a metropolitan reporter and went to the Montgomery County bureau, the most affluent suburb of Washington. My subject was the school system. I'm not a person who will get a story first. I've probably broken a story six times in my career. I'm a person whose instincts are to take a longer time, think about it, try to figure out how to explain it better and more vividly than anybody else.

I started gearing toward, "Let's look at Item 6 on the agenda, let's see what's behind that, let's see if we can bring the people in this battle to life." So by the time I had been there a year and a half, I was getting labeled a writer as opposed to a reporter.

Q. *How did you get back to California?*

A. I never felt at home in Washington. So I came back to California and we worked out a superstringer deal. In 1979, they figured out this deal where the Style section would have me as a full-time correspondent.

Q. *What else have you done for the* Post?

A. In 1980 they asked me to go to South America. My husband took a leave from his law firm and we lived in Buenos Aires and traveled all over the continent. When we came back I was pregnant and took about a year and two thirds leave, and came back as a contract writer, which is now my status. Originally, it was because I wanted to work a four-day week and there was no precedent. They've since become more enlightened. A lot of women at the Style section work part time because they have small children.

Q. *Do you still want to work for a magazine eventually?*

A. I've found what I could do at magazines I can do at more length, with more readers, better editing, and for much better pay at the *Washington Post*. At magazines, the pay is dreadful, the editing is sometimes stellar and often, really stupid.

Q. *Have you made any personal sacrifices for your career?*

A. If I were in another line of work, I would be working more part time than I am. My kids and my husband would be happier if I were in a job that didn't involve travel.

I would never have been a homemaker. I loved my maternity leaves but by the end of them I was raring to go back to work.

Q. *On the flip side, have you made professional sacrifices for your family?*

A. Had I not had a personal relationship that mattered, I would have stayed in South America another year or two. I might have gone on to be a foreign correspondent.

Q. *Did having children change you as a reporter?*

A. It changed me for the better. Having children was the first thing I did where I was fully a participant and not just standing around on the outside taking notes. I became much less desperate as a reporter. Things didn't matter quite as much.

Not only did I not mind writing about things that were in the female province; I wanted to do it. I wrote essays, nearly all about working women and kids.

In some ways I'm a worse interviewer because I'm more interested in people now. I see them less as objects for consumption to be routed into a newspaper story. I've lost a certain edge. I sit with people in their kitchens, hold their babies, and sometimes I don't get their quotes quite right. I understand their lives better but the mechanics of reporting are not as well honed.

Q. *Did you ever think you were jeopardizing your career by taking leaves?*

A. I never did. I quit; I didn't take leaves. The important thing is, you have to mean it. I was hoping we would be able to work something out later, but if we didn't, it was fine.

Q. *Do you think you've had to work harder than your male counterparts to get where you are?*

A. No way. I'm right on the cutting edge of generational change for women in the newsroom. I know women in the newsroom who are 43 or 44 who feel rightly that that is absolutely true.

My mentor when I came to Washington was Eileen Shanahan. She was at the *New York Times* then. Eileen had gone ahead of us with a machete, clearing the way. By the time I got there, clearly something had changed. It was as though someone had said, "Women, we're going to try this. We're going to treat you the same way we treat the guys."

There was one editor in particular. He was probably in his 50s. A crusty, swearing kind of editor. He thought I was great and you could tell this was a revelation to him, a delightful, astonishing, new concept. "Send her to the White House, send her anywhere."

They sent me to a housing project to check on a couple drug murders. This nice lady said to me, "You have to get in your car and leave, you're not safe here." And I remember thinking, "Gee, things have really changed."

The dividing line was about four years ahead of me. The women who were 40 when I got there were pretty tough cookies. They had fought to get out of the women's pages, to get good beats. I was getting the benefit of it. I'm one of these people who gets furious with the young women who don't understand the women's movement and what it did.

Q. *Do you think women are different as interviewers? More empathetic?*

A. Women are trained to be better listeners. But empathy doesn't necessarily makes you a better interviewer. The qualities that make up a good interviewer also have to do with processing information, preparation, a willingness to go for the jugular if you need to.

If I were a newspaper editor and somebody had to go interview a mother whose child had just been run over by a car, my instincts would be to send a woman. The woman opening the door would feel better.

Q. *Have you encountered any sexism in your career?*

A. Almost none. What I have encountered has been in the nature of stuff that you could laugh off. People saying, "Don't tell me you're the reporter for the *Washington Post*." And me saying, "I feel a sexist comment coming on. Let's just deflect it right here." Everybody laughs and you go right on.

Q. *Do you ever use feminine wiles to get a story?*

A. Do I wear eye shadow if I'm going to interview a man? Yea, I do. Have I ever suggested to an interviewee that I would consort with him after the interview? No.

Indeed, in Washington it was assumed for a long time in the newsroom that I was a lesbian. This had to do with questions of carriage; I wore pants; I crossed my legs like this. I was from Berkeley, what did I know? I wasn't distraught about this until I realized it wasn't as it would have been in Berkeley. It was, "Ooh, she's a dike." Then I got upset and wanted it understood that I was heterosexual. I started wearing more skirts.

I had the reputation of trying to come on too tough. I was trying to come on tough because I was terrified. I was 22 years old and my name was on the front page of the *Washington Post* being read by the President.

There have been situations where I was aware that the person I was interviewing found me attractive and that affected the chemistry that was developing in the interview. That happens between male reporters and female interviewees as well.

There's the famous Sally Quinn line, "Would you let a man put his hand on your butt if you knew you'd get a good story?" No. I would not. You tend to use less feminine wiles than charm. Charm is something we all use shamelessly. But that can be female-female. It does not feel to me like feminine wiles but the wiles of a reporter.

Q. *What advice would you give women coming into the business today?*

A. Start thinking about how family's going to work with it. It's complicated. The ways in which you're expected to grow up as a reporter are not ways that are conducive to having a family. You become an editor and you're supposed to stay there til 8 or 9 and you don't get home to tuck your kids in.

You can't have anybody cover for you if you're on deadline. If your kid is barfing somebody else is going to have to take care of him. All these things are inconceivable to you when you're 23.

Q. *How do you choose your stories?*

A. Last year I invented a beat called family and society, focusing on the changing American family and how that was coming up against the law and society at large. I wanted to develop some expertise on this.

I couldn't figure out how you become a middle-aged reporter, how you make use of your accumulated experience. Reporting is a fabulous job when you're in your 20s. You sit at people's knees, get knowledge and transfer that to your reading audience. But there comes a point when you become impatient because you know as much about your subject as some of the people you're interviewing. You're tired of simply quoting people. This is why a lot of people become pundits, a lot of people become editors.

Q. *Let's talk about your working methods. How did you approach the research for the court-ordered cesarean piece?*

A. I worked as though I were preparing an amicus brief myself. I asked for copies of briefs. I went to the law library. I didn't look up every case, but they computerize legal journal articles so all you have to do is punch in your key words—in this case, fetal rights, maternal/fetal conflict.

In addition, with each person I interviewed, I asked, who else is thinking about this, writing about this?

Q. *Are you a self-taught legal researcher?*

A. Actually, one of the classes that most stayed with me from college was Journalism and the Law. I remember some of the libel and privacy cases but what I really remember is how to do research in a law library. I love it. It's like a detective game — tracking down cases and tracking down legal arguments.

Q. *What's the best place to start in legal research?*

A. The best place to start would be with legal journal articles. They are fairly easy to understand, though some of them get fairly arcane. They make an argument, explain the logic, give you extensive footnotes. A lot of the cross-referencing I did was generated from footnotes. That led me to the Madyun case.

Q. *Do you use electronic data bases other than the law library's computer program?*

A. The *Post* has access to LEXIS but it's expensive so I generally don't use it. Besides, I like doing the research. I probably am much more computer-ignorant than a modern reporter should be.

Q. *How much of the interviewing did you do by phone and how much in person for this piece?*

A. Basically, all the reporting was done by phone. I'm much more comfortable with that than I used to be. Reporters always have back problems from sitting with the phone scrunched up by their ear. I got a headset like secretaries have. I can type as fast as people talk so I just had zillions of pages of computer notes.

Q. *Do you use a tape recorder?*

A. I use a tape recorder only when I am doing a profile of a person and I'm going to need long, complete quotes. Otherwise, I use a tape recorder only as backup. I don't trust tape recorders. So I always take notes as furiously as if it weren't on.

Q. *What do you do between the reporting and the writing?*

A. I'm usually given three days to three weeks to write a piece. First, I go through my notes, numbering the pages of my notepads. Sometimes, if I'm feeling ambitious, I go through each one line by line and circle quotes.

Q. *Do you index your notes?*

A. Yes. Either on the top page of that notebook or on a separate index page: "So and so, Pages 1 to 22." Occasionally, it will be more elaborate. "Mr. Jones, Pages 1 to 29, (great quote about abortion law in Wisconsin)."

Q. *What do you do next?*

A. I look through piles of material I've accumulated. I make about six piles around my chair. I stare at the blank computer screen a while, twirl around in my chair, call a couple friends, look at the ceiling, get an intense urge to make a cup of tea, discover an important lengthy article for the piece that I must read, call another friend, make an appointment for my kid at the dentist.

The weird thing about this is, I'm writing as it's going on. Things are floating around in the back of my head. Normally, it's one to two days of fighting it and trying madly to do anything in the world but sit down and write. Once I've done that, all I want to do is write.

Q. *Do you use an outline?*

A. Not really. My outlines are more in the way of scribbles on a pad that say 1, 2, 3, 4, 5. I don't suboutline at all. I use lists.

Q. *What are you looking for when you're choosing the lead?*

A. The lead is an invitation to the reader. It tells you that you are going to be so seduced by my wonderful writing that you're going to read this piece. A lot of writers will start doing jumping jacks in the first four paragraphs. I find it tiresome. They fill their paragraphs with wonderful metaphors, fabulous turns of phrase.

My leads are more measured, more straightforward than they used to be. I find it easier to gently gather momentum.

Q. *What do you do if you get stuck?*

A. Often, the place I'm stuck is not really the place I'm stuck. Dr. Seuss taught me that — Ted Geisel. He told me, when you're stuck, the problem is that you're obsessing on this one passage when really, the difficulty is four or five pages back.

Q. *Do you tend to use short paragraphs after long ones for emphasis?*

A. Paragraphing means a lot to me. I get in big arguments with editors all the time about that. A paragraph is the place where the reader mentally pauses. It is a completed thought.

I write paragraphs that are very long. I get accused of wanting the reader to work too hard to read my pieces. That may very well be true.

Q. *Who is your reader?*

A. I used to say that I wrote to myself, which was to say I wrote to a person who was interested in a lot of things and not terribly well informed about anything. I wasn't a specialist in anything.

The most interesting problem I'm having now is I'm developing a little too much expertise. I guess my imaginary reader has gotten older as I have and has become more patient, more willing to attend to things, to spend a long time with stories.

Q. *How would you describe the tone of the cesarean piece?*

A. Complicated. I can see people over their corn flakes, saying, "This is law school. I don't want to be doing this." But one thing that helps get people into the stories is they hit us where we live. This is life and death and childbirth.

The letters I've got about this say, "My wife and I argued about this for three days." My goal is to start arguments, stimulate thinking.

Q. *What do you want in an editor?*

A. Somebody extremely smart. I think editing is a much more difficult job than writing and reporting. Good editors are much rarer. They have the ability to see what's wrong, what's missing, and a willingness to get involved with the writer. It's an intensely emotional relationship. You have to be a friend, a companion, a hand-holder, a psychological counselor, a person who's willing to get yelled at, a person who understands how intensely you care about every single word.

A lot of bad editors don't understand that ultimately, the words on the paper are all we've got. They get furious at us for caring about punctuation. They cut five lines without telling us and don't understand why we're mad.

I have a reputation as somebody who's prickly to edit. The reason is that I care so passionately about every single word. I will rewrite when asked. But what drives me crazy is when I'm rewritten or things are cut or changed without letting me know.

Q. *Some writers say when they finish a good piece they fear they'll never write anything good again. Do you ever feel that way?*

A. I don't think I've had quite that feeling. I always feel, in the beginning of a piece, that this is the piece I will not be able to write. There's a period that lasts from a half hour to a week and a half during which I stomp around and say, "This is the one. I can't do it."

People will say, "Why don't you just write the middle?" I can't do that because the opening sets the sound of it. Sometimes you can't figure out who's talking until you've written the first few paragraphs.

Q. *Tell me about the essay on canning.*

A. That resonated with a lot of people. I wrote it in about two hours. It's about that whole problem of taking on too much and constantly trying to find out how to make it work and blowing it all the time in major ways while being convinced this is the proper path to pursue.

I did can the following year. I got many calls from Washington about that.

6 Anna Quindlen

COLUMNIST ■ *New York Times*

© Jill Krementz

WHEN Anna Quindlen gave up her job as one of the highest-ranking women at the *New York Times,* she planned to stay home with her two young sons and work on a novel. Instead, she ended up writing a weekly syndicated column for the *Times* called "Life in the 30s."

In winning a nationwide audience for her writing, Quindlen capped a fast-rising career at the *Times.* Hired at age 24 as a general assignment reporter, she had become a deputy metropolitan editor in six years.

The New Jersey native is a graduate of Barnard College. Before joining the *Times,* she worked at the *New York Post.* She has received the Meyer Berger prize given by Columbia University for the best writing about New York City. Her work has appeared in *Ms., McCalls, Woman's Day, Ladies Home Journal,* and other magazines.

Quindlen, 37, stopped writing "Life in the 30s" when her daughter was born in November 1988. That same year, a collection of her columns, *Living Out Loud,* was published by Random House. In 1990 she began a new weekly op-ed page column for the *New York Times;* the column deals with political and social concerns.

POWER

At two o'clock in the morning I am awakened by the appearance of a person no taller than a fire hydrant, only his black eyes visible over the horizon of the mattress. "What do you want?" I whisper. "Nothing," he whispers back.

What can have woken my younger son and brought him down from the third floor to stand here in his blue pile Dr. Dentons? It usually boils down to some small thing: a glass of water, a night light, a token rearrangement of the blanket. I always suspect that, if he could put it into words, the explanation would be something else entirely: reassurance that he is not alone in a black world, that nothing horrible is going to happen before daybreak, that someday he will sleep the sure, steady, deep sleep that his elder brother sleeps in the twin bed next to his own. His search for reassurance leads him to our bed, where two terribly fallible people toss and turn, the closest thing he knows to God.

This is what no one warns you about, when you decide to have children. There is so much written about the cost and the changes in your way of life, but no one ever tells you that what they are going to hand you in the hospital is power, whether you want it or not.

I suppose they think you know this, having been on the receiving end all your life, but somehow it slipped to the back of my mind. I was the eldest in a large family; I was prepared for much of what having a baby required. I knew how overwhelming were the walks, the feeding, the changing, the constancy of the care. I should have known, but somehow overlooked for a time, that parents become, effortlessly, just by showing up, the most influential totems in the lives of their children.

We have only to study ourselves, our friends, and the world of amateur and professional psychologizing in which we all live to know that parents someday will be cited as the cause of their children's (choose as many as you like): inability to open up, affinity for people who belittle and hurt them, vulnerability, inferiority. Occasionally — very occasionally — their accomplishment and their strength. We need to find our weaknesses outside ourselves, our strength within. I knew that. I read *Portnoy's Complaint,* D. H. Lawrence, and Eugene O'Neill. And yet I had managed to depersonalize the message until nights like this one, when I wake up with the moon shining through the window and stare back at a person who, staring at me, seems to be saying, "You are, therefore I am."

I am not comfortable with this, which is a little like saying I don't like having green eyes. "Remember that you are the world to your child," one pamphlet I was given says. Oh, great. After a lifetime of yearning for egalitarian relationships, of trying to eschew power plays with other human beings, I find myself in a relationship which, by its very nature, can never really be equal nor free from a skewed balance of power.

We dwell so often on the harm that can be done by exercising that power malevolently, by those people who hit their children, or have sex with them, or tell them day after day that they are worthless and bad. Free of those things, I am more troubled by the subtleties. Raising children is a spur-of-the-moment, seat-of-the-pants sort of deal, as any parent knows, particularly after an adult child says that his most searing memory consists of an offhand comment in the car on the way to second grade that the parent cannot even dimly recall. Despite what the books suggest, you usually do not have several weeks to puzzle out how to separate battling siblings or what to say about death. So it is inevitable that, after a hard day, I occasionally sit back and think about whether I made any crucial mistakes between the chocolate pudding and the hide-and-go-seek. The answer is probably no. But still I consider the question—of passive power, of the power of suggestion, imitation, reaction.

Perhaps I have been preoccupied with all this lately because, despite the difference in their ages, my sons have both fallen in love with me. I can see it in their eyes. For the elder one, this is the grand passion before he lets go, flies off into the male world, switches his identification to his father. For the younger, this is the cleaving to me absolutely which anticipates that process. It is all in the books. Spock says it's fine as long as the child does not become "too close" to the parent of the opposite sex. "In that case, it's wise to get the help of a child guidance clinic," he adds.

There's not much to cure what ails me. I am aghast to find myself in such a position of power over two other people. Their father and I have them in thrall simply by having produced them. We have the power to make them feel good or bad about themselves, which is the greatest power in the world. Ours will not be the only influence, but it is the earliest, the most ubiquitous, and potentially the most pernicious. Lovers and friends will make them blossom and bleed, but they may move on to other lovers and friends. We are the only parents they will have. Sometimes one of them will put silky arms around my neck and stare deep into my eyes like an elfin Svengali and say with full force of the heart, "I love you." The vowel in that middle word dips and lengthens, like a phrase in a Brenda Lee song. My first reaction is to be drowned in happiness. My second is to think: don't mean it so much. Don't feel it so deeply. Don't let me have so much influence over you. Of course, I have no choice. Neither do they.

A SICK FRIEND

The way he told it, it really was a funny story. He was sitting at the kitchen table, his second beer in hand, talking about having minor surgery. He said the inside of the office looked like a gathering of ghosts, with the doctor and his assistants draped, masked, gowned, gloved. The trays, the floors, the chair, the countertops: everything

was swathed in white. And there he was in the middle of it, feeling as
though he should have a bell in his hand, so that when he could talk
again he could clang the thing and cry "Unclean."

You've got to trust me on this; he made us laugh at the whole
thing. The time to cry was long past, the time when we all found out
that he tested positive for the AIDS antibody, the beginning of the
time when he knew that to have a mole removed or a tooth out would
be a major undertaking, fraught with feelings of fear and anger and
shame.

And then it got less funny. I noticed a deep cut, and asked how he
had gotten it. He had had an accident at home, but didn't go for
stitches. He couldn't stand the idea of the fuss that would be made if
he told them he was exposed. He couldn't stand how he would feel
about himself if he didn't tell them.

And it stopped being funny at all when I came downstairs after
he was gone and picked up my beer to finish it. And stared from the
bottle in my hand to the bottle on the table and realized that I didn't
know which was mine and which was his. And, feeling horrible, hyp-
ocritical, paranoid, pitched them both in the trash.

Things are bad all over on the AIDS front, even in our house,
where we have routinely done what some of the folks of Arcadia,
Florida, and Kokomo, Indiana, and a host of other towns went to
extraordinary lengths to avoid. Our friend plays with our children,
eats at our table, is never permitted to leave without a hug and a kiss
on the cheek. It would never occur to me to do otherwise. I know I
will not be exposed through him.

I know.

I think.

I hope.

I wanted to jump right on the people who have been bigoted
about this, the people in Arcadia who wanted to keep those three little
boys out of school and who refer to gay people as "queers," the ones
in Kokomo who made Ryan White's life so unbearable that his family
left town, the parents in Texas whose pediatrician closed up shop last
week because his little patients were taken home when it turned out he
was antibody positive. The people who won't eat at restaurants where
gay waiters work or won't give blood. Except there is a little bit of
them in all but the very best of us. We call them ignorant, and they
are. But I suspect we all feel at least a little ignorant where AIDS is
concerned.

The problem is that we would love absolute certainty on all aspects of this issue. We are a nation raised on True or False tests. We want doctors to give us the answers, which shows how short our memories are. After all, it was the doctors who told us that smoking wouldn't kill you and amphetamines during pregnancy didn't do a bit of harm. We want to know precisely how this disease spreads and why some people who are exposed get it and some don't and whether being exposed means inevitably getting sick. First we hear that the biggest argument against transmission through casual contact is that health-care workers don't get it. Then we hear that health-care workers have gotten it. And we don't know what to believe. All we know for sure is that getting sick means dying, at least so far. And that you can't get it from a beer bottle that's been sitting around for an hour. I know that.

I think.

I hope.

There is a very small cadre of smart and deeply committed people who have an unwavering commitment to never letting one small bit of the misinformation about this filter into their psyche. And there is a larger cadre of those who are using their poor children as an excuse to spout venom and lies about groups of people they despise and feel threatened by. And then there are a lot of people in the middle, people trying to be smart and rational about this, people who read the latest stories and statistics and try to be sensible and yet who watch a mosquito coming toward them and wonder where it's been and whose blood is inside it. When our friend first found out he had been exposed, he offered to stop visiting our house. I was indignant. What did he take me for? In medical parlance, it would be necessary for there to be "an exchange of bodily fluids" for him to infect my children. There was no risk to having him to dinner, more of a risk to cutting him out of our lives and depriving ourselves of his friendship and of our own self-esteem. So I smiled as he roughhoused with the older boy, and all the time somewhere in my mind I was thinking, "Please, God, don't let the kid accidentally bite him."

Columnists are usually in the business of opposites, of us and them. And that's what this started out being, a column about us and them. I continue to think about myself as different from people who torment first graders whose only crime was a bad blood transfusion, who are probably more likely to become mortally ill from well kids than the other way around. I continue to think of myself as different from those people who would leave a dying man on the sidewalk if he were bleeding in certain areas of New York and San Francisco. But I've watched the mosquitos, on occasion, I must admit. And one

night not too long ago I threw away the butt end of two perfectly
good beers because one was mine and the other wasn't. Sometimes,
when I'm feeling self-congratulatory, I think about that and I am
ashamed, and I realize that maybe there is someplace between us and
them, and that this is it.

MAKING NEWS

For most of my adult life, I have been an emotional hit-and-run
driver — that is, a reporter. I made people like me, trust me, open their
hearts and their minds to me, and cry and bleed onto the pages of my
neat little notebooks, and then I went back to a safe place and made a
story out of it. I am good at what I do, so often the people who read
those stories cried, too. When they were done, they turned the page;
when I was done, I went on to another person, another story — went
from the cop's wife whose husband had never come home to the
impoverished eighty-year-old Holocaust survivor to the family with
the missing child. I stepped in and out of their lives as easily as I did
into a pair of shoes in the morning, and when I was done I wrote my
piece and went home, to the husband who had not been killed, the
bank account that was full, the child safe in his high chair. Sometimes
I carried within me, for a day or a week or perhaps even longer, the
resonances of their pain. But they were left with the pain itself.

It was not always as bad as I've made it sound. On occasion I
covered people who wanted to be covered and wrote about things that
were not arrows to the heart: pothole programs, town meetings, the
cost of living, the GNP. But I was good at something called human
interest reporting, just at the time that human interest reporting became the vogue, and so I have spent a good deal of time in the homes
of vulnerable strangers, setting up a short-term relationship, making
them one-shot friends.

While they were lowering their defenses, I was maintaining my
objectivity, which made it possible for me, in a kind of shorthand
reminiscent of the "if u cn rd ths" ads on the subway, to put in my
notebook observations like "strokes baby's head and starts to cry" or
"removes pictures of parents from drawer and tells how they were
killed by SS."

I am proud of what I do, and I am ashamed of it, too. I am reasonably sensitive and not too ruthless, and so I have sometimes saved people from their own revelations and sometimes helped them by giving them the feeling that they were talking to someone who thought they were unique. I have never really understood why they talked to me. I am in one of the few businesses in which a service is provided, not to the people we deal with directly, but only to the faceless thousands who read about them. Sometimes reporters call our house to talk to my husband, who has tried newsworthy cases, and I do not miss the irony of the fact that I find them more or less a nuisance, depending on whether they call in the middle of dinner and how officious they are about the absolute necessity of their task.

Some people I have interviewed told me they thought they could help others know they were not alone, and I suspect they were right, and some people said they thought publicity might help them, and they were right, too. Occasionally I would write a story about a person in a bad spot and I would get checks for them in the mail, and I'd pass them along and think, "Well, that's good." But that wasn't why I did the stories. I did them for me.

I still do, although not on a regular basis. I still write stories and some of them are pithy explorations of unspeakable pain. I did a magazine piece not long ago about breast cancer and I sat one night in a conference room listening to eight women talk about the feeling of taking off their blouses and seeing the zipper of the scar, and I sat there, my two perfectly good breasts slowly swelling with milk for the baby at home, and felt like the worst sort of voyeur, a Peeping Tom of the emotions. Afterward some of them came to me and said how glad they were that I was writing about them, so that others would understand, and I tried to take solace from that. But all I felt was disgust at myself.

I know there are good reasons to do what I do. The more we understand worlds outside our own orbit, the better off we will be. I know there are people who do not believe reporters feel any of these things, that we file our feelings with the clippings, that both are soon dried out beyond saving. That's not true. The problem is that some time ago we invented a kind of new journalism and then tried to play it with old journalism rules. We approached a rape victim with the same feelings about objectivity and distance that we had brought to a press conference, and that was not fair—not so much to the rape victim, but to ourselves.

Some years ago, I did a story about Stan and Julie Patz. Their names are probably familiar; their son, Etan, age six, disappeared in 1979, and they have opened their door to reporter after reporter because anything might bring him home. I interviewed Julie several years after he had gone, and at some point during our conversation my eyes filled and tears began. I thought I felt her pain—now that I have children of my own, I realize I hadn't a clue to what her pain was—but I was also angry at myself for being, after years of practice and journalism review articles, so unprofessional. I thought that what was the right response for a human being was the wrong response for a reporter.

Years have passed, and Julie's son is still missing. In the meantime, I have had two sons of my own. For a while I looked for Etan's face in every playground and schoolyard, but then I stopped. I am ashamed of that. I am proud of the story I wrote. I had the story, and Julie had the life. I still think of her sometimes, and of her pain. Now that I work as a reporter less, I am capable of bringing my emotions to it more.

Perhaps there are no unwritten rules that say you are not to feel these things. Perhaps I made them up out of my own insecurities and stereotypes, the way I insisted on drinking Scotch shots when I first got into the newspaper business, so that everyone would know I was serious stuff, not just a kid. Some of this is changing for the better, I think. The day the space shuttle exploded, at the end of the evening news, it looked to me as if Dan Rather was trembling on the verge of tears when he signed off. For a moment I was able to forget the cameras hovering over the faces of Christa McAuliffe's parents as they looked up to see their eldest child blown to bits, and to forget that if I were still in the newspaper business I might have been there too, scribbling, "Mother lays head on father's shoulder." It appeared that his emotions and his profession were merging, and it made me feel a little better about myself. But the part of me that still looks at every disaster as a story wondered for just a moment if his contact lenses were bothering him, or if the light was in his eyes.

A Visit with Anna Quindlen

Virginia Young: *When did you decide to become a journalist?*

Anna Quindlen: I decided to become a writer when I was a real little kid. I was good at it, I thought it was easy. During high school, I realized the typical writer was starving in a garret somewhere. And I am not the starving-in-a-garret type. I'm very interested in creature comfort.

I was working on my high school newspaper and I suddenly thought, here's a way to support myself until I can write a novel or short stories. I won an award from my local newspaper and badgered them about a job. I said, "I'll sweep floors, work in the cafeteria." Finally they gave me a job as a copy girl.

Q. *You were still in high school?*

A. I was 18, I had just graduated from high school. The *New Brunswick* (New Jersey) *Home News,* a good medium-size daily. Eventually they gave me assignments to do in my spare time and I built up a number of clips. During my third year at Barnard I started baby-sitting for a couple who were both reporters, he at the *Times,* she at the *New York Post.*

Q. *Did you seek out reporters to baby-sit for?*

A. Yes, I went through the baby-sitting file, picked out the by-lines (laughing). I was an excellent baby-sitter, too. But I was on the make. I didn't think it was possible to get a job in New York journalism without being pushy. I was pushy. And they both got me interviews.

Actually, I only had an interview at the *Post* because the *Times* wouldn't consider me for anything except a copy girl's job and I was real arrogant and thought, "Gee, I've already been a copy girl." I wanted to be a reporter, even though I was 19. I got a summer reporting job at the *New York Post.* I came back after I graduated in 1974 and worked there until the end of 1976.

Q. *How did you get a job at the* New York Times?

A. My city editor, Warren Hoge, had gone to the *Times* and he managed to convince them that they should hire me. They were trying to introduce brighter writing and they were trying to hire women. They were in the process of settling a class action suit alleging that there weren't enough women on the staff. I started work there in February 1977.

Q. *How old were you?*

A. I was 24. I worked general assignment, City Hall, then general assignment again. I was given the "About New York" column; then, in June 1983, I became deputy metropolitan editor.

Q. *Why did you take an editing job?*

A. The thing I found compelling about the job was, it made me one of the highest ranking women in the news department. It put a woman at the Page 1 meetings when sometimes there weren't any. I thought it would be good for women at the paper.

I would be able to hire women, give them good assignments. I don't have any problem with that kind of behavior the way some women do. If I had a choice between two equally qualified people and one was male and one was female, I always chose the female. I'm very comfortable with redressing the injuries of centuries.

Q. *Did you expect to climb even higher in the* Times *hierarchy?*

A. You don't go into a job like that wanting to be No. 2 forever. I expected to become metropolitan editor and it seemed quite likely that was going to happen except I had a baby, went on maternity leave, came back, and five months later, I was pregnant again. As soon as I was pregnant with the second one, I knew I couldn't have two kids and be metropolitan editor. It wouldn't have worked for me.

Q. *How did you get started writing "Life in the 30s"?*

A. Christopher was born in June of 1985 and I quit the paper. I started on a novel. But then the *Times* asked me to write the "Hers" column for eight weeks — at that time only free-lancers could do it. I liked it and got a lot of offers to do a regular column.

I went back to (*Times* Executive Editor) Abe Rosenthal and said, "I've got all these offers, except that one day in a fit of incredible emotion I promised you I would never work for another newspaper. Were you serious?" And he said, "Yes, but don't worry because you can do a column for us." That's where "Life in the 30s" came from. He told me I should write about what I was talking about with my friends on the telephone.

Q. *How has being a woman affected your career?*

A. Early on at the *Times*, it helped me.

When I had my interview with the managing editor of the *New York Post*, I wanted the job desperately and I was trying to be mouthy and glib because I thought that's what would be expected of me there. He said, "Why should I hire you?" And I said, "Because I'm a woman." He shook his head, took me to the door of his office, pointed, and said, "My staff is 50 percent women." He didn't need more women on his staff. He hired me because I was mouthy and glib and because he thought I'd be good.

But at the *Times*, I don't think I'd have gotten hired if I hadn't been female. They made it clear that I was a lot younger than they were used to hiring and I didn't have enough hard news experience. Most of my clips were features because when you are a good stylist, they tend to use you for that. And afterward they say, "You don't have enough hard news experience."

Q. *Do you think the business is harder on women's personal lives?*

A. All jobs are harder on women because some women automatically think, I've got to work part-time, I've got to stop working, I can't take certain kinds of assignments. Men in general don't think that. Most men wouldn't have thought that having two children was an impediment to becoming metropolitan editor.

Q. *Did you feel torn when you quit writing "Life in the 30s," being at the pinnacle of your profession?*

A. No. If I hadn't been so secure in my career, it might've been harder because I might've thought, "Gee, will I be able to get back in?" If I'd had my kids at 25, it would've been a real problem. But luckily, I got started early in the business so I could take time off and do what I wanted to do.

Q. *Have you made any personal sacrifices for your career?*

A. No. Unacceptable. I wouldn't do that. My husband and I have a difference of opinion about this. He thinks that I am investing myself too much in my life with the kids. But we're going to go on having a difference of opinion about that for a couple more years.

Q. *Have you had to work harder than your male counterparts to get where you are?*

A. I probably did but it's hard for me to separate out how much had to do with ageism and how much had to do with sexism. When you're as young as I was at a paper like the *Times*, a lot of the rap against you is you're too young. By the time age didn't matter any more, I was well enough established there.

Q. *Did you ever worry about failing?*

A. When I was deputy metropolitan editor, I was afraid of making a mistake for fear that it would reflect badly on women. I wanted to go into that Page 1 meeting and make a good presentation and look sure of myself because I didn't want to look like "The Girl." And I didn't want anyone to think I was impeded by the fact that there was another person living inside my stomach.

There are certain things I never would have done in the office because they would be perceived as "girl" things. I would never have put on makeup at my desk. I would have my ripped my tear ducts out rather than cry.

You didn't want to hang back. In some sense that's fake machismo. I remember being in a funky area of the South Bronx, working on an "About New York" column when I was five months pregnant and thinking, "This is insane." You're not just messing around with Anna Quindlen's life, you're messing around with somebody else's life and you're not going to do that any more.

Q. *Are women different as interviewers?*

A. I'm different from the stereotypes. I try to have an interview that's more of a conversation. I don't mind letting go of stuff about myself if I think it'll move us along and make the person more comfortable. I tend not to be confrontational unless I absolutely have to be.

That's one of the things I found hardest when I first got into the business — asking the hard question, the question I knew would anger somebody, embarrass them, the questions I'd been raised to believe were impolite.

I do not find it hard at all now. I just do what works. If I'm going to ask a question that I know is going to make them angry, I wait until the end of an interview so they'll give me everything I need before they order me out of the room.

Q. *Are women more empathetic interviewers?*

A. No. I've worked with women who can chew glass and I've worked with men who had incredible empathy. I think women reporters sometimes bend over backward not to do that.

I remember being out with the cops when they pulled a floater out of the river. The whole time I'm thinking, "I will not get sick, I will not get white, I will not react to this." They got the floater out and one of the guys from the wires just blew his cookies. I didn't blame him but I was not going to do it because I was bending over backward not to be "The Girl."

Q. *Do you network with other women journalists?*

A. All you have to do is look at the acknowledgments section of my book. Cynthia Gorney and I have shared the names of editors at magazines that are good to work with, have shared sources for 12 years now. Ditto for me and Janet Maslin, the film critic at the *Times*, ditto for me and Leslie Bennetts, who was at the *Times* and now is a contributing editor at *Vanity Fair.* We all trade stories and give advice and listen to leads.

When I was first at the *Times* it was a necessity. Not only were there very few people of my gender but there were very few people of my age. That's how I met Kathy Slobogin, a senior producer at West 57th Street. She was Tom Wicker's news clerk. And I just glommed on to her at the Xerox machine one day.

Q. *Don Fry of the Poynter Institute has coined the phrase "phallic journalism" to describe tough-talking editors bossing people around. Has that been your experience and if so, how do you deal with that?*

A. There isn't so much of that at the *New York Times.* At the *Post* there was, but it was an acting job and I loved that. The executive editor used to come out and rant and rave and use profanity and I used to think, "God, this is what I knew it would be like." I think the darkest day in any newsroom is the day they lay the carpeting. I like that crazy melange.

The part I don't like is the posturing that accompanies the scramble up the ladder, the watching-your-back mentality, how did I do in that meeting, was I impressive?

When I was deputy metropolitan editor, people were trying to convince me what a great future I had at the *New York Times.* They would say, "Some day, you could be managing editor of this paper." That's interesting because managing editor isn't the No. 1 job at the paper. Executive editor is. But no one ever said, "Someday you could be executive editor."

Q. *Do you think it's becoming more and more possible that a woman could be in the top newsroom position?*

A. Yes, every year it's becoming more and more possible. Do I think it's going to happen in my lifetime? I'm not sure.

To have more deserving women in high positions, the heretofore inviolate tracks are going to have to change. You didn't used to get to be executive editor of the *Times* unless you had done a foreign assignment, probably done Washington, won a Pulitzer, run a major desk. Now you could probably get away with not having the foreign assignment or not having the Pulitzer.

Q. *Have you ever used feminine wiles to get a story?*

A. I'm not good at feminine wiles. People have tended to perceive me as mother, sister, or daughter, three relatively nonthreatening roles.

Early on there were people who thought I was too stupid to understand the import of what they were saying so they said things in front of me that they shouldn't have said. And there were people who felt like I had a shoulder you could cry on, people who unloaded on me who wouldn't if I were male. But none of it had to do with being sexy.

Q. *Some writers say that when they finish something good they fear that they'll never write anything as good again. Do you ever feel that way?*

A. I usually think that it's not that good when I finish it. My problem is always between fantasy and reality. I come up with an idea and I think of various ways it's going to shake down. And I think, "God, it's going to be great." But when I finish it, it's not as good as the fantasy.

Q. *When you get an idea for a column how do you develop it?*

A. It's usually a combination of an idea in general and an anecdote in specific. Oftentimes the two are very distinct until I realize how one can serve the other. A good example is the column called "Power." The image of my younger son coming into the room and standing next to the bed in the middle of the night was something I knew I was going to use.

Once I knew I was going to write a column about the power parents have over their kids, I realized that vignette would make a perfect beginning. Once I have a beginning like that, I'm home free. I'm one of those people who, once they have the lead, knows where she's going from there. I also tend to write in a circular way. The ending comes back to the lead. I don't feel comfortable unless I've completed the circle.

Q. *What do you do when you have writer's block?*

A. I don't get blocked much. I make myself write even if I feel blocked, just about something entirely different or letters or anything, just to get it going. Once you get it going, the block goes away. I don't mind writing something bad just so I'm writing. Afterward I can say, this is bad but it's got one good sentence in it that I could build around.

Q. *How long does it take to write a typical column?*

A. It depends. Some of the issues columns I revamp and revamp. There are others that I've just been able to write, zip. It's either because it's been living in my head for so many years that the column is essentially written—I'm just transcribing—or it's something I feel so passionately that I can hit the ground running.

I wrote a column about my grandmother dying. It couldn't have taken more than half an hour. It was just this burst of passion, like that kind of sex where you don't take your clothes off, you fall on the ground. It came straight from the heart to the typewriter and it didn't have to stop at the mind.

Q. *Do you always use specific vignettes or do you sometimes use composites?*

A. I approach this column very much as a reporter so if it didn't happen, I can't make it happen. I've been good at seeing the ordinary stuff that has importance because that's what I always used as a reporter anyway. Half of my notes on a story were always the neon signs in bar windows, what was in a trash can, what somebody was wearing—weird details, like the fact that their slip strap was hanging out of an armhole or their underwear was showing at the top of their pants waistband. That's the same thing that has served me well in the column.

Q. *Do you file incidents in your mind or do you put them on paper?*

A. The first year I was so paranoid about forgetting things that I wrote them down on odd strips of paper that littered my desk. But after a while I found I could remember them quite accurately, particularly if I knew what they were going to attach themselves to.

Q. *Do you always start out with, "I have this point in mind, this message I want to leave?"*

A. No, I usually have a general point in mind. Like I'll say, I want to write about the incredible power people have over their children. It's only as I'm writing that I discover the permutations of that. As you logically progress in a column, you come to the realizations that even you hadn't realized until that moment.

Q. *Who do you think of as your reader?*

A. I think of me as my reader. I write for myself and there have been maybe a dozen columns that I thought could be of no interest to anybody except me and then dozens and dozens of people would say, "Oh, I've always felt like that."

Q. *Has there been a subject too painful or personal to write about?*

A. There have been subjects that were off limits. If I were having problems in my marriage I wouldn't have written about it. If something real hard and personal were happening to one of my kids, I might not have written about it. There haven't been many things too painful. If I could write about my mother then I could write about anything.

From week to week I made choices. But I can't tell you what those choices were because it was a subliminal thing. It was like that screen that whales have that they strain the plankton through in their mouths. You got all the plankton, I don't know what was in the water that went by.

Q. *Was it emotionally draining to lay your life out so honestly?*

A. Yes. It was ripping your guts apart once a week. One reason I used to write an issues column was for relief. There were certain of these columns that I felt like I'd been run over by a truck when I finished them.

Q. *What do you want to accomplish in your writing?*

A. I want to make the reader be there. The thing that I've always liked about journalism is you get to go places you wouldn't go otherwise. You get to watch open heart surgery or meet the president or go to New Delhi or go to a crack house. But in order to earn your passage there, you have to take your reader with you. If you're not capable of taking the reader with you, you shouldn't be in the job. The great frustration for me has always been that the best I can give the reader is a mirror image. A mirror image is good but it is not the real thing.

Q. *Do you revise much?*

A. Most of my revision goes on mentally. I go over stuff in my head and throw it away so that by the time I sit down I've already revised; it just hasn't been done on paper. There are certain columns that I've beaten into submission but not many.

Q. *Do you think in terms of a nut graph, where you spell out the point?*

A. Sometimes a nut graph works but in a column like mine, it's useful to make the reader do the mental gymnastics with me. If you're writing about the death penalty, for example, you don't say to them right away, "I'm against the death penalty." You take them through your own thoughts: what people want the death penalty to do, how it's applied, and then, by the end, you say, "So you can see by what I've just shown you that it doesn't work."

Q. *How do you structure a column?*

A. The structure followed the structure of my thinking process. For example, I'd think, "What's so bad about having power over another human being? Well, there's this and this. What's good about it?" That tended to be the way I wrote it.

Q. *Do you read your work aloud?*

A. Sometimes. When I read it in my head it's aloud because I write very much by ear. If something doesn't sound right it gets changed. The meter has to be right. I've always felt strongly that words had a rhythm, that they were like music. I'm Irish; we had to feel that way.

Q. *What advice would you give someone who wants to write a column?*

A. You have to make a threshold-level decision to give part of yourself away to the reader. Then you've got to stick with it. That's a hard decision to make and I can understand anybody who doesn't want to do it. It's odd to have all these people think they know you, think they're your friends. There's something wonderful about it but there's something weird about it, too.

It doesn't mean you have to give them everything. They got about 70 percent of me. But that part that you're going to give them, you have to really give them. You can't be cagey or self-protected.

Q. *I know you got lots of fan mail, but did you get much negative mail?*

A. I got real negative mail sometimes from feminists. When the book came out, there was a big feminist brouhaha, people saying I was neoconservative, this was the new traditionalism, how could you call yourself a feminist if all you cared about was your husband and your kids.

Q. *How did you feel about that?*

A. People are missing the boat. The 1970s part of the movement was seeing that women be admitted to places they hadn't been admitted before. That was enormously important and changed all our lives. But that sometimes was denigrating to the ways women had done things before.

People get excited if you say there are differences between men and women. I'm comfortable with that. I'm not comfortable saying there are differences and therefore, women shouldn't be allowed to do all this good stuff or make decent money. But I'm comfortable saying most women have better nurturing skills than most men.

I'm a feminist. I've worked for the rights of women for many years and I'm going to continue to do it.

Q. *Have you found writing fiction different from writing for a newspaper?*

A. It's exactly the same. I'm looking for that same combination of small details. I'm served in good stead by all the years I've worked as a reporter because I know how dialogue sounds. That has made a big difference.

It's like reporting. You just have to create the scene in your head, then report it. So you look up at the trees, look down at the ground, and look at what people are wearing. The only thing is, you've made it all up.

Q. *What advice would you give women coming into the journalism field today?*

A. Do what works for you. Don't recoil from life-style stuff or features if that's what you love the most and do best just because there are men in the organization who don't value it as much as the harder news.

Don't be afraid to move if you can. Women tend to get invested in a place. Instead of thinking of it as an office, they think of it as a surrogate home.

It's a great job for women, and it's a business that's more and more sex-blind all the time. We're in a period of complacency right now, a plateau period. But people get to the end of a plateau and climb a mountain again. I'm hopeful. I'm very hopeful.

7 Molly Ivins

COLUMNIST ■ *Dallas Times Herald*

IN 1967, Molly Ivins broke new ground. She was the first woman assigned by the *Minneapolis Tribune* to cover the police beat. Years later, she found herself covering another male institution: the Texas legislature.

"And, there is no place in this country more sexist than Texas," the 44-year-old columnist said during an interview in her Austin office.

The Texas native has a bachelor's degree from Smith College and a master's from Columbia University, where in 1976 she was named the School of Journalism's outstanding alumna. That same year, she joined the *New York Times* as a political reporter. Six years later, she began writing a column for the *Dallas Times Herald.*

She is a humor columnist for *Ms. Magazine* and the *Progressive* and appears regularly on National Public Radio and the McNeil/Lehrer television show. Ivins has served on the board of the National News Council and remains active in Amnesty International's Journalism Network. Her specialty is taking shots at politicians, especially those who run her state.

Following are two columns that illustrate diversity of subject and style. The first appeared in *Ms. Magazine,* the second in the *Dallas Times Herald.*

THE MEMORY LINGERS ON

As the Gipper rides slowly into the sunset, the rest of us are left with so many magic moments to remember. We all have our own favorites. Such as the time he appointed a Commission on AIDS consisting of 13 fruitloops including a sex therapist who said AIDS could be transmitted on toilet seats and another who charged that homosexuals engage in "blood terrorism" by deliberately donating infected blood.

Or the time they made him go into McDonald's during the '84 campaign and he sat down and asked, "What do I order?"

Everybody remembers Reagan's famous comment, on visiting the Bitburg Cemetery in Germany, that the Nazi SS soldiers buried there "were victims just as surely as the victims in the concentration campus." Ah, but how many of you recall the immortal remark he made to the Lebanese foreign minister? After the minister finished a half-hour lecture on the intricate relations of his country's many political factions, Reagan said, "You know, your nose looks just like Danny Thomas's."

But perhaps my all-time favorite episode in the entire eight years came early on with the great bee doody crisis. In 1981, Secretary of State Alexander Haig accused the Soviet Union of using chemical warfare on Southeast Asia, of having sprayed a lethal "yellow rain" on remote tribesmen that led to terrible sickness and even death. Chemical warfare! Practicing it in remote mountain areas so no one could catch them at it! The brutes, the evil, conscienceless Commies.

The substance called yellow rain by our State Department was later identified as bee shit by scientists here and in several countries. It seems that bees occasionally leave their hives, fly up to a considerable altitude, and defecate en masse. The resulting clouds of poop apparently frightened people, but never made anyone sick. The Reagan Administration not only failed to apologize for the original charge; they never withdrew it.

What I like about this episode is that it has all the grand lunacy of the Reagan Administration at its finest. It has a great plot, great drama, great villains (Commies, of course). And it's so divorced from reality, it has that patented Reagan element of berserker comedy. Followed by that patented Reagan stubbornness, perhaps even defiance, in the face of facts.

It doesn't matter how often you tell Reagan something he doesn't want to believe. The man still thinks that you can buy vodka with food stamps, that he never traded arms for hostages, and that the Soviet Union has sent billions of dollars of weapons to the Sandinistas. He has been President for eight years now and he still believes that money spent on the military does not increase the national deficit. Honest to God.

Now, all of this would be amusing if it weren't for the reality Reagan is so fond of ignoring. If Reagan were merely, in the words of former Secretary of Defense Clark Clifford, "an amiable dunce," we could collect his bloopers, his fantasies, his lies, and the evidence of his ignorance with the dedication and delight that all true collectors bring to their harmless passions.

Jane Mayer, coauthor of the book *Landslide,* said, "I was in Beirut when the Marine barracks were bombed. You can't see something like that without realizing that there are actual repercussions when there is chaos in Washington. Seeing all those young men dead made me realize how much all this really matters."

No one who went through the war in Vietnam can forget how much ignorance really matters.

As one who is congenitally optimistic to the point of idiocy, it seems to me we got off quite lightly from our eight years with Ronald Reagan as President, considering what could have happened.

True, Bill Casey set up a secret government and a bunch of rich right-wingers bought themselves a secret foreign policy, but it could have been worse. True, the rich got richer, the poor got poorer, and the middle class shrank (and not because, as George Bush maintains, so many moved into the upper class), but it could have been worse. True, we have lost precious time in starting to work on critical problems in the environment, education and housing, but it could have been worse.

Congress stopped it from being worse again and again—the plan to cut $800 million from child nutrition programs, to destroy Legal Services, to tax unemployment benefits, to dock the Supplementary Security Income payments of the disabled if they received any private charity—Reagan has been foiled again and again. His most enduring governmental legacy will be a national deficit the size of a modest black hole.

But the Reagan years have left even me with a rather sour taste in my mouth from too much sugar-sweet optimism. Perhaps the hardest thing to get over will be the extent to which Ronald Reagan has muddled our collective grasp of reality. A few years ago, when he was told the Congressional Budget Office was showing a dramatic redistribution of income from the poor to the rich, Reagan replied, "I don't think it's true."

That was his entire response to the evidence in front of our collective nose on a whole range of problems. All the pundits have been thumb-sucking over this sorry Presidential campaign, wondering where this new level of untruth came from, why politicians now believe they can get away with outright lies.

Why? I know the American press is ahistorical, but the guy is still sitting there in the White House. And the rest of us like his game of "Let's pretend." We like imagining ourselves in some nice old-time movie where we always get to wear the white hats and we always win and everything is simple. But reality is still out there, and it's gaining on us.

SHORT STORY ABOUT THE VIETNAM MEMORIAL

She had known, ever since she first read about the Vietnam Memorial, that she would go there someday. Sometime she would be in Washington and would go and see his name and leave again.

So silly, all that fuss about the memorial. Whatever else Vietnam was, it was not the kind of war that calls for some "Raising the Flag at Iwo Jima" kind of statue. She was not prepared, though, for the impact of the memorial. To walk down into it in the pale winter sunshine was like the war itself, like going into a dark valley and damned if there was ever any light at the end of the tunnel. Just death. When you get closer to the two walls, the number of names start to stun you. It is terrible, there in the peace and the pale sunshine.

The names are listed by date of death. There has never been a time, day or night, drunk or sober, for 13 years she could not have told you the date. He was killed on Aug. 13, 1969. It is near the middle of the left wall. She went toward it as though she had known beforehand where it would be.

His name is near the bottom. She had to kneel to find it. His name leaped out at her. It was like being hit.

She stared at it and then reached out and gently ran her fingers over the letters in the cold black marble. The memory of him came back so strong, almost as if he were there on the other side of the stone, she could see his hand reaching out to touch her fingers. It had not hurt for years and suddenly, just for a moment, it hurt again so horribly that it twisted her face and made her gasp and left her with tears running down her face. Then it stopped hurting but she could not stop the tears. Could not stop them from running and running down her face.

There had been a time, although she had been an otherwise sensible young woman, when she had believed she would never recover from the pain. She did, of course. But she is still determined never to sentimentalize him. He would have hated that. She had thought it was like an amputation, the severing of his life from hers, that you could live on afterward but it would be like having only one leg and one arm. But it was only a wound. It healed. If there is a scar, it is only faintly visible now at odd intervals.

He was a biologist, a t.a. [teaching assistant] at the university getting his Ph.D. They lived together for two years. He left the university to finish his thesis and before he could line up a public school job—teachers were safe in those years—the draft board got him. They had friends who had left the country, they had friends who had gone to prison, they had friends who had gone to Nam. There were no good choices in those years.

She thinks now he unconsciously wanted to go even though he often said that it was a stupid, f---in' war. He felt some form of guilt about a friend of theirs who was killed during the Tet offensive. Hubert Humphrey called Tet a great victory. His compromise was to refuse officers training school and go as an enlisted man. She had thought then it was a dumb gesture and they had a half-hearted quarrel about it.

He had been in Nam less than two months when he was killed, without heroics, during a firefight at night by a single bullet in the brain. No one saw it happen. There are some amazing statistics about money and tonnage from that war. Did you know there were more bombs dropped on Hanoi during the Christmas bombing of 1971 than in all of World War II?

Did you know that the war in Vietnam cost the United States $123.3 billion? She has always wanted to know how much that one bullet cost. Sixty-three cents? $1.20? Someone must know.

The other bad part was the brain. Even at this late date, it seems to her that was quite a remarkable mind. Long before she read C. P. Snow, the ferociously honest young man who wanted to be a great biologist taught her a great deal about the difference between the way scientists think and the way humanists think. Only once has she been glad he was not with her. It was at one of those bizarre hearings about teaching "creation science." He would have gotten furious and been horribly rude. He had no patience with people who did not understand and respect the process of science.

She used to attribute his fierce honesty to the fact that he was Yankee. She is still prone to tell "white" lies to make people feel better, to smooth things over, to prevent hard feelings. Surely there have been dumber things for lovers to quarrel over than the social utility of hypocrisy. But not many.

She stood up again, still staring at his name, stood for a long time. She said, "There it is," and turned to go. A man to her left was staring at her. She glared at him resentfully. The man had done nothing but make the mistake of seeing her weeping. She said, as though daring him to disagree, "It was a stupid, f---in' war," and stalked past him.

She turned again at the top of the slope to make sure where his name is, so whenever she sees a picture of the memorial she can put her finger where his name is. He never said goodbye, literally. Whenever he left he would say, "Take care, love." He could say it many different ways. He said it when he left for Vietnam.

She stood at the top of the slope and found her hand half-raised in some silly gesture of farewell. She brought it down again. She considered thinking to him, "Hey, take care, love," but it seemed remarkably inappropriate. She walked away and was quite entertaining for the rest of the day, because it was expected of her.

She thinks he would have liked the memorial. He would have hated the editorials. He did not sacrifice his life for his country or for a just or noble cause. There just were no good choices in those years and he got killed.

A visit with Molly Ivins

Sherry Ricchiardi: *How did you get into journalism?*

Molly Ivins: I sort of fell backward into it. I wanted to write the great American novel. But it occurred to me around my freshman year in college that quite a few of us were planning to do that and, inevitably, some weren't going to make it. It also occurred to me that I might be among those who wouldn't.

Current affairs was the only other thing that excited me. If the only thing you can do is write and what's going on in the world is one of your great interests, journalism is a natural thing to do.

Q. *Who were key influences along the way?*

A. I had a wonderful high school English teacher named Robert P. Moore. I'm still in touch with him, bless his heart. And, some editors influenced me. The late Frank Premack at the *Minneapolis Tribune* was a picky son of a bitch and I think I hated him when I worked for him, but I sure did learn a lot. I. F. Stone is one of my heroes in journalism.

Q. *How has being a woman affected your career?*

A. I was an exception to what happens to most women in

journalism and I think it had a lot to do with my size. In high heels, I stand about 6-feet, 2-inches tall. No editor ever looked at me and said, "Oh, you poor, sweet, fragile little thing. We couldn't send you out to cover a riot." It was always, "Ivins, get your ass out there."

As a matter of fact, I never worked for an editor I didn't tower over. I think that's why the *Minneapolis Tribune* made me a police reporter instead of giving me the elementary education beat.

Q. *Do women coming into the field today have it any better?*

A. I don't believe they face discrimination at the hiring level or with assignments. But they hit discrimination when they try to get promoted. They ought to be prepared for that and ready to fight.

Q. *Have you had to work harder than your male counterparts to succeed in the newsroom?*

A. There's no doubt about it. For women to have an equal chance with men, we also have to have more credentials. I felt that in addition to being six-feet tall, I had to have a master's degree from Columbia University. That, I believe, also saved me from some of the discrimination women my age were experiencing in journalism.

Q. *Have you made personal sacrifices for your career?*

A. It's relatively easy for women to have a job, but it is relatively difficult for us to have a career. That is a problem we all face.

A lot of years have passed and I'm not married. I would have loved to have had a child. Occasionally, I've thought of adopting. But, there isn't enough structure in my life for that. If you are going to take on the task of being a single parent, the very least you would owe the child is to be home every night.

And, there's a problem with the men you meet. I believe strongly that it is not smart for women reporters to become romantically involved with their colleagues, their competition, or their sources. That leaves the occasional plumber who comes to fix the toilet as the only available male.

Q. *Has being a woman affected the subject matter you write about? Does it make you more empathetic, sympathetic, sensitive?*

A. I, like most people in this business, have long ago realized there is no such thing as objectivity. Who you are affects the way you see. Being a woman obviously affects the way I perceive the world. There is no question that it makes a difference in what I write about.

I'm a female chauvinist. That's embarrassing to admit, but it's true. I have seen a generation of older women in this profession who truly have suffered. The sexism they experienced and the low esteem in which they were held by editors has eaten into their souls and into their self-concept. It's astonishing that so much kindness remains in them.

Q. *How did this affect you?*

A. These women tended to be stuck in women's sections, which were always called the snake pit. I determined very early that I was going to be on the city desk. I was never going to be assigned to the women's section, God forbid!

It took me years to notice a remarkable phenomenon. For a long time, the best journalism about women, family issues, and social issues, came out of those sections. These reporters were writing about abortion, wife and child abuse, incest—stories far out on the cutting edge. Their stories got into the paper because nobody was paying attention to what they did.

Q. *Are women in newsrooms today more competitive than when you came into the business?*

A. Women who obtain real power in newsrooms have to be twice as smart, twice as shrewd and twice as tough as their male counterparts. Women at the top are going to be utterly steeped in male values because they've had to compete in a male world.

When I was at the *New York Times,* I worked mostly with men who were extremely more competitive than I was. Now, at age 44, I have become sort of a mother figure in the newsroom.

Q. *Do you have any regrets about your career?*

A. One day a young female reporter came up to me and said, "Molly, I've been offered this new assignment. Do you think it would be a shrewd career move?" I tried not to laugh in her face because that wouldn't be polite.

If there is an epitaph on my tombstone, I would like it to read, "Molly Ivins never made a shrewd career move."

You are talking to a woman who left an excellent established newspaper to go to a small, alternative paper that paid one-fifth of what I was earning at the *Minneapolis Tribune.* You are talking to a woman who left the *New York Times.* But, regrets? Not really.

Q. *Why did you leave the* New York Times?

A. I was Denver (Colorado) bureau chief, covering nine states. One day I wrote a feature story about a small town where once a year they hold a community chicken slaughter.

They sit around and drink a lot of beer, listen to music and pluck chickens. It's not a bad deal. Everybody winds up with a freezer full.

In the course of the story I called it a "gang pluck." I knew full well it wouldn't make it into the *New York Times,* but I liked to put things into my stories to amuse the guys on the national copy desk.

Well, word of it got around and I was told to report in for re-assignment. Abe Rosenthal called me into his office and started talking about how I tended to stick my finger in the eye of the *New York Times,* as he put it.

We went through several incidents and he said, "You tried to get the words 'gang pluck' into a story in the *New York Times.*"

I said, "Well, yea Abe, I did."

He said, "Gang pluck."

I said, "Well, Abe, I thought it was a good play on words. I knew it wouldn't make the paper."

He said, "Gang pluck. That is a synonym for gang fuck. You were trying to get our readers to think of the word 'fuck.' "

I said, "Damn it, Abe, you're a hard guy to fool." And that was the end of my career at the *New York Times.*

Q. *What advice do you have for women coming into the field?*

A. I tell young reporters when someone offers them a new opportunity they should consider three things: Will it be any fun? Can I do any good? Can I learn anything?

Journalists get paid to go out and learn something new every day. What a fabulous thing! I can't imagine approaching journalism with the idea of getting ahead.

Q. *Have you ever experienced overt sexism in the line of duty?*

A. When I was a police reporter for the *Minneapolis Tribune,* I experienced just about everything there was in the way of sexism. What got me most about working in an all-male institution was the dreadful gossip. I don't know how women got the reputation of being gossips—men are just awful.

At one time or another, I was simultaneously rumored to be sleeping with the police chief, three police captains, five lieutenants, and God knows how many sergeants. The fact is, I never slept with a cop; I never went out with one; I never looked meaningfully into a police officer's eyes.

Q. *Was that the worst of it?*

A. No, Texas politicians are the worst. When I returned to Texas, I arranged interviews with some prominent political leaders strictly to find out what was going on.

I'd enter the room in a very serious manner and attempt to interview these guys. What astonished me was that several of them would say, "You pretty little thing. Don't worry your pretty little head about that. Why don't you come over here and sit on my lap?"

In those days I wore high heels that made me 6-feet, 2-inches tall. I would sit there and think, "If I sat on your lap, I would squish you like a little bug."

Q. *How did you deal with this kind of treatment?*

A. At times, it infuriated me. At times, I felt denigrated by it. I once heard a Texas legislator order a lobbyist to "Get me two sweathogs for tonight."

Returning to Texas was like stepping back 20 years in time. Texas is so socially backward, particularly if you've been some place like New York City where the women's movement made strong advances.

Q. *Are there other incidents that stand out in your mind?*

A. A few years ago, I was over at the legislature with a *Dallas Morning News* reporter on one side of me and a *Houston Chronicle* reporter on the other side — both men, of course. In those days, in fact it's still true today, the senate pages all were young women.

As one of them passed, the *Dallas Morning News* hit me in the ribs with his elbow and said, "Jesus Christ, look at the ass on that girl." The *Houston Chronicle* hit me from the other side and said, "Look at that pair of knockers." It was at that moment I decided I could not be one of the boys.

Q. *As more women move into leadership roles in the newsroom, are we helping to reshape the news?*

A. There's no question about it. If women ran newspapers, the toxic shock syndrome stories instantly would have been on Page 1. As it was, it took quite awhile for that to happen.

If an after-shave lotion was killing men, you better believe it would have been front page news. But, writing about menstruation and tampons was taboo. The handling of those stories truly revealed male squeamishness and the blindness of sexism.

Wife abuse, family violence, divorce, incest — those topics never made the newspapers until women began covering them. Now, we see them on the front page.

Q. *How did you get into writing a column?*

A. I was working for the *New York Times* when I got a call from an editor asking, "How would you like to come back down to Texas and write a column?" I don't know whose idea it was to hire me.

When I accepted the job, I only asked one thing. I wanted complete freedom. The editors promised I could write about whatever I wanted and say whatever I wanted. I began writing the column in 1982.

Q. *Tell me about how you get your ideas.*

A. My life is spent going, "Oh my God! What am I going to write about?" As soon as I finish one column I'm suddenly in the "Oh my God" stage again. Once I get an idea, it's easy.

Mostly, I write off the news. I go through the newspaper and see what makes me mad. That's a pretty good indication that I need to write about something. And I automatically cover anything that happens in Texas politics.

Some of my columns are what I call thumb-sucking. That's a piece where I say what I think about something without doing any research or interviewing anybody. I clip stuff constantly. I pay part-time staff out of my own money to help with this.

I also write about things that happen to me. I have funny encounters with funny people, hundreds of them, thousands of them. Sometimes I write the kind of stories I've been telling my friends over dinner for years.

Q. *What process do you go through after you get an idea?*

A. I have absolutely no set process. I sit down at the computer, put the code in at the top. I type dateline AUSTIN and start from there. I don't outline; I don't have any set plan.

Q. *How much time, on the average, do you spend on a column?*

A. My deadline is around noon, and I hate it. For me the ideal situation would be to have a 6 P.M. deadline like a normal reporter. I could read newspapers before I come in to work, decide what I wanted to write about, spend the morning doing research and calling people. In the afternoon, I would write.

Now, I get up around 6 A.M. to read the paper. By 9 A.M., I'm still in the "God, what am I going to write about?" stage. If the situation is absolutely dire, I can write a column in little over an hour, but it won't be very good. If I have three hours to write, I can produce quite a nice piece of prose.

Q. *Once you start writing, do you have any formula?*

A. Every now and again I say, "This is shit." I delete it and go back to where I was last on track. No, I don't really have a formula.

Q. *Do you rework sentences and paragraphs?*

A. I rewrite as I go along. I reread a chunk at a time and rewrite. If I have time, I'll read the whole thing and make more changes. I polish right up to the end right on the computer screen.

Q. *What is the average length of your column?*

A. Around 1,000 words. After you've been writing a column long enough, you can't write any other length. You write letters that turn out to be 1,000 words. You write recipes that come out to 1,000 words.

Q. *Are you edited much?*

A. Lately there's been a little more editing. Of course, I loathe being edited. When I worked for the *New York Times,* I wrote a line that said, "He was a man with a beer gut that belonged in the Smithsonian." Editors changed it to, "He was a man with a protuberant abdomen."

Nine times out of 10 anybody who has touched my copy has made it worse. On the other hand, the tenth time, they usually save me.

Q. *Tell me about the Vietnam column. It's a different style than you usually write.*

A. I wrote that in my head on the plane trip back from Washington, D.C. I find it very easy to write in my head. Frequently after a long drive, I sit down at a computer and the whole story just comes out.

Q. *Did you plan to write the Vietnam column when you visited the memorial?*

A. No, I decided that afterwards. I'm interested in how angry I still am about Vietnam. I've talked to a lot of veterans who have come to a peace about it, but I have not.

Q. *Why did you write it in third person?*

A. It was too personal. I couldn't do it in first person. It was very emotional; I was crying the whole time I wrote that column. I still have a hard time talking about it.

Q. *Who is your reader?*

A. Texas is very conservative. Almost anybody elected to office is conservative. To be a liberal here is to be a member of the embattled minority.

I say all the things that a liberal Texan wants to say to the people in power. I either am very popular with some readers or very unpopular—but they read me.

A lot of people read my columns because they're funny. A lot read it for the Texas language. Some truck drivers once told me they read my columns because I write Texas. I have always said if I didn't write with a Texas accent, I would have been lynched by now.

Q. *How do you use humor?*

A. I use humor to open peoples' ears. That's what happens when people laugh. They open their ears and hear what you have to say.

Occasionally, I use humor as a weapon. I view satire as a weapon of the powerless against the powerful.

The times when I feel so terrible and wish I was dead occur when in an attempt to be funny, I inadvertently hurt somebody. You have to be terribly careful with humor. Of course, when my humor is aimed at Texas politicians, it's a free fire zone.

Q. *Are there any secrets to writing humor?*

A. There is a tremendous difference between spoken and written humor. There is a tone to the way something is spoken. To write so that timing is part of the line is extremely difficult. You have to write a sentence that makes people pause.

I write pause into a sentence by inverting the form of a sentence or by sticking "he said" or any other parenthetical phrase into the middle of it. There has to be a rhythm.

There are very few rules. I always assume my readers are as smart as I am. I never write down to them. I don't hesitate to use a long or esoteric word if it's the right word for that place. But, I don't use big words to show off.

I'm not very self-analytical. It makes me uncomfortable to stop and talk about my writing.

Q. *Does being humorous come naturally to you?*

A. I can't imagine actually trying to be funny. I have trouble writing for *Ms. Magazine* because they label my column "humor." I'm paralyzed by it.

God gave me Texas politics to write about. How can I not be funny?

8 Christine Brennan

SPORTS ■ *The Washington Post*

IN 1985, Christine Brennan walked into the lives—and into the locker room—of the Washington Redskins. She was the first female reporter assigned to cover them. But this Toledo, Ohio, native was accustomed to being a groundbreaker.

Four years before, at age 23, she became the first woman sportswriter for the *Miami Herald.* During college, she interned at the *Toledo Blade,* the first woman to cover sports in that area.

Brennan, now 32, majored in journalism at Northwestern University, earning bachelor's and master's degrees. Immediately after college, she joined the *Miami Herald* sports department. In September 1984, a *Washington Post* offer lured her to the East. Her chief assignment: the Washington Redskins.

Four years later, she covered the Olympics in Calgary and Seoul. That same year, 1988, she was elected president of the newly organized Association for Women in Sports Media, with a membership of 150.

Following is a story Brennan calls one of her favorites and excerpts from a first-person piece she wrote for the *Washington Post Sunday Magazine.*

MANN AT WORK

DREAMING OF GLORY (SOMEWHERE IN CHARLES MANN'S SUBCONSCIOUS)

7:45 a.m. The football is snapped. Bodies crack into bodies. A defensive end wearing a burgundy No. 71 on his white jersey, charges around the end of a line of 10 men pushing and shoving and comes face to face with his prey. The quarterback, the star of the show, is about to fall to the ground in the arms of a bigger, stronger man. The big man wraps him up. He takes him down. A sack. A quarterback's nightmare. A defensive end's dream.

GETTING READY FOR WORK

8 a.m. The wake-up call is startling in the silence. It's Sunday morning at the Dulles Marriott. Autumn has arrived, and it's cool outside, good football weather, which is why the phone is ringing.

149

Crackling through the receiver, the voice of someone at the front desk is telling Charles Mann it's time to go to work.

He's up in a flash, suddenly impatient. He had to wait all night to get up for what he dreams will be the greatest day of his life. Mann snaps on the light, yells at roommate Ken Coffey to get out of bed, then disappears into the shower. In no time, Mann is pulling on his T-shirt, shorts and sneakers, then striding downstairs into a meeting room big enough to hold 45 football players and all the food they eat for breakfast. But he isn't hungry. He picks at the bacon, scrambled eggs, toast and sliced potatoes that have accumulated on his plate, and then pushes himself away from the table.

"The guys who know they're not going to play, they are the ones who pig out," he says.

Charles Mann knows he is going to play. He has the best job in the world, even if he is known as the guy on the other end of the line from Dexter. He plays football for a living, left defensive end to be more exact, for the Redskins in Washington. Every player ever drafted knows it's one of the greatest places a pro could ask to play; a consistently good team; fans who adore you; teammates who, by and large, are regular, dependable guys; loads of opportunities to make yourself famous on the side. At 26, Mann makes good money, too — about $250,000 a year, which breaks down to about $15,625 per game. That's how the checks come, 16 of them a year, every Monday during the season.

Mann gets paid well for what he does because he's a real professional. He prepares for his work as carefully as a doctor or lawyer. Although many people think that a defensive lineman is just a big, powerful brute, lunging spontaneously off the line to sack quarterbacks, his moves are actually part of a complicated choreography, carefully rehearsed. Every play is the result of meticulous observation and anticipation born of constant practice and numbing study. For the fan, each Sunday in the fall is a break from drudgery of the work week. For Charles Mann, it's just another hard day at the office.

COMMUTING

10 a.m. Mann drives home from the Dulles Marriott in his Chevy Blazer, the vehicle of choice for defensive linemen, changes into a suit and tie, picks up his wife Tyrena and heads to the office — RFK stadium. His mind is racing. His head is on the field already. How will he

do? An offense runs about 60 plays per game. His goal is simple: one sack.

A football player, Charles Mann says, is nothing without his dreams. Years ago, when he first started playing on the sandlots in Sacramento, Calif., Mann realized a play could only be made after it had been dreamed about, mapped out, step-by-step, in one's brain. Thousands of things can happen during a play, especially when one considers there are 22 men on the field, each making moves based on what he sees — or predicts — are other men's moves. Each man has so many options.

"If you haven't thought about a play," Mann says, "you're not going to make it."

For instance, last season, Mann spent a week thinking about Denver's John Elway, perhaps the most elusive quarterback in the National Football League. Hours and hours, eight a day at Redskin Park, countless others at home, were spent obsessed with Elway. It sounds almost passive, but Mann's job was called "contain," a verb turned into a noun by football coaches, meaning a player should not let Elway get outside of him. It worked so well that Mann got three sacks, 30 percent of his total in an injury-ridden, disappointing year.

The first sack was unreal. Mann was lined up, the offensive tackle in front of him. The ball was snapped, and the offensive tackle was gone. He left to double-team Dave Butz. Now, Mann had two things in front of him: 10 yards of grass and John Elway. Mann is fast for a lineman, with 4.8 speed in the 40-yard dash, but he was slowed by 10 to 12 pounds of equipment. Then again, Elway was wearing his gear, too. "I'm licking my chops," Mann says.

Part of the reason for Mann's glee was simple. Elway, who is right-handed, was setting up to throw the ball to the left side, something that doesn't happen very often. Mann thought he could blind-side Elway, which is the way Dexter Manley, rushing from the other side, gets most of his sacks on right-handers. This time, for a change, the quarterback wasn't staring Mann in the face.

But Elway heard footsteps and turned to see Mann bearing down on him. The center, back to block for his quarterback, turned into Mann, upsetting his feet. Mann started to fall. "If I don't make the play, I am in trouble," he was thinking. "Elway gets around me and he's gone. The coaches will get mad at me on Monday for not having contain."

So Mann did the only thing he could think to do. As he flew by

Elway, lunging over the blocker, he kicked out his left leg, karate-style. His shoe met the ball and sent it spinning into the air, away from Elway. A pileup ensued. Denver recovered the fumble, but for an 11-yard loss. A sack. But was it legal? "It must have been or they would have called a penalty," Mann says, laughing.

ARRIVING AT THE OFFICE

10:45 a.m. If there were ever a time for thinking, "visualizing success," it would occur in the locker room. It's a long walk from the parking lot out front of RFK Stadium, past the autograph hounds and security guards, into the bowels of the stadium, where the locker-room door opens onto a long hallway before the wide expanse of the dressing room reaches out to greet a player.

The locker room is slowly coming to life when Mann gets there. Witness Mann's odyssey through it: He enters, goes to the door of the training room and on a piece of adhesive tape writes his number — 71 — which is the football equivalent of taking a number at the ice cream parlor. Waiting to be called to have his ankles and right knee taped for battle, he strips off the nice clothes, throws on shorts and grabs a cup of coffee. Usually, it's only one cup, just enough to get edgy.

"I don't want to be out on the field on third down and long early in the game and thinking, 'I've got to use the bathroom.' And if that happens, you hold it. We've got strong bladders in the NFL." There are four stalls and four urinals in the home locker room at RFK. There is a mad dash to use them at halftime.

Keoki Kamau, the assistant trainer for the Redskins, tapes Mann when it's his turn. It takes Kamau just 8 to 10 minutes to wrap 90 feet of tape on two ankles and one knee. Mann tapes his wrists and fingers in ways taught to him by teammates — wide strips on the wrists, thin strands in figure eights on the fingers. Total cost to the Redskins in tape: $15. It will take Mann 45 minutes to an hour of walking around the locker room to loosen his taped knee enough so he can run. "You've heard of mummies. . . . "

Before they begin to put on their equipment, most players sit on the benches in front of their lockers, or on the floor, reading the Game Day program — and saving it for the scrapbook if they appear in it — wearing Walkman headsets, swapping stories. Mann doesn't wear a Walkman and doesn't say much. When he sticks an arm into the air, he notices he is shaking. Just slightly. Just right.

For entertainment Mann, like everyone else in the locker room, watches Dexter Manley. Manley puts on a headset and screams and dances to the music, working up a sweat. The players used to wonder if this might not take something out of him before a game. They don't worry anymore.

DRESSING FOR SUCCESS
12:05 p.m. For the fourth time today, and it's just about noon, Mann changes clothes. This time, he is dressing for battle. He puts on his jock, then his socks and his football pants. He pulls on a gray half-T-shirt, then puts his shoulder pads on top. If he wore no T-shirt, his shoulders would be raw by the second quarter. He places a foam neck pad behind his head, to guard against whiplash, he says.

Next comes one of the hardest parts of the day—putting on the jersey. Most players get started themselves, then stand there blindly, tied up in their jersey, their arms stuck straight in the air, waiting for someone to put them out of their misery.

Mann carries his helmet, one with four bars especially close together around the eyes so stray fingers don't find their way through, onto the field with him. He should wear a mouthpiece to protect his capped front teeth, but that hasn't worked well. "I get tired. When I get tired, I want to open my mouth and be able to breathe good. I can't get enough air with my mouthpiece in."

MEETING WITH THE BOSS
12:45 p.m. All dressed, Mann lies on the carpet in the locker room and stretches. There is a pep talk from Coach Joe Gibbs. And pretty soon, Mann is on the field, and the national anthem is playing.

No disrespect intended, but Mann has something else on his mind when the anthem is playing. His eyes are scanning the unbroken line of players on the opponents' sideline, searching for the right offensive tackle. That's his man. In the locker room at Redskin Park that week, pictures and bios of all the opponents have been pinned to a bulletin board. Every player knows who his man is, where he went to college, if he's married or has kids. Mann wants to see how his opponent looks, if he is bigger than he thought or smaller. "You try to stare him down, too, but at that distance you can't tell if your eyes ever meet his eyes."

On the field, a football player's mind should never wander, Mann says. But there on the sideline Mann is imagining who is watching the game, especially if it's on national TV. Which people he hasn't heard from in years are suddenly remembering they once knew Charles Mann?

Often Mann is one of the captains who go out to midfield for the coin toss. Coach Joe Gibbs likes the psychological edge of having more captains than the other team. Sometimes Redskins win 6 to 1. "We will never be outcaptained," Mann says.

Mann runs back to the sideline to wait the final minutes before he will go in and play. This is a strange time of the day. It's a lull, Mann says, when nervous energy runs out and physical exertion has yet to commence. "It feels like if you slept too long and you're kind of groggy," he says. "When you see guys hitting each other on the shoulder pads, what they're doing is trying to shake themselves up, get themselves ready."

On the very first defensive play of the 1985 season at Dallas, Mann was so exuberant he was called for a late hit on quarterback Danny White. He broke free of his man and into the backfield. White unloaded a pass, and Mann had time to stop, but he didn't and crashed right into White. "I'm thinking, it's a shame I got through and he threw the ball, so I hit him anyway. That settled me down and the rest of the game went well."

Mann doesn't like the reputation he has gained for getting personal fouls or late-hit penalties, but he has had his share. He once pushed Los Angeles Raider running back Marcus Allen out of bounds, and was hit with a personal foul call, good for 15 yards. "I'm 6-foot-6, 270 pounds," he says. "I can't stop on a dime." Gibbs has told his players that if they get in that kind of situation, they should get their hands up in the air, as if they didn't mean it. A sympathetic official might let you off. "I use that a lot," Mann says.

Last season, he leveled Green Bay quarterback Randy Wright, hitting Wright's helmet with his own helmet. Wright received a concussion and spent a night in the hospital. Mann received a $2,500 fine, which he appealed, futilely. "Last year and the year before last, I was known for getting late hits on quarterbacks. I've been back there so many times and so excited, only to watch the quarterback let go of the ball. I want sacks so bad, sometimes it's hard to stop. It's not malicious."

In fact, Mann says things will be different this season. He is one of several Redskins who attend chapel services the night before each game, and he studies and memorizes Bible verses before he goes to bed every evening. He is part of a support group of four players — with Ken Coffey, Darrell Green and Keith Griffin — who meet once a week to talk about their lives, families and how they can "learn to love one another . . . we hold one another accountable," he says. "A lot of people think religious people can't be strong and play hard. Well, they can. If Jesus were here, He would not be a wimp."

This year, Mann wants to cut out penalties. "When you see a guy getting penalties like I was, you are looking at a guy trying to get the respect of other players by playing tough. Well, no more. I realize kids are watching me. I realize as a Redskin I can be an example. I believe I can knock a guy down legally and then pick him up, like Butz does. What if I did it? People would say, 'Hey, Charles Mann knocked down a guy. Hey, Charles Mann just picked him up.' "

TAKING CARE OF BUSINESS

1 p.m. As fans are settling into their seats around the stadium, the tension on the sideline is unbearable. It's time to get out there, to play. It's time to be in a huddle.

On first and 10, there is so much for a defensive end to worry about. It's not second and long, or third and short, when the play seems obvious and a defender can cheat this way or that. On first and 10, no one knows.

The 11 men break the huddle with a clap of their hands, in unison, a tradition most have known since junior high. They slowly trudge to the line, in no hurry because the offense still is huddling. The football sits by itself, a marker for the line. Butz and Grant, the two tackles, walk to either side of it. Mann and Manley leave 1½ feet between the tackles' outside shoulders and themselves. When the offensive linemen walk toward them and lean over the ball, Mann goes into his stance. He looks for the offensive tackle's right shoulder. He draws an imaginary line between the right shoulder and his right shoulder, and begins to lean over. Already, he is outside of his man, just as he likes it.

Mann's left hand reaches toward the ground as he stretches his body out, on tiptoes, rear end high in the air. If the Redskins are playing on a baseball field, and the ball sits on the skin of the infield, Mann desperately tries to find grass on which to plant his fingertips. He hates dirt. No traction.

Mann calls his stance the "high-booty" method. "You can see my behind miles away," he says. "My wife has no problem seeing me out there, and it's not because I'm tall." When he arrived at Redskin Park from the University of Nevada at Reno for his first practice in 1983, his stance was even more pronounced. Defensive line coach Torgy Torgeson told him to push his toes back farther, to use his legs more.

As he lines up, pawing at the ground with his cleats, ready to hurl himself into a man just as big to fight over a few yards of grass, Mann hears his own husky breathing and little else. A word or two is being spoken: "Watch for the stunt . . . Six, six (indicating that a running back is coming to the six-hole, located between the tackle and tight end, where Mann is) . . . I'll take him . . . " Jordan is yelling changes to the linebackers and defensive backs. All the secrets are now out.

CHATTING WITH A CO-WORKER

2 p.m. Although Manley is all the way down the line, past Butz, Mann worries about him. Mann doesn't do much talking at the line, but if he does, it's a good guess he's talking to Manley. As defensive ends, they have the same desires and responsibilities.

As the play is about to begin, Mann's eyes search for clues. He looks at the running backs first, to see if they are lined up his way. Then his eyes move to the offensive tackle's feet. If he is up on his toes, it's a signal the offense is going to run, because the tackle is getting ready to come forward. If his heels are down, it signals pass, because his first step will be backward, to set up.

Mann's favorite thing on a football field is getting a sack. Tackles are nice, but nothing compares to the kick of a sack. But you don't just get a sack. Bulling past the line, grabbing Elway, pulling him down . . . it builds over months. It builds in the weight room on a Nautilus machine that looks like a shoe store footrest chair. To get a sack, Mann says, the most important part of his body is his left hand. It gives him the "strength to grab."

Because Mann reaches with his left hand, it must be strong. So every other day he sits on this little machine in the Redskin Park weight room, his hand gripping a handle tightly, pulling 35 pounds of cold, hard weights up and down, 12 times in all, with his left hand.

CLEARING THE DESK

3:45 p.m. If it were all strategy, no one would invite fans to watch. Mann knows his stuff, but he wouldn't be ready for every play were it not for the emotion of the moment. In that first Giants game, right in the middle of it, Grant ran onto the field and regained the first-string spot he had lost the season before when he had suffered a knee injury. What a lift this was.

"He's back, and we know he's probably 80 percent," Mann says. "He and I compete on things, how many tackles we have, how many fumble recoveries." Competition, even jealousy, between Redskins is real, just like on any other job. Grant's return drove deep into Mann. He had something to prove. He wanted to outdo Grant again. "Remember the guy in 'Hoosiers' who wants the ball at the end? On third and one, I want the guy running right at me."

The same thing happens to Mann when Butz gets going. This is so rare, it's amazing. When the younger players get Dave Butz, 37, high-fiving his teammates, they know they've got something good going. Butz is emotional against St. Louis, his old team. He picks one other Sunday at random during the year, it seems, to go wild. The players can't wait for the moment.

Butz is a stalwart, a big man to lean on. Literally. During the Redskins' wild-card win over the Rams last December, Mann made a big mistake. He snacked at halftime, taking one of the Jay Brunetti's peanut butter and jelly sandwiches and wolfing it down. In the second half, he felt his stomach cramping up. There was nothing to do except drape himself over Butz and moan between plays. "Dave, I'm not going to make it. Dave . . . " Mann kept looking to the sideline, looking at fresh players who couldn't wait to go in. But he would die before he left the field because of peanut butter and jelly.

The pitfalls for a football player are innumerable. It's third and one, the running back runs a "dive" play toward Mann, and the ball squirts loose. Players go after the ball hard but almost don't want to be the first one with their hands on it. The pileups Mann has been in have looked like street muggings. Players know to grab at the fingers of the man holding the ball and peel them away from the ball so they can steal it from him before the refs see it. Mann says, smiling sneakily, "I may have peeled back a few fingers in my career."

It's a game of survival. In four years, Mann has missed only one game. But from head to toe he has suffered injuries to 14 different areas of his body; cuts on his forehead from his helmet ripping his skin; a black eye when an oversize helmet he was wearing slid down and hit him in the eye; a root canal when he got hit in the mouth two years back; a pinched nerve in his neck; a sprained right shoulder; a swollen left elbow; numerous sprained wrists; sprains in every finger on both hands; an abdominal pull; two pulled groin muscles, both at

the same time in 1985; a bruised left knee; two arthroscopic operations on his right knee; a twisted left ankle that will always be bigger
than the right one; and a toenail on his middle toe, left foot, that can't
withstand the pressure of training camp and falls off once a year.

Injuries have a funny effect on a big guy like Mann. In the fourth
game of the 1986 season, at home against Seattle, Mann got pushed
into a blocker by linebacker Angelo Snipes and twisted his knee. As
he lay on the ground, trying to get up, assistant trainer Keoki Kamau
ran out and bent over him. "Relax, man, stay down," he said to
Mann. But Mann knew he couldn't stay put, for a most unusual
reason. "I'm at RFK. So is my wife. If I'm carried off, she will go
crazy."

Mann got up and went back in, and he had the knee drained the
next day, when he learned a ligament was stretched. The following
week, the Redskins traveled to New Orleans. Tyrena made Charles
promise her he would not play. He wanted to, but he kept his word
and never went in. The trainers and coaches had a say in the decision,
too.

By the next week, he was playing and he did not miss another
start, although his knee wasn't in good shape the rest of the season.
Mann had been hoping the '86 season would be Pro Bowl year, but
now he had missed the first game and was not playing at full speed.
"Talk about depressing." After the bad performance against the
Giants, Mann couldn't sleep for a week. He was a nervous wreck. He
went to see team doctor Donald Knowlan twice for tranquilizers.
Knowlan said no and suggested aspirin. It was the pressure. He wasn't
playing as well as he had hoped. Manley was going great guns. They
compete, both of them admit. It hurt.

"I never abused drugs or alcohol," Mann says, "but for the first
time, I understood why people did."

He began to play better, getting two sacks against Minnesota and
one against Dallas in November, before the three at Denver. He obtained pictures of them, framed them in clear plastic and hung them
on a wall with the others in the basement of his three-bedroom Reston
home. It's his sack wall, just what every defensive end needs. He's got
to get some of the game's biggest guns yet, guys like Joe Montana and
Jim McMahon. "You can say you sacked them, but it's better to have
a picture to show it," he says.

WORRYING ABOUT TOMORROW

4:15 p.m. The post-game prayers and game balls shared and dinner at Houston's in Georgetown complete, Mann goes home to watch the TV highlights—if he can stay up that late. The game will not officially be over until Monday, when he gets his report card on the game, every play written down with a "+" or "−" next to his name. On a sheet of 60 plays, he'll average eight minuses. You get one for stepping with the wrong foot, for getting taken out of a play by a block, for slipping. Mann's eyes come back to these things later, for when he first sees his sheet, he looks for sacks. The game statistics kept in the press box might give him a sack, but until the coaches, after watching the team's tape of the game, give it to him the next day, it's not officially his. Players have been known to come in early and lobby for a half sack because they were close to the tackle or a full sack if they were given partial credit. This is serious business. Contracts have sack clauses.

This, after all, is a job. Mann has his real estate license and is trying some acting, but that's only for fun. Ask Charles Mann on a Monday morning at 8 a.m. where he is headed, and he won't necessarily say Redskin Park. He'll say, "I'm going to work."

Or ask him on a Sunday, after the wakeup call. His answer will be the same.

Following are excerpts from a January 1988 Washington Post Magazine *story by Chris Brennan titled, "My Three Years Covering The Redskins."*

In 1985, I enthusiastically walked into the lives—and the locker room—of the players, coaches and management of the Washington Redskins. I was then and still am the only woman who has ever covered the Redskins. To do my job, I spent practically every day from July to January with the team; training camp, practices, home and away games.

Some on the team and in the media thought this was a big deal, but, to me, there was no reason to fuss. I had been a sportswriter for nearly four years at the *Miami Herald* before coming to the *Post* in 1984. I covered the University of Miami during its first national championship season. I covered the Dolphins off and on and was one of the first women in their locker room. I covered four consecutive national championship games . . . I had been in men's locker rooms about 50 times. Dealing with the unusual demands of being a woman in a man's world was no particular problem for me.

I even had the cocktail-party stories down pat. The two most-asked questions of a woman sportswriter:

1. Do you get into the locker room?
2. What do you see?

Yes.

Not a whole lot.

Perhaps my troubles began because I am a woman. Perhaps they started because I ask a lot of questions. Perhaps it's because I work at the *Post,* a newspaper that is not exactly universally loved by men and women who work at Redskin Park.

You see, I thought I was just doing my job when I asked the owner of the Redskins if the team was considering trading a key player. I didn't expect such a simple question would cause me to be declared persona non grata by one of the world's richest men for months.

I thought I was well within my rights to write about the contract that the team's general manager was about to sign. I didn't expect him to get angry and refuse to give me a private interview for nearly two years.

And I figured if a former star player on the management staff said something on television, I could report it in the sports pages of my newspaper, right? Wrong. I did that and it ended a fine working relationship I had with that good man — just like that.

I've come through my stint on the beat in one piece. I enjoyed it — mostly. I'm unscathed. I still think I have the greatest job in the world. But, I'll tell you this: The past three years, I ran into the strangest occupational hazards.

For a while, unbeknownst to me, I was the alibi for a player who was cheating on his wife. One of the player's buddies on the team stopped me one day and said that if the player's wife ever asked, I had called their house to interview him.

I didn't get it.

"You see, (Madame X) called one night and (Player X) told his wife it was you."

"Oh, great," I said.

Another time, a player told me word was out in the locker room I was having an affair with a local sportscaster, who is married. I wasn't, but that didn't stop players from giggling every time they saw the unsuspecting announcer talking to me. I later told my TV friend. He told his wife. I told the guy I was dating. I think we had the last laugh.

I probably had a dozen football players ask me out. Some were married, some weren't. Maybe I should have expected this. I didn't, at first. Politely, I said no. The tendency was to tell some of them to take a hike. I didn't. What if I had to interview them the next day?

Sometimes, my job got outrageous. Three-hundred-pound defensive tackle Dave Butz laughingly told me if I insisted on interviewing him while he was naked, I should be naked, too. Actually, I avoid naked football players at all costs. I prefer it when the people I interview have their clothes on. A woman in the locker room is a hot topic for some, but consider this: I spent only about four hours of my 60-hour work week in the Redskins' locker room at practice and after games.

In the locker room, I tried to act nonchalant. I maintained eye contact. I made beelines to lockers. I carried large notebooks that conveniently blocked my view of certain areas, should I look down.

But you can't plan for everything. The players knew to expect reporters from noon to 1 p.m. before practice. A few minutes before noon one day, I opened the large, red locker room door and stepped right in.

Whoa!

It was Mark Moseley. Barechested. Pulling on his football pants. Mooning me. (He didn't mean it.)

"Sorry, Mark," I said, turning away.

"We're going to have to put a cowbell around your neck," he said.

A Visit with Christine Brennan

Sherry Ricchiardi: *How did you first get interested in sports?*

Christine Brennan: As a child I was taller than all the boys and I was good in sports. I never threw like a girl. I was very athletic, and actually, I still am.

I had a baseball mitt when I was five years old. That's what I wanted for my birthday. I had a few dolls, but the baseball mitt was much more important to me. On the night of my tenth birthday, my parents gave me a scorebook. I listened to the Toledo minor league baseball games and kept score. I was fanatical.

I still have a shoe box in my parents' attic with all my baseball cards in it.

Q. *When did you start thinking about being a sportswriter?*

A. I loved sports and lot of my friends would say, "You know you're going to be a sportswriter someday." But there weren't any role models. I graduated from high school in 1976 and there probably were some female sportswriters in New York City or Boston, but I didn't know about them. I just figured it was a field women weren't into.

In the summer of 1978, I was a city desk intern with the *Toledo Blade,* my hometown paper. About six months later, I got a letter from the editors. They asked if I wanted to write sports for them the next summer.

It was total joy to go to sporting events and to write about them—my two loves. I covered the Toledo Mud Hens baseball team. In 1980, I applied for the *Miami Herald* internship and got it in sportswriting. That led to a full-time job there later on.

Q. *How did you land a job at the* Miami Herald *right out of college?*

A. It would be naive to believe I got that job simply because I was a fabulous writer. I'm aware that had I been a white male coming out of Northwestern University with the same degrees—everything else being equal—I wouldn't have landed one of the plum assignments at the *Miami Herald* at age 23.

My guess is that I would have been at one of the bureaus, covering high school sports or some minor college sports. Being a woman opened a few extra doors. I felt I deserved the opportunity.

I'm very grateful to the generation of women sportswriters who went before me. I've fought a lot of battles, but they fought even more.

Q. *Did you ever worry about failing?*

A. Had I failed, I would have set back the cause of women getting into sportswriting in Florida by years. Editors would say, "Remember Christine Brennan? She was that disaster we hired. If she couldn't do it maybe we should wait before we try another woman."

Q. *Was that an extra burden on you back then?*

A. I didn't look at it that way. Being tall—I'm 5 feet, 11 inches—my parents always said, "Stand up straight. You're going to be watched." My parents always told me I could do anything I wanted and for some reason, I believed them.

I also think that because I was so young, I didn't realize what might have been at stake.

Q. *Were there times it took plain guts to succeed?*

A. Yes. The first football game I covered for the *Miami Herald* was in mid-September 1981. I was supposed to go to the University of Florida locker room afterwards. The editors had cleared it. Reporters started filing in and a state trooper was watching to make sure everyone had a credential.

All of a sudden, the state trooper grabbed my arm and said, "No women allowed in here." I said, "Hey, I'm supposed to be in here." And he said, "No, you're not" and wouldn't let me pass.

I yanked my arm away from him. By that time, several of my sportswriter friends, all men, saw what was happening and shoved me along in a wave with them. I wasn't in the business of defying state troopers, but I said to myself, "This is wrong. He can't keep me from doing my job."

Q. *Are there many disadvantages to being a woman in a man's world?*

A. The locker room still is a problem for some female reporters. And attitudes, especially in those last bastions of male supremacy such as the NFL (National Football League), make it tough. I used to tell myself, "No, that's not sexist. That coach really didn't like my story." But, my guess was that he didn't like a woman being there. He didn't like a woman's byline on the story.

There are two buzz words for women sportswriters — equal access. Back when I started, equal access didn't exist.

Q. *Who served as your mentors along the way?*

A. Paul Anger, the executive sports editor of the *Miami Herald* who hired me in April 1981, taught me so much about writing. I was a raw talent. And George Solomon, our assistant editor at the *Washington Post*, has meant a lot to me.

Behind every successful woman sportswriter you will find a decent man. They are the ones who have the guts to push you and put you on the beat.

My parents still are my biggest advisers. During family vacations, I remember my dad buying all the newspapers possible. I fought with my brother over the sports pages. I knew the bylines of all the sportswriters in my hometown. They were my heroes.

Q. *How have you been treated by the athletes you cover?*

A. Black athletes tend to be more understanding of the trials and tribulations women sportswriters face, such as dealing with unruly players or coaches who don't understand why a woman should be covering them. It's easy to see why, in general, black athletes would be more sensitive. They've gone through some of the same things.

Doug Williams of the Redskins fought for years to be accepted as a black quarterback in the NFL. I have to believe he has a stronger sense of what it's like for me to wander into the locker room and deal with antagonistic players.

Q. *How do you handle being a ground breaker in this profession?*

A. Whenever I'm asked to do interviews or speeches, I do them for two reasons. I picture a seven-year-old girl seeing me and saying, "Hey Mommy, I love sports. She does that job; I could do it, too." If I could reach even one little girl, that would be wonderful.

I also picture a 40-year-old guy with a beer gut, Doritos on one side of his armchair, a can of Bud Lite on the other side. He's sitting in front of the TV, yelling at his wife to get him another beer. Then, he looks up and sees me being interviewed about going into the Redskins' locker room. I'd like to think that a little glimmer of light would hit and he'd realize that a woman can do anything.

I feel there's a greater good out there. I can help knock down stereotypes.

Q. *What personal sacrifices have you made for your career?*

A. I lead a crazy life. At times on dates, I excuse myself and go to a pay phone for half an hour and make calls on stories. That doesn't go over real well with some guys.

The kind of guy I end up wanting to spend time with is one who understands my job. If he doesn't understand, it's not the right person and that's okay. Today, some people wait a long time to marry and have kids. I feel no sense of urgency.

Q. *Do you feel that being a woman affects how you report?*

A. I'd say, speaking in general terms, that a woman is more sensitive and more attentive to detail or to the intricacies of a scene. You know, not just looking at the play on the field, but noticing the coach on his knees in prayer before a play.

A Redskin player was on TV talking about me one day and he said, "She gets behind the issues a little bit more. She really digs deeper."

Q. *Are there common obstacles women sportswriters must overcome?*

A. In general, it's acceptance from male administrators of teams, male athletes, and sometimes male reporters. When other female sportswriters read the first-person piece I wrote for *Washington Post Magazine* on covering the Redskins, a lot of them said, "Change the byline, fill in different names and that's my story."

Q. *Do you think it's fair for women to fall back on feminine wiles to get a story? Do you ever resort to that?*

A. I like to smile, I like to laugh, I like to be happy. If I tend to smile at an athlete a lot, that's just me. When I go into a men's locker room, I want to blend in as much as possible. So, I don't wear a red leather miniskirt and boots.

It's wrong to play dumb if you're not dumb. If you honestly don't understand something you can say, "Sorry, I don't understand what you're talking about." I guess I'm saying no acts.

Q. *Have you done much networking with other female journalists?*

A. I enjoy networking, but I haven't sought it out. Being president of AWSM (Association for Women in Sports Media) is something new for me. I'm not a joiner. Sometimes I'm the only woman in the press box, but that doesn't bother me anymore. It goes back to the days when I was a little kid playing with boys.

Q. *Let's talk about your piece on Charles Mann. Where did the idea come from?*

A. Jay Lovinger, the *Washington Post Sunday Magazine* editor, called me at the end of the 1986 season and said, "We've got an idea for a story. We want you take a player and dissect what he does. Make it like a day at the office. Describe every detail. Go into everything — what he does, what he wears, what he thinks."

I loved the idea. It was my kind of journalism. I love asking somebody, "What were you thinking at that exact moment?" I love recreating. That is the wonderful part of this job. Sports involves so many memories and trivia and so much reminiscing.

Q. *How did you decide on Charles Mann?*

A. We didn't want a quarterback or a running back. We wanted somebody who is caught in that mass along the offensive or defensive line, somebody who isn't so obvious. At that point, my thoughts went to one person — Charles Mann.

I wanted a player who was intelligent and articulate, not a player who said the typical cliches after a game. I wanted someone on the verge of greatness.

It was to be a cover story for the magazine to kick off the football season. My deadline was midsummer of 1987. I wanted somebody who still was a mystery to the fans.

Q. *When did you start the interviewing?*

A. I did an interview or two that spring. I was just trying to get some biographical material from him. In high school he was a tall, thin kid who thought he'd never play college football. I wanted to be prepared with a running commentary on his life so if something clicked, I could throw in a piece of his past.

I wanted to flush him out as a human being. I knew that was the key to the story.

Q. *How much time did you spend with him?*

A. We did 18 to 20 hours of interviewing on the phone or in person. I talked with the trainer, Kioki Kamau, who worked with Charles in rehabilitation and did the taping before games. At one point, I asked Kioki, "How much tape do you estimate you put on Charles?" I went after little details like that.

I talked to other players and to coaches. I talked to Dexter Manley because he was the defensive player on the other side of the line.

Q. *How did you come up with so much rich detail?*

A. A lot of it was from my own observations. I've seen around 300 football games in my time—high school, college, professional. During the National Anthem, the players stand there like wild, caged animals. I thought to myself, "These guys aren't paying any attention to the song." So, I asked Charles, "What do you think about? What do you look at? Do you look at the flag?"

I wanted to crack that safe, so to speak, and get inside his brain. I kept firing questions about what he did, what he thought in certain situations. I asked questions to gain insight into the obvious.

Q. *What was your ultimate goal?*

A. To get a great story. I picture a guy eating his Wheaties at the kitchen table and reading my story or a woman riding the metro to work with it in front of her. I want to knock peoples' socks off with my stories.

Q. *Do you imagine the shape of a story as you interview?*

A. No, I'm kind of scared of that. I end up with all these volumes of notebooks and tapes and I sit there thinking, "Oh my God! What am I going to do with this?" That's when I begin thinking about style and shape.

Q. *How did you determine what writing strategy to use for the Mann story?*

A. After I'd gone though the "Oh my God" stage, I decided on a chronology. I felt it was the perfect way to get him through a work day, and that was the theme I wanted to use. I knew I could backtrack and throw in pieces of his past.

Q. *How did you decide on the lead?*

A. At first I thought I wanted to start with him eating breakfast or showering or popping out of bed. It sounded nice, but it wasn't too dramatic. Finally I thought, why don't I have him dreaming about the game?

During the interviews, I asked him, "Do you dream about sacking the quarterback?" And he said, "Sometimes I find myself waking up in the morning remembering I just had a dream about sacking John Elway (quarterback for the Denver Broncos). I get a fumble and score a touchdown."

At the time he said that, I thought it was hokey, but I put it in my notes anyway. In the end, I decided the dream was a fun way to start the story. It was an honest-to-goodness dream he had described to me.

Q. *Do you write from the lead of the story down?*

A. Yes, but I go back to the lead many times. I had a good 40 to 50 inches of this story in the machine when I finally perfected the lead. Computers are great because you can move things back and forth. I could never use a typewriter now. I'm spoiled that way.

Q. *What do you do between the reporting and the writing stage? Do you create an outline or mark up your notes?*

A. I look through my notes and rip out pages. For this story, I made little piles, different ones for the pregame, game and postgame. I had a pile for the biography and for certain interviews. I started to jot notes to myself about the good quotes. I transcribe my own tapes because I don't trust anybody else to do it.

I jot down labels in the margins of my notebooks so I don't have to keep leafing through them. I want to have everything physically in one spot.

Q. *Do you get edited much?*

A. No, not really. Very little was changed in the Charles Mann story.

Q. *Do you have any magic tricks for writing or reporting?*

A. I ask the obvious questions during an interview. "Why do you do this, Charles? What if there is dirt on the field instead of astroturf. Does that change the game for you? How do you decide where to put your hand when you set up for a play?"

Another thing is to show real interest in the subject, to be genuinely interested in what this person says and does. That always works for me.

Q. *Do you ever clean up quotes?*

A. Yes, if the language is jarring to the reader. I'm not going to help a guy who is hopeless. If someone fractures the English language constantly, I let it ride. But, if a player says, "I played good," depending on my mood, I might change it to "played well."

Football players swear all the time. You know, the s-word and the f-word. Of course, I clean up those quotes, but I don't change the context.

Q. *How did you capture the rich detail on the play where Mann caused Denver's John Elway to fumble?*

A. I asked Charles to describe some of his great plays and he mentioned that one. I went to a television station and got a video tape of the play and took it to his house. We watched it 20 to 25 times.

I had my tape recorder running to record his comments. I'd stop the film and ask "What were you thinking of right there?" I guess you could call it high tech journalism.

9 Sara Terry

INTERNATIONAL REPORTING ■ *Christian Science Monitor*

WHEN she was 13, Sara Terry dreamed of being a classical ballet dancer, swirling across a stage in a cloud of lace. She recalls a "total aversion" toward the media when she was growing up.

But a longing for international travel drew her into Newswriting 101 at California State University at Long Beach. Gaining skills as a free-lancer might pay her way overseas. She had no idea it would change her life forever.

Since 1978, Terry's assignments for the *Christian Science Monitor* have taken her into the back alleys and brothels of the Third World; into the lives of Iraqi children forced onto the battlefield as human minesweepers; into Afghan refugee camps.

In Zambia she was held hostage at gunpoint; in the Philippines she was offered a special prize, the sexual favors of a 14-year-old boy. Quite a switch from a middle class childhood in San Pedro, California.

Home-based in London, Terry's reports appear in the newspaper and are broadcast on Monitor radio and television. For three months in 1987, she traveled the world's poorest countries with two other journalists for the series, "Children in Darkness," which became a Pulitzer prize nominee.

The series won third place in the Scripps-Howard National Journalism competition and first place in the Sigma Delta Chi Public Service category for the broadcast version. Terry, 35, calls the assignment "the toughest thing I've ever done."

PAWNS OF AN ADULT WORLD –
A World Where Survival Is a Daily Battle

Kham Suk is 13 years old. She is a small child, with a delicate face. When she giggles, she sounds like any little girl at play. But Kham Suk doesn't have much time for fun. Three months ago, her mother walked her across the border from Burma into Thailand and sold her to a brothel for $80.

Kham Suk's family desperately needed the money. Kham Suk is still paying the price: $4 a customer.

Jafar Ibrahimi was only 10 years old when Iranian soldiers took him away from his village in northern Iran and put him on the front line of the Iran-Iraq war. He was sent into battle as a human mine-sweeper. "In front of me, children were being killed," he remembers. "I can't say how many, but too many." Miraculously, he survived two or three days in the mine fields before Iraqi soldiers captured him.

For more than five years, Jafar has been living in a prisoner-of-war camp in Iraq. He is prisoner No. 8085.

Sunil Butt left his home in Pakistan when he was five years old. His stepmother was so cruel to him that he got on a bus one day and never went home. Today, the 12-year-old works as a waiter in New Delhi, in a grimy dhaba, a teahouse in an alley behind the *Times of India* building. Sunil sleeps in the street. He gets up every morning about 4 or 5 o'clock and works without a break until 9 p.m. Sunday is his day off. He earns about $11.72 a month.

When asked whether he misses his family, Sunil waits a long, long time before answering. "When I think of my family," he finally says, "I go crazy."

These are children who live in darkness, the darkness of poverty, ignorance, greed — and indifference. There are tens of millions of children like them in the world today. They are the pawns, the possessions, and the products of an adult world that all too often exploits childhood for its own ends.

A few — very few — of these children are being rescued from society's shadows by small grass-roots programs around the world. But the increased awareness of the needs and rights of children that was triggered in 1979 by the United Nations' International Year of the Child is being overwhelmed by sheer numbers.

Children under 15 years old represent as much as 40 percent of the total population in some developing countries. Their numbers are growing steadily, especially among the poor. And a constant flood of poor peasants into packed cities means that millions more children will be on the streets — living in conditions where the poor have a hard time getting clean water, let alone sending their children to school or breaking out of the relentless cycles of poverty that make children especially vulnerable to exploitation.

"These children are bearing the responsibilities of adults," says Jennifer Schirmer, an anthropologist at Wellesley College in Massachusetts, who has worked with exploited children in Latin America. "The kinds of burdens they bear are a type of daily violence — the

daily, grinding violence of poverty. . . . What we're creating is prema-
ture adults."

Experts say that children are at risk in virtually every country in
the world (sexual abuse of children in Western families is one often-
cited example). And they argue that children invariably wind up at the
bottom of almost all national agendas for political and social action.
Yet, within this sphere of universal indifference, the problem of exploitation is most pressing in the developing world.

Most, if not all, developing countries have laws on the books and
lofty statements enshrined in their constitutions about the rights of
children. But without a strong social consensus to enforce them, these
legal documents are what one Guatemala juvenile-court judge calls
"dead letters."

Public will to enforce these laws is largely lacking because much
of the developing world has not had the economic breathing room to
enjoy the luxury of a debate on childhood—and from that debate, to
develop and enforce a social consensus about the right of a child to a
time of innocence and protection.

For millions of children squeezed between poverty and indifference, that absence of protection means being pushed to the very
margins of society.

Adults are often the enemy in a world where survival is a daily
battle. Adults like the taxi drivers in Guatemala City, who have been
known to pour gasoline on the heads of sleeping street children and
set them on fire. Adults like the middlemen who scour the impoverished countrysides of India and Thailand, offering needy parents
$50 or $100 for their children—and who then sell the children at a
substantial profit to a brothel or to a small factory, where boys and
girls often work in conditions of virtual slavery.

Sometimes the enemy is even a greedy mother or father—as in
the case of Marivic, a brown-haired, brown-eyed girl who wound up
in Manila's red-light district when she was only 10 years old. Her
mother was dead and her father was a drunkard, who forced her to
beg—and eventually to prostitute herself—so that he would have
money to buy liquor.

"He wanted me to steal, but I wouldn't do it," says Marivic, who
learned she had venereal disease and—frightened that she might die—
found her way more than a year ago to a small home for former child
prostitutes in Manila.

According to advocates of the fledgling children's-rights movement, the world risks a great deal with its present course of indifference and inaction. The costs, these activists say, are both personal and global — a price to be paid not only by the individual but by mankind as well.

"There's a wonderful human ingredient in these children that you can't find anywhere else," says Peter Tacon, director of CHILDHOPE, a newly formed, Guatemala-based international organization aimed at helping street children, "and that is the ingredient of prophecy, of hope.

"These children are in fact prophetic by their very existence — prophetic of what will happen to our race if we do nothing to work with them, prophetic of the depths of human despair and suffering that can result from selfishness and greed," he says.

"At the same time, they are prophetic of a very wonderful new world that can be had if we will lend a modicum of dignity and respect to their lives."

What worries activists like Mr. Tacon is the number of children who are growing up with a limited and hostile sense of the world. For many of them, the future is tightly hemmed in by horizons so narrow that moving out of poverty seems unthinkable.

Fourteen-year-old Mauro is a good example. He collects passenger fares on buses in Cuzco, Peru, earning about 75 cents a day. When he has children, he says, they will be like him — they'll have time for school, but they'll also have time for work. Why? "Because maybe there won't be enough money. . . . If you're poor, then your kids have to work, of course."

These children also represent what one Geneva-based expert on street children calls "a time bomb in society." Governments that now place a low priority on children's needs in favor of addressing debt burdens and guerrilla war could well find those problems compounded in the years to come by street children who have become street adults. The result: an undereducated, underemployed population, straining social services and threatening social order.

"The main reason for protecting children is the continuance of community," says Judith Ennew, an associate lecturer at Cambridge University and leading expert on street children. At its most extreme, she adds, "a community which fails to look after its children ceases to exist.

"So at the most pessimistic level," she says, "you're talking about the total crack-up of society. Obviously, society's not totally cracking up, but maybe it's changing in ways that we don't want."

There are no quick fixes for these children. In fact, because the problem is tied to economic growth and social awareness, the answers are likely to be evolutionary instead of revolutionary.

Despite the long-term nature of the problem, however, children's-rights activists do say that, since the International Year of the Child, they have witnessed an awakening in the world to the urgency of the problem. One of the main indications, they say, is the UN Convention on the Rights of the Child, which is still in its draft stages.

The document will be the most sweeping agreement ever on children's rights — drawing together many fragmented policies and statements that are now scattered throughout some 80 different documents.

The convention, which is expected to be ready for the UN to debate within the next few years, will be "an absolutely vital instrument to have," says Nigel Cantwell, director of programs at Defense of Children International, a children's-rights organization.

"It's not that the convention itself will change anything," explains Mr. Cantwell, whose Geneva-based organization monitors abuses of children's rights in much the same way that the London-based Amnesty International tracks human rights violations.

"But it will give us greater force, greater strength in our action, greater moral support," he says. "We can then say, 'This is what the international community has laid down and we're here to see how you guys are implementing it.' "

As important as such international documents are in upholding standards — and as imperative as national policies and laws are in carrying them out, legal paths alone are not the way out of darkness. As Ms. Ennew of Cambridge University puts it, "You can't legislate for love."

Advocates for children's rights say that the cornerstone of change must be laid in the hearts and minds of individuals. Until a community provides the caring and the will to rescue children from the darkness of indifference, they say, lasting change will never come.

"People may say, 'Well, this isn't my child. I didn't bring him forth, so what responsibility do I have for him?' " says Neera Kapur, a trustee of a Bombay organization called Child Relief and You (CRY).

"But I think the time has come. . . . There's a demand being made not just on the society, but on the world. There's a demand being made that selfishness has to slowly wear off.

"Every individual needs to make his contribution, not just a monetary one, but as one human being to another, to see the needs of another individual, to recognize them," Ms. Kapur says. "It's a change in mental attitude that can go a long way."

Children's-rights activists say that the indifference they are battling is rooted in consumerism, materialism — and fatalism, the feeling that the problem is just too big to be tackled, so why try? Advocates concede the numbers seem overwhelming. But over and over they respond to skeptics with a modest yet urgent plea: One child at a time. If there is hope — a way out — for one child, they say, there must be hope for another. And another.

Reducing the problem to a one-to-one relationship is also one way of bringing individuals to what many experts in the field see as a profound turning point in world history — the wider recognition of a child as a human being with inalienable rights.

The time has come, children's-rights advocates say, to stop viewing children as personal possessions; to stop abusing their dependence on adults; to stop taking advantage of the fact that they have no political or social power, that they have no means of their own to stand up to adults who exploit their innocence.

The time has come, they say, to treat a child as an individual who has rights that must be respected by all mankind. It is a demand that cuts through cultural barriers and straight across the gap between developed and developing countries.

"There is a lack of consciousness of the rights of a child as an individual, as a person," says Michel Bonnet, an activist for children's rights and an expert on child labor. "That problem is exactly the same in the third world and in the first world.

"It's a problem of rights."

SEXUAL EXPLOITATION –
*When All You Have To Sell
Is Your Body*

Ray is pretty savvy for a nine-year-old. He's taught himself a little French, he's managed to save a little money, and he knows his way around town—especially around the bars and back streets of Manila's red-light district.

Ray uses words like "pedophile" when he talks about his life. It's not just a big word he's picked up on the street. He knows exactly what he's saying, because for two years now, Ray has been selling himself to white, middle-aged men who come to Manila to buy boys for an hour or evening of sex.

"It's a dirty job," says Ray, who uses the money to buy clothes and pay for books and uniforms for public school. Referring to his child-prostitute friends, he adds, "We only need money. That's why we go with the foreigners. All the people here don't like this job, but they need money.

"This job is not easy to do, you know," says Ray, who makes about $10 for a full evening of work. He speaks in a flat, matter-of-fact tone. "You must do some services to foreigners, and sometimes you have a customer who has some sickness—AIDS, like that.

"And when it's transferred to you," he continues, "what will you do? You cannot live anymore."

The sexual exploitation of children by adults is ugly and vicious. It is also a fact of life for tens of thousands of third-world children like Ray, struggling to survive the brutal realities of poverty—and the greed of adults who take advantage of a child's desperation.

Unlike many of the teen-age prostitutes in Times Square or on Hollywood Boulevard, child prostitutes in developing countries generally are not runaways; they are fighters. For many of them, the way to survive—or at least to get a meal to last them until tomorrow—is to sell the only thing they have: their bodies. And they quickly learn that what they have is marketable. There are plenty of adults—male, female, Western, and non-Western—who are only too willing to buy.

The Philippine government estimates that of Manila's 15,000 street children, 30 percent are involved in prostitution. In Thailand, officials of children's-rights groups say, the figure is even higher — as many as 40,000 prostitutes under the age of 14. Although the problem is generally considered to be most severe in Asia, child prostitutes can be found walking the streets — or sometimes locked up in brothels — from Bombay and Taipei to Nairobi and Santiago.

In fact, although exact numbers do not exist, children's-rights advocates say that wherever there is poverty — and wherever children are living or spending most of their time on the streets — it is almost inevitable that they will fall prey to the sexual appetites of adults.

"For most of these kids, it's not a question of right or wrong," says Enrico Enriquez, who helps run a small home called New Beginnings for ex-child prostitutes in Manila. "If they do what the pedophile asks them to do, they'll be given money. . . . It's a means of making money for them and their families."

Fourteen-year-old Mehgie supports her younger brother and bedridden mother. She tried to get a job in a grocery store, but she was too young. So, on Feb. 28, 1987, she sold her virginity in the back room of a Manila bar for $125.

Since February, Mehgie has worked — from 7 p.m. to 4 a.m. — at a disco in Manila's bawdy Ermita district. She makes roughly $3 a night for dancing, $20 an hour for sex — money that she uses to help her family and to pay for private school. Good grades are important to Mehgie. She wants to go to college and learn to be a computer engineer.

"If we have no dance, we have no money," she says in broken English. "But I don't like. When I finish my study, I'm not dancer."

Mehgie goes to church every Sunday. She prays that she will finish school, and that the men that she is with don't have diseases. She talks to the priest about her problem. He tells her to pray to the Lord.

In some ways, children like Mehgie and Ray are better off than other children are — circumstances may have forced them into prostitution, but adults have not. For many others, however, prostitution has a nastier dimension: Adults make them do it.

Sometimes it is a parent who prostitutes his or her own child; grassroots workers, like Mr. Enriquez, say that parents have shown up at New Beginnings to demand their daughters back because a customer has been lined up for them. Other times, a parent may sell a child to another adult — the case for many Burmese girls working in brothels on the border between Thailand and Burma. The price a brothel owner will pay for a young girl is almost equal to a year's earnings for a poor Burmese farmer.

There are also cases of adults who trick children into prostitution—or even kidnap them. For Ar Soh, a soft-spoken Thai teenager, a two-year nightmare of forced prostitution began when a man she knew came to her village and offered her a job in a nearby town. Ar Soh was 13. She trusted, and followed, him.

The man took Ar Soh from her village in the north to a town near Bangkok. There he sold her to a brothel. For two years, Ar Soh was kept in virtual slavery—and forced to have sex with as many as five men a day. Finally, one customer tried to help her escape by digging a hole with a spoon in the dirt floor under her bed. When the owner discovered it, he beat Ar Soh with a steel rod, locked her in a closet for three days, and moved her to another house, where she was locked in a room two floors up.

Ar Soh was desperate to escape—and she did. She squeezed through a window and jumped to the pavement below, breaking her back. With help, she made it to the police and a hospital. Today, at 18, Ar Soh makes artificial flowers. The man who enslaved her is in jail.

"These girls are treated as sex objects, they are seen as flesh trade," says Khunying Kanitha Wiechiencharoen, a lawyer and activist who helped Ar Soh recover through an organization she started for distressed women and children. "It's really difficult to get those children out of all those greedy hands."

Children's-rights advocates like Mrs. Wiechiencharoen worry about the toll that prostitution takes on a child—about the physical damage inflicted on young bodies through adult sex and sadism; about the emotional confusion suffered by a child plunged into sexuality while still discovering his or her own identity; and about the distortion of values imposed on a child who learns early in life that sex can be sold for survival.

"That particular part of a person's life, between the ages of 11 and 12, is the most vulnerable," says Jennifer Schirmer, an anthropologist at Wellesley College in Massachusetts and a children's-rights advocate. "That period of time creates who you are for the rest of your life. It's the most vulnerable part of your life because you are at the mercy of adults. You need protection by adults from adults."

Child prostitution is illegal in virtually every country in the world. But children's-rights experts say that generally the penalties are not severe enough to be effective. Some fines imposed on brothel owners for using children are as low as $20 to $30.

Laws that are not backed by the will of a government are equally futile, experts say. In the Philippines, for example, local activists say their work was made especially difficult because child prostitution was at least tacitly supported by former President Ferdinand Marcos. His regime, they say, was eager for revenues brought in by "sex tourists" — foreigners who get their tips on where to find child prostitutes through gay sex guides like *Spartacus,* or through travel agencies that tailor trips to the sexual interests of both heterosexual and homosexual clients.

Turning the tide against child prostitution is not an easy task. Some people view the answer in simple — if challenging — economic terms: end poverty, end prostitution. That's the way Norma sees it. She is a young Chilean mother and former prostitute, who lives in one of Santiago's poblaciones, or poor neighborhoods.

In recent years, as Chile's economy nose-dived under the military rule of Gen. Augusto Pinochet Ugarte, thousands of girls started streaming out of the poblaciones every evening, heading for the traffic circles and downtown strips where they knew that for 15 minutes of sex in a car they could make $3 or $4 — enough to buy a meal. Even though Chile's economy has begun to improve in the past year, thousands of girls still work the streets.

"Of course I worry about my daughter," says Norma, who has two sons and a seven-year-old daughter. "I hope she turns out well, but you can't know for sure . . . if I have food for my kids, if she isn't hungry, she'll never want to go to the streets. . . . But if she is hungry, she'll struggle for the little she can earn herself."

Although advocates of children's rights agree that economic well-being is essential to strengthening the fabric of the family — and providing a safety net for children — many also say that part of the battle against the sexual exploitation of children involves shifts in individual and social attitudes.

Internationally, that shift has begun only in recent years, notably in the wake of the UN's International Year of the Child in 1979. For years, groups like UNICEF, the UN's main agency for helping children, have focused their relief efforts on health measures that became known as the "child survival" revolution — aimed at saving the lives of children through hygiene and immunization programs. In recent years, however, the growing children's-rights movement has tried to push child relief efforts beyond health issues. They ask the pointed question "Survival for what?"

"Lowering infant mortality rates might be considered brilliant," in the short term, says Peter Tacon, director of CHILDHOPE, a Guatemala-based group that helps street children. "But we have to realize that while we may be saving them for a period of time, what's really happening is that they're condemned to an existence that is anything but life.

"You're also condemning the world to a real legacy of human degradation, of human deprivation. And as stewards of our sons' and daughters' futures, I don't think this is something we would want them to inherit from us."

It has taken time, but gradually the international community is responding. UNICEF, for example, has broadened its scope to include children in "extremely difficult circumstances," and individuals within the organization are pushing for a more active involvement in matters of child exploitation.

Although few national governments have tackled the issue head on, there are signs of change. The Philippines, for example, under President Corazon Aquino, is setting up programs for sexually exploited children. Unlike former President Marcos, who publicly denied that child prostitution existed, Mrs. Aquino and her administration have been very open about the problem—even to the point of declaring June 1986 to 1987 "The Year of the Exploited Child" in the Philippines.

At the local level, too, some individuals around the world are taking a stand. Their numbers are not very large nor are their efforts necessarily well known—in fact, one home for ex-child prostitutes in Santiago shuns news coverage to protect the privacy of the children who live there.

New Beginnings is one of the grass-roots efforts aimed at getting children off the streets. The Manila program is set up for sexually abused and exploited girls between the ages of 8 and 13.

"We are trying to give them a home where they can learn something useful, where they can have education, Christian teachings and where they will be part of a loving family environment," says Enriquez. "We are hopeful that if they stay with us long enough, we can change their outlook on life so that when they leave, they are new people. They can have a 'new beginning' on life."

The work isn't easy. Some of the girls run away—because they miss the excitement and freedom of the streets, or because they feel responsible for earning money for their families. What's more, as of this September the agency that has funded most of New Beginnings' first two years of work will no longer be able to pay, leaving the program $10,000 short—and its future in question.

"Of course, we can only help a dozen or 15 children out of thousands who are being prostituted," Enriquez admits. "But as they say, the first mile begins with the first step, right?

"Well," he says gently, "that's where we are now."

A Visit with Sara Terry

Sherry Ricchiardi: *Who influenced you to become a journalist?*

Sara Terry: As I look back, my career has been almost entirely influenced by men. From an early age, my father always said, "Sara, you should go into communications." I had absolutely no interest in anything remotely related to the media, but I always wrote very well. I actually wanted to be a classical ballet dancer.

Q. *So, how did it happen?*

A. My sophomore year in college, I began looking for a major. I wanted something that would allow me to travel internationally. I finally decided on journalism, not because I had any great change of heart regarding communications. I figured it would allow me to free-lance, which I could use to pay my way overseas.

From the very first day in Newswriting 101, I fell head over heels in love with journalism. As corny as it sounds, I knew I had found my niche.

Q. *Did you have any mentors along the way?*

A. Back then, the most important influence on my career-to-be was Ben Cunningham, a journalism professor at California State University. He questioned modes of thought and the ways people perceived the world. He pushed me. He pestered me. He questioned me.

He pushed me into thinking about some of the most fundamental issues in journalism, such as ethics, the importance of the First Amendment, a reporter's responsibility to self, to the medium, to the world.

My second mentor was Doug Hardie, managing editor of the

Anaheim Bulletin, the newspaper I worked at straight out of college. He made me work to write better leads.

I remember one of his examples. First, he typed something like, "Last night the City Council voted to set a 2 A.M. closing time for local bars." Then, he typed a second lead: "Councilman Bob Jones thinks that 2 A.M. is a fine time for tipplers to down their last drink."

I've used that example as a guideline for almost every lead I've written at the *Monitor.*

My last mentor was David Anable, who at the time was overseas news editor at the *Monitor.* I learned fine-tuning from him. None of these men realized that I looked to them as mentors. I never spoke of it with them.

Q. *Did you ever have female mentors?*

A. I've always been aware that I've never had a woman mentor. I can't explain that, except there were no women professors at my university and no female news editors at the *Monitor* until Kay Fanning took over in 1983.

Of course, there was a women's page editor, and I do say that with a bit of sarcasm. There were quite a few women writers at the *Monitor,* but quite frankly, I didn't want to emulate them.

Q. *Why was that?*

A. In part, they seemed unapproachable. Also, in a subconscious way, I didn't identify with them, which was partly generational, considering that I am a product of the post–women's liberation movement. I didn't want to emulate their life-styles. They were either divorced or they had been single all of their lives. I felt it was a price they had paid to be successful journalists.

Q. *How has being a woman affected your career?*

A. I don't know that people in the newsroom have ever treated me differently because I'm a woman. I've never been discriminated against because I'm a woman, nor have I been harassed. I've always been judged—at least during my years at the *Monitor*—on my merit as a reporter.

I do feel guilty about that. I know women who passed before me in this profession paid the price. I skated in on the backs of those women.

Q. *Have you made any personal sacrifices for your career?*

A. I wouldn't say I have made sacrifices, but I have made many choices. In the early years, by choosing to pursue a career so actively, I gave second priority to a romantic relationship. I worked long hours and traveled frequently. During my early to mid-20s, I found that some men my age were threatened by a woman who did well in her career.

I often dated older men but never on a long-term basis. I was afraid that being successful in my career might doom me to a life as a single person.

Q. *How did that change?*

A. By the time I reached my late 20s, when I felt less driven by my work, I consciously chose to make room for a romantic relationship. I met a man whom I fell in love with. We've been happily married for around four years now.

I've postponed motherhood. Now, I've reached the point where having kids is something I'm thinking about.

Q. *Does being a woman make a difference in how you report?*

A. Absolutely, without question. I don't mean the mere physical fact of being a woman. I mean drawing on the qualities I associate with womanhood—compassion, sensitivity, being a good listener, the ability to set ego aside.

I don't think these qualities are exclusive to women. I know male reporters who are tender and caring, and I know female reporters who can be harsh and cynical.

I think because I'm a woman, I'm more inclined to be open to the situation—to allow myself to be moved by someone's emotional pain.

I saw that in myself during the "Children in Darkness" series. It was an emotionally devastating experience to spend three months traveling in some of the poorest parts of the world, witnessing some of the greatest travesties human beings are capable of committing.

Q. *How did it happen that three women, yourself, Kristin Helmore, and photographer Melanie Freeman, were assigned to the series?*

A. Kay Fanning, who was the editor at the time, made a point of saying that we were not chosen because we were women but because we were considered to be the best ones for the job.

Q. *Was being female in Third World countries a help or a hindrance?*

A. In developing countries, men are the authority figures—white males even more so. Women are frequently patronized. When we showed up in Iraq, after having filled out visa forms that clearly stated our desire to visit the Iraqi POW camp for Iranian child soldiers, I was approached by a government press officer who said, "So you want to visit nurseries for Iraqi children?"

Because women are viewed as insignificant in these countries, government officials often were more inclined to speak openly. We were not viewed as a threat to their power.

Most of the children we met absolutely craved affection. We responded, as women, in a very nonthreatening way. For a child prostitute, there was a comfort zone in holding a woman's hand or hugging a woman that would not have been there with a man.

Q. *Who decided how the series would run?*

A. After our return, we had a meeting about the direction the series would take. We three women sat down with four male editors. During the conversation, I kept stressing that I thought our readers would be very disturbed by the series and that I didn't want to start writing and then be told that the subject matter was too unsettling.

One of the editors turned to me and said, "Look I know this was rough. But I don't want to see you or your writing get emotional."

I hit the roof. I said, "I do not ever want to hear the word 'emotional' used again in the course of discussing this series. I think that's a very male accusation. It implies that I, as a woman, am allowing my feelings to run away with me. What I'm saying, as a human being, is that you cannot be human and not respond deeply, and with pain, to this series."

The word "emotion" never came up again.

Q. *Were you asked to change much of what you wrote?*

A. With the exception of one word, I was never asked to change anything on the basis of it being too shocking or painful. The one word, by the way, was in the lead of the first story. I wrote, "Kham Suk's family desperately needed the money. Kham Suk is still paying the price: $4 a trick."

The editors felt the word trick was simply too harsh, too much like rubbing the reader's face in the horror of the situation. I protested vigorously, but the word trick was changed to customer.

Q. *Do you feel you've had to work harder than men to get ahead?*

A. No, I truly don't think so. As far as a reporter is concerned, the proof really is in the pudding. Either you can report and write a story or you can't. I've always been measured as a reporter among reporters when it's come to advancement and assignment.

Q. *Have you had to work harder to prove yourself to the men in the newsroom?*

A. I know some female reporters have faced patronizing by male colleagues. It's a sort of prove-you-can-hack-it thing. It especially seems to come up around political reporters, particularly older ones. Perhaps that's because politics historically has been such a good-old-boys' network.

Among women reporters of my generation, I don't find a sense of having been discriminated against on the basis of sex. That may be different for women reporters who are older.

Q. *Do you feel it's proper for women to use feminine wiles during interviews?*

A. For starters, I don't consider the use of sexuality to be a legitimate way to get a story. By sexuality, I mean anything from flirting to overt sexual overtones to sleeping with someone.

Now, as for using femininity, that's something else. I've used my femininity and the simple fact of my womanhood every way possible, as long as the result is to get the story I'm after and if it doesn't involve coming on sexually to someone. For example, if a corporate head or a politician treats me patronizingly because I'm just a "girl" and "too pretty to worry my head about it," I'll let him do it—as long as it serves my need.

Q. *Can you give me an example?*

A. When I was 23, I covered Kevin White's last race for mayor of Boston. He took a liking to me early on. He'd sort of preen when he spoke about his accomplishments, and actually spoke rather candidly about his campaign strategy. Once, he threw his arm around my shoulders and said something like, "I'm going to teach you all about politics."

Fine by me. It meant I had more access to him than most of my male colleagues. He was more unguarded with me and said things he probably wouldn't have said to male reporters on the beat. He perceived me as a harmless young girl.

I didn't deceive him. I didn't act stupid or naive. It was his perception of me and I used it to my advantage. It didn't last long, though. After I started covering the campaign regularly, writing stories, showing up at press conferences, asking some tough questions, he put his guard up around me.

Q. *How do you use your femininity?*

A. I use what I call "dress psychology" if a situation warrants it. If I want to create the impression that I am approaching a man as his equal, I usually show up in pants. If I feel I need to persuade him to give me some information or to trust me, I wear a dress. Nothing with a plunging decolletage or anything, but something that emphasizes the fact that I'm a woman.

The message that you can send by how you dress is a wonderful tool to have at your disposal as a reporter.

Q. *Do you feel women bring a special dimension to the newsroom?*

A. A lot of women let their sensibilities be co-opted by men for the sake of being businesslike. When a woman really draws on her womanhood, she can bring a wonderful sense of mothering to a newsroom, especially a woman who is an editor. Kay Fanning did that at the *Monitor.*

Women also tend to care about their colleagues who are going through hard times. It's not just a brisk, "How's it going?" but "Are you OK?" Women are more likely to draw someone out.

Q. *Is networking with other women journalists important to you.*

A. No, it really isn't. I don't like joining organizations. I don't mean to sound harsh, but I don't see the need for women journalists to look out for each other. I don't need an organization or a network to help my career. Either I can cut it as a reporter or I can't.

I remember when Kay Fanning first came to the newsroom, some of the women reporters laughed about the fact that they'd run into her in the bathroom. They'd say, "Gee, this is what it's been like for men all these years."

Q. *Do you have any advice for young women entering the field?*

A. I would tell them they don't have to dress like a man in proper little suits. They don't have to stifle compassion or creativity. Their sensibilities as a woman might lead them to a story in a different, and perhaps, better way. It's okay to cry when a story hurts. It's not unprofessional to respond like a human being, like a woman.

Q. *Tell me about "Children in Darkness." How did the series come about?*

A. The idea had been kicking around the newspaper for three or four years. All the correspondents who had been in the Third World, and they were all men at that point, kept saying, "We have to do something about children."

I saw the proposals from the men and they were very neatly packaged. It was sort of a masculine way of looking at it as a quantifiable problem. In the end, they sent three women.

Q. *How specifically did being a woman make a difference on this assignment?*

A. I never thought I'd be glad for sexism, but in this case, I was. Officials would come right out and say, "Of course people break the child labor laws here. We don't care. That's the way it is."

There was a frankness because they thought, "What can these insignificant women do or write that could threaten my position or affect me?" They would tell us anything because they didn't believe we had any power.

And, there was a side benefit to being female. In some of these countries, there are taboos against hurting women. In a way, we felt protected.

Q. *Were you ever in danger?*

A. Only in Uganda and Zambia. We were hauled in to the police station and accused of bribing child soldiers in Uganda. We were talking to these kids outside the Ministry of Defense when one of their commanders came up and shouted at them.

The children, to protect themselves, said we offered them money. The authorities chewed us out and tried to search us. This one guy tried to confiscate Melanie's film.

Later on in the trip, we made an unscheduled landing in Zambia where the military held us hostage at gunpoint for four or five hours. At first they demanded money, then they let us go.

Q. *How did you prepare for this assignment?*

A. I went through 10 years worth of *Readers' Guide to Periodicals* and newspaper searches. I still have the first articles I found on child labor, child prostitutes, and child soldiers. The stories were almost nonexistent. Nobody had put it together under this broad umbrella of childrens' rights.

I spent two weeks interviewing experts on childrens' rights. I asked, "What are the key issues? Which countries should we go to? Do you have any contacts there?"

We broke new ground with the series by raising the issue of childrens' rights in Third World countries in a mainstream newspaper, which nobody before us had done.

Q. *What kind of response did the series bring?*

A. UNICEF, which historically has been more interested in inoculating children than dealing with their exploitation, ordered a copy for every employee and every member of the Convention on the Rights of Children.

A Jesuit priest wrote saying he nominated us for a Pulitzer prize. Some people sent $10; some sent thousands. Foundations phoned to ask, "How can we get involved with this?" An American, married to a Burmese woman, called to say they were going to the Golden Triangle to get Kahm Suk out of the brothel.

The response was phenomenal. It restored my faith in the human heart.

Q. *Where did your travels for the series take you?*

A. We spent three months in 13 countries, including India,

Thailand, Chile, Peru, Guatemala, Pakistan, and the Philippines. It was the most grueling reporting I had ever done, and it was the sweetest when it was over because of the response.

We had to let down all our defenses, set aside all our western opinions, prejudices, life-style, and background. I don't know if men would have let themselves be vulnerable in quite the same way.

Q. *Where did you find the 14-year-old male prostitute you interviewed?*

A. A taxi driver took us to a club filled with boys, most under 18. It was run by a gay man called Madame Joey, an outrageous, flamboyant character. They sat us down at a table in front of the boys, who were preening for us, flexing their muscles and smiling. I felt so humiliated.

Madame Joey assured us they all had been checked for AIDS and venereal disease. He said they were all masseuses and knew how to act in a 5-star hotel. He asked what age I wanted.

I asked, "Who's the youngest?"

"The youngest are more aggressive," he said and pointed to this 14-year-old. Then Madame Joey added, "He ejaculates five or six times a night."

I said, "Yes, thank you. He's fine." As I was leaving, Madame Joey said, "Call me tomorrow. I will find a 10-year-old for you."

Q. *What happened after you left the club with the boy?*

A. We got in the car and this kid grabs my hand and starts to give me a massage. I thought, "At what point am I going to be able to explain this to him?"

When we got him back to the room, the translator worked with me. I got down on my knees in front of him and said, "Look, I'm traveling all over the world, talking to children everywhere." I tried hard not to be intimidating. We told him if he wanted to leave we would take him back.

He thought about it for a while, then just started to talk. His family didn't know what he was doing. He was using the money to pay school expenses. One night he was beaten by a sadist for three hours. The man paid him an extra $10 after the beating. The boy said he complained to Madame Joey, who said, "That's tough."

Q. *Did you pay him?*

A. We always paid the child prostitutes something because we were using their time.

Q. *Did you tape these interviews?*

A. We taped everything because eventually we did a program for the *Monitor's* public radio program.

Q. *How did you find these children?*

A. From my research, I knew we would find child prostitutes in the Philippines; I knew we would find them in Thailand. But doubt was always hanging over our heads. At times we felt like we weren't going to find them and the editors would have spent thousands of dollars for nothing.

We couldn't just pick up a telephone and say, "Hi, can I please have a number for child prostitutes." We had to make connections through the local people.

In each country there was some sort of street organization. We would ask, "Where do these kids hang out?" We'd hear about a pick-up place and stake it out. We began to get a sixth sense. I would say to Melanie, "That guy's a pedophile." We would follow him for an half an hour.

Q. *How did you organize the volumes of material you collected after you got home?*

A. I had three parts to write. I had the overview, the child prostitutes and the child soldiers. I had to take them one at a time or I would have gone crazy.

I kept a separate piece of paper for each part of the series. I separated my notes into piles. I had a clean notebook to make notes on how I wanted to write. I would mark, "Use this in part 1."

On that separate piece of paper I wrote quotes, facts, settings that would go in the first part. I ended up with this very condensed single page.

That single page was a life-saver because I checked things off as I wrote. Everything I listed on that page was crucial to that particular story. For each part of the series, I started the process over again.

When I read through my notes, I used a yellow Hi-Liter for quotes I wanted to use or for facts I wanted to refer to. Sometimes I took a red pen and wrote at the top of the page: "This is a good quote about. . . . "

Q. *How did your emotions figure into this?*

A. It was particularly hard with part 1. I wanted people to understand what was at work here, not just that there were child prostitutes in the world, but that there were children who truly lived in darkness — the darkness of poverty, of ignorance, greed, and indifference.

I waited 10 days before I started writing part 2. I didn't want to deal with it. When I finally sat down and wrote the first two paragraphs, I burst into tears.

Q. *Did you write at home or at the office?*

A. At the office, usually. I had to separate this from my home.

Q. *Were you on a deadline?*

A. We came back in mid-May. The series started on June 28. It was a very tight deadline. The editors wanted it even faster; they didn't want to hit the summer lull. We knew another team of reporters was out doing something similar. We didn't want to get beat.

Q. *How did you find Kham Suk, the child who opens the series?*

A. Melanie and Kristin heard of a village in northern Thailand filled with girls from Burma. We had 48 hours left before we had to leave for India, so we decided to go.

We arrived in the village that night and found that it was Thai New Years and all the brothels were closed. It was a village of around 3,000; there was a map of the 21 brothels in town.

We saw a door that was padlocked. We knew it was a brothel. We walked a little further and found an open patio. We walked into the courtyard and saw all these little girls. I don't remember how we communicated, but I walked over, threw down some money, grabbed two of the children and left.

We took them back to a guest house where the owner spoke Burmese. We sat down with these two little girls and they started to giggle. The sound of Kham Suk giggling seemed so out of place with the fact that her mother had walked her across the border and sold her for $80.

Q. *How did you decide on Kham Suk for the lead?*

A. I made very conscious choices. I wanted a girl for the first paragraph, a prostitute. Then I wanted a soldier and a laborer. The lead was written in three capsules. There is a paragraph, about four lines long about each child. Then a new paragraph with two lines. It's written like a "go for the gut" sort of thing.

Kham Suk's mother sold her; she was a little girl. It reflected the complexity of the issue. Her family needed the money. Eighty dollars was like an annual income for a Burmese farming family. Her mother got it in one shot for selling her daughter.

All of the contrasting images of childhood, the mother/daughter relationship, the terror, the money, the role of the child in the family — it all came down to Kham Suk. I needed something tight and small that said volumes.

I was manipulating the reader's attention, but I didn't manipulate the facts. I was consciously saying, "This is going to be so powerful that you will keep reading through the rest of the series."

Q. *Do you write from the lead down in your stories?*

A. I absolutely cannot write without the lead. It was funny. I sat down and started going through my notes and there was Kham Suk.

Q. *Did the strong emotions you were feeling cause writer's block?*

A. Apart from bursting into tears when I didn't want to write part 2, it was amazing. I never had writing just flow like it did once I got past my personal involvement. I kept asking myself, what am I seeing? What are the universal threads here? What's the same in this country as in the other countries?

Q. *Overall, what was the most difficult?*

A. It was the fact that I had to be open to all the horror and all of the pain. These were such delightful children; I was really taken with them. I had to be completely open to the worst suffering I had seen in my lifetime.

Q. *Did you make conscious choices about writing strategy for this series?*

A. I'm a perfectionist as a writer; I don't leave it to an editor to make my writing better. There was one device in these stories — I used short sentences as often as possible.

Q. *Why?*

A. Because the stories were about children. I didn't want to be too intellectual, too abstract. The whole lead is short sentences. You can't escape from the impact of what is being said like, "Kham Suk's family desperately needs money."

There is no flowery language; the situation itself was urgent and compelling enough. I just needed to tell it simply and in a straightforward way.

I think cadence is powerful. That's something I was very conscious of with this series. Unfortunately, a lot of reporters and editors don't "hear" a sentence.

Q. *Do you have any magic tricks for writing?*

A. I read my writing aloud; I feel that's very important. It's a cliche, but I ask myself, "What would I tell my best friend about the story?"

I would have told about Kham Suk and about this little boy who was sent to battle as a human minesweeper. I would have told about the child who goes crazy when he thinks about the family he was forced to leave behind.

10 Common Threads

The selections in this book were written by five women in their 30s, three in their 40s, and one 50-year-old, and in some ways, their attitudes about reporting and the roles of journalists reflected the age difference.

Some of the older women have battled sexism at its rawest. They've been denied prime assignments and had to fight to be taken seriously.

Not true for most of the younger women. They've received the same treatment as male colleagues and, in fact, some got their jobs partly because they were female.

On the issue of whether they had to work harder than men to succeed, answers ranged from:

Lucy Morgan, 50: "If we have gotten somewhere in a male-dominated world, we have done it because we were willing to work harder."

To Cynthia Gorney, 36: "The dividing line was about four years ahead of me. The women who were 40 when I got there were pretty tough cookies. They had fought to get out of the women's pages, to get good beats. I was getting the benefit of it."

Almost all talked about the personal sacrifices they made for their careers. But the generational difference again was evident. Of the nine women, four are married, two are divorced and three are single.

Said Molly Ivins, 44: "A lot of years have passed and I'm not married. I would have loved to have a child. Occasionally, I've thought of adopting but there isn't enough structure in my life for that."

Bella Stumbo, 46: "I spent 15 years wanting to establish myself in a good job with a good salary. I spent so long with those kinds of goals that I sacrificed the other side of life, the family."

Sara Terry, 35: "By the time I reached my late 20s, when I felt less driven by my work, I consciously chose to make room for a romantic relationship. I met a man whom I fell in love with. We've been happily married for four years now. I've postponed motherhood and now I'm thinking about it."

Christine Brennan, 32: "It's the 80s. And people wait a long time to marry and have kids. I feel no sense of urgency.".

On whether being a woman makes a difference in how they report, almost across the board they agreed that women tend to be better listeners and more compassionate interviewers who have the ability to empathize with their subjects.

Jacqui Banaszynski, 37: "I think it is okay to use your femininity in a way that puts people at ease. People are more comfortable talking to women. They expect us to be softer, more understanding and less demanding than men."

Brennan: "I'd say that a woman is more sensitive and attentive to the intricacies of a scene. You know, not just looking at the play on the field but noticing the coach on his knees in prayer before a play."

All said being a woman has worked to their advantage in interviews.

Anna Quindlen, 37: "Early on there were people who thought I was too stupid to understand the import of what they were saying so they said things in front of me that they shouldn't have said. And there were people who felt like I had a shoulder you could cry on, people who unloaded on me who wouldn't unload on me if I were male."

Terry: "If a corporate head or a politician treats me patronizingly because I'm just a 'girl' and 'too pretty to worry my head about it,' I'll let him do it — as long as it serves my need."

Several noted the problems of juggling home and career.

Morgan: "Almost everyone is struggling with something other than the job. That's more common to women because more falls to them such as child care and care of their elderly parents. A lot of men don't seem to have those responsibilities. I have often said, I need a wife."

Alice Steinbach: "I was a single parent and my two sons were young enough to need supervision when I started in this business. It was damned hard work."

One common piece of advice: Don't be emotional in the office.

From Banaszynski: "I see too many women getting pegged as flaky, inconsistent and emotional."

And Quindlen: "I would have ripped my tear ducts out rather than cry in the office."

11 Progress — Or the Lack of It

By the year 2055, projections indicate that women will attain levels in newspaper editorships on a par with their level in America's population—53 percent. That prediction comes from Dorothy Jurney, who in 1988 completed her tenth annual survey of women in directing editorships for the American Society of Newspaper Editors.

But progress has been slow in coming.

Research by Jean Gaddy Wilson, director of New Directions for News, indicates that newspapers continue to employ women at percentages much lower than their proportion in the population despite the fact that 66 percent of all journalism students today are women.

"The next 10 years will show us. Since 1977 women have outnumbered men in journalism schools. If education is a key to management, then women are ready—they have been for a decade," Wilson said.

The following information was distributed at an April 1989 conference in Washington, D.C., titled, "Women, Men and Media." The study, funded in part by the Gannett Foundation, Women in Communications, and the Knight Foundation, was presented under the heading *The Press: The Pay Gap—The Power Gap*. Among the findings:

—A woman editor earns significantly less than a man in the same job at the same size newspaper, television, or radio station. The cost to the female editor in the yearly paycheck is: newspaper, $7,793; television, $9,074; radio, $3,323.

—Americans continue to receive their news through a white male filter. Only 6 percent of the country's newspapers have a female publisher. Women hold about 25 percent of the midmanagement jobs.

195

Women lack control over content, policy, and direction of newspapers.

—The smaller the newspaper, the higher percentage of women employed. At newspapers with less than 5,000 circulation, women hold 57 percent of the jobs; at papers of 100,000 or more circulation, they hold 29 percent of the jobs.

12 Women Worth Watching

Many women could have been featured in this book. More trailblazers, award winners and brilliant writers surfaced during the research; a list of 25 of them follows. Their careers — and their work — are worth watching.

SUSAN AGER, *Detroit Free Press;* winner of 1988 National Headliner Award for feature writing for three stories including "Daddy Hurt Me," about false allegations of sexual child abuse; 1985 National Headliner Award for stories on AIDS, Alzheimer's Disease, and discrimination against homosexuals; National Endowment for the Humanities Fellowship for Journalists at University of Michigan, 1980–1981.

TAD BARTIMUS, Associated Press enterprise writer in the West and Midwest; nominated as finalist for 1989 Pulitzer Prize in feature writing; founded the Journalism and Women Symposium (JAWS) in 1985; became the first woman in AP's history to head an AP domestic bureau when appointed Alaska bureau chief in 1975; one of three women assigned by AP to Southeast Asia during the Vietnam War.

NINA BERNSTEIN, *New York Newsday,* special projects team reporter; while with the *Milwaukee Journal,* won a 1986 Investigative Reporters and Editors Award for "Justice Denied," an expose of the Milwaukee municipal justice system; 1984 Nieman Fellow at Harvard University.

RITA CIOLLI, *New York Newsday,* national correspondent specializing in the law; juris doctor degree, Georgetown University Law Center 1977; adjunct professor New York University, teaching courses on media and law; 1983 Alicia Patterson Foundation Fellowship to research book censorship in schools; won the American Bar Association's Silver Gavel Award for her 1982 series, "The Island Tree Case: The Book Ban that Made History."

TRACY DODDS, *Los Angeles Times,* sports reporter; first woman to join the sports staff at the *Milwaukee Journal* in 1973 and the *Houston Post* in 1980; investigative reporting award from APSE in 1975; twice included in *Best Sports Stories of the Year,* a collection; first to win an award for newspaper reporting from the Women's Sports Foundation; vice-president of the Association of Women in Sports Media; one of the first women in the country to cover sports as a daily beat.

CELIA DUGGER, *Miami Herald,* urban affairs reporter; while at *Atlanta Journal and Constitution* in 1983, won, with a colleague, George Polk Award for regional reporting; Georgia AP public service award for state capital reporting.

LYNN DUKE, *Washington Post,* general assignment reporter covering drug problems; while at *Miami Herald,* won 1987 J. C. Penney-University of Missouri award for an article on crack; 1988 Pulitzer Prize finalist for feature writing for same story.

KATHERINE ELLISON, *San Jose Mercury News,* Mexico City correspondent; together with two colleagues won a 1987 Pulitzer Prize for international reporting and George Polk Award in the same category; authored book on Imelda Marcos; won Overseas Press Club fellowship in 1980.

LISA GETTER, *Miami Herald,* investigative team; Sigma Delta Chi award for best magazine article by a college student while at Northwestern's Medill School of Journalism; nominated as 1989 Pulitzer Prize finalist for general news reporting.

DOROTHY GILLIAM, *Washington Post,* columnist; chairs Robert F. Kennedy Journalism Awards Committee; Woodrow Wilson Fellow; board member of the Fund for Investigative Journalism and the Institute for Journalism Education; Columbia University Graduate School of Journalism Alumni of the Year Award; author of *Paul Robeson, All American,* a biography.

KRISTIN HELMORE, *Christian Science Monitor;* won Overseas Press Club Award for series called "The Neglected Resource: Women in the Developing World"; won third place from National Association of Black Journalists for 1986 series on poverty in the Afro-American community; co-authored with Sara Terry series on child exploitation.

KAREN ELLIOTT HOUSE, *Wall Street Journal;* 1988 Overseas Press Club award for a series on Islam; 1984 Pulitzer Prize for international reporting for a series on King Hussein's dilemmas; fellow at the Institute of Politics, John F. Kennedy School of Government at Harvard University; board member, Council on Foreign Relations; member of advisory board of the Georgetown Center for Strategic and International Studies.

ATHELIA KNIGHT, *Washington Post;* 1986 Nieman Fellow at Harvard University; while on the *Post's* investigative team she wrote a series, "Pursuing the Legacy: A Year at McKinley High School," which won a second place award from the National Association of Education Writers.

CHERYL LAVIN, *Chicago Tribune,* feature writer and columnist; finalist for American Society of Newspaper Editors award 1987; nominated for a Pulitzer three times; authored a book, *Tales from the Front,* based on the syndicated column she writes, with Laura Kavesh, about romance.

MYRA MACPHERSON, *Washington Post;* Fulbright grant winner to study sociological trends from World War II to present in Japan, 1987; author, *Long Time Passing: Vietnam and the Haunted Generation,* and *The Power Lovers: An Intimate Look at Politicians and Their Marriages;* fellow at Rutgers University Eagleton Institute for Policy Studies, 1973.

EILEEN MCNAMARA, *Boston Globe,* political and general assignment reporter; 1988 Nieman Fellow at Harvard University; her year-long project on how Massachusetts judges treat battered women resulted in one judge leaving the state and four others undergoing investigation; began at the *Globe* as a secretary.

EVELYN RICHARDS, *Washington Post;* with the *San Jose Mercury News* until 1988; finalist for Gerald Loeb Awards for Distinguished

Business and Financial Journalism, 1988; Overseas Press Club award for economic reporting, 1987; Knight Fellowship at Stanford University 1986–1987; International Press Institute, Japan, 1983; Davenport Fellowship in Business and Economic Reporting, University of Missouri, 1980.

KAREN DORN STEELE, *Spokesman-Review* and *Spokane* (Washington) *Chronicle;* dual appointment as 1986–1987 Knight Fellow and Arms Control Fellow, Center for International Security and Arms Control, Stanford University; 1987 William Stokes Award for Reporting on the Environment (honorable mention) for coverage of secret irradiation of eastern Washington in the 1940s and 1950s; 1986 First Place, Daily Government Reporting, Northwest Chapter, Sigma Delta Chi.

OLIVE TALLEY, *Dallas Morning News,* general assignment with emphasis on projects; won, with a colleague, Dallas Press Club, Texas Medical Association, Women in Communications Inc. and American College of Emergency Physicians awards for series on indigent health care, 1987; UPI Award for spot news, 1987; was a Pulitzer finalist for a series on the criminal justice system in 1990. She recently was elected to the Board of Investigative Reporters and Editors.

LORETTA TOFANI, *Philadelphia Inquirer;* 1983 Pulitzer Prize for local investigative reporting; 1983 Investigative Reporters and Editors award; 1988 best news story, Sigma Delta Chi regional competition; best story and best feature story 1988, Pennsylvania Associated Press Managing Editors Association; 1988 National Headliners Award; Fulbright Fellowship to Japan, 1983–1984.

IRENE VIRAG, *New York Newsday;* 1984 Pulitzer Prize for general local reporting for team coverage of "The Baby Doe Dilemma"; 1986 Pulitzer finalist in feature category; 1987 New York State Associated Press Award for best feature, "The Survival of Cindy," about a welfare mother; 1985 John Hancock Award for excellence in business and financial journalism for "Property Taxes: The Unbalanced Burden."

SUSAN WATSON, *Detroit Free Press,* columnist, former city editor; first black female city editor at a major metropolitan daily;

National Newspaper Guild award 1978 for an investigation into the abuse of retarded children and adults at a state-operated facility.

VIVIENNE WALT, *New York Newsday,* general assignment reporter; nominated for Pulitzer Prize in 1986 and 1987 while foreign correspondent for *Newsday* in South Africa; native of South Africa; fluent in French, Hebrew, Dutch/Afrikaans.

NANCY WEAVER, *Sacramento Bee;* while at the Jackson (Miss.) *Clarion-Ledger,* won 1983 Pulitzer Prize for public service for series on schools; 1987 World Hunger Award; 1987 Robert F. Kennedy Journalism Awards, honorable mention, for "Hunger in California."

IRENE WIELAWSKI, *Providence Journal;* 1987 finalist for Pulitzer in specialized reporting for 20 medical stories; J. C. Penney-University of Missouri award, 1986, for six-part series on experiences of three new doctors in their first year of hospital training.

CREDITS